ATTIC
IN
GREECE

ATTIC
IN
GREECE

Austen Kark

Little, Brown and Company

A *Little, Brown* Book

First published in Great Britain in 1994
by Little, Brown and Company

Copyright © Austen Kark 1994

The moral right of the author has been asserted.

A CIP catalogue record for this book
is available from the British Library

ISBN 0 316 91065 1

Typeset by M Rules
Printed in England by Clays Ltd, St Ives plc

Little, Brown and Company (UK) Limited
Brettenham House
Lancaster Place
London WC2E 7EN

In gratitude
to John, Xaroula and Zafiris
in Athens
to Babis, Kostas and all my friends
in Nauplion and,
of course, as always, to Nina

THE FORMER YUGOSLAV
REPUBLIC OF MAKEDONIA

BULGARIA

ALBANIA

M
A
C
E
D
O
N
I
A

Drama

Kavalla

Thessalonika

Thassos

Mt Olympus

Lemnos

Corfu

Joanina

Larissa

P
I
N
D
O
S

Trikkala

THESSALY

Volos

Pelion

D

Preveza

Lamia

SPORADES

Aegean

Skiros

Levkas

S T E R E A

Sea

Cephalonia

E
V
I
A

Kalkis

ELLAS

I
O
N
I
A
N

Patras

P

Corinth

Pirgos

Mycenae

ATHENS

Andros

Piraeus

Zakynthos

Argos

Epidauros

Tinos

Nauplion

CYCLADES

Ionian

Kalanata

Sparta

Naxos

Sea

Monemvasia

Milos

Santorini

Kithira

MEDITERRANEAN   SEA

Sea of Crete

Khania

Heraklion

C R E T E

0   100 Kilometres

0   20   40   60 Miles

GREECE

Prologue

It was, I think, December 1961, and for various complicated reasons Nina and I were travelling in the Greek Prime Minister's second-best car, driven by Dimitri, the Prime Minister's alternate chauffeur.

We had been visiting Salonika, Kavala and the north-eastern border with Turkey and, on our way back to Athens, had arrived in Lamia in central Greece after nightfall. For once the system failed. Normally Dimitri went into the best hotel with his cap on, a large polished crown gleaming above the peak, and we were given a grand room at what then seemed a pretty fancy price. The only other time Dimitri put on his cap was when we approached a village. Ordinarily a careful, moderate and rather un-Greek driver, he had two disquieting habits. One was a tendency to turn round and address us, while driving on winding and often precipitous roads, whenever he thought we had not got the point – which was often. The other was when he had a village in his sights. He would put on his cap, glance to make sure that the flag was fluttering proudly, look rigidly ahead, his usually mobile face stern in a glare, brigand moustache bristling, and increase speed till villagers, dogs and chickens scattered. As soon as we were well clear of the village he would take off his cap, smile at a job well done and return to his stately and talkative progress .

Later, when he had left us at the hotel and gone off to see some friends, we would sneak out and find the nearest cheap taverna and fill up on cabbage soup. We were paying for food and hotels out of a not very generous BBC subsistence allowance, admittedly intended for one person but barely sufficient even for that, and we were only allowed, because of exchange controls and currency regulations, to take £25 spending money with us.

This time, in Lamia, there were no rooms. Not at the Grand Hotel, not at the not so grand. The National Theatre was performing, a cabinet minister was in town and, not that it had much effect on the hotels, prisoners were rioting in the gaol. Dimitri found us a room in a large, respectable house, not only in the centre of town but very handy for the gaol. The house was dimly lit and forbidding, and the prison discomfortingly noisy. Dimitri, perhaps to reassure us, said, "A home is better." To be accurate, with teeth flashing and eyes crinkling kindly he said, "*Ein Heim ist besser*", being of the misguided belief that since we patently did not speak Greek (I could just about decipher the street-names and mutter a courtesy or two), we must speak German. He, having been deported to Germany in 1942, had a loose but easy acquaintance with the language.

The room was large, dark and mysterious. An oil lamp illuminated an icon of the *Panayia*, the Virgin Mary, placed high in a corner. It flickered as, to a different rhythm, did a central electric light in ornate, dark blue glass with slits of ruby red. The bulb, when functioning properly, gave out perhaps five watts' worth of light. Beside the bed, a high, hard, narrow wooden affair, was a candle. There were two other similar electric lights, one in the entrance hall below, which had been turned off as soon as we climbed the stairs, the other flickering high up, as though on some distant landing near the dark sky. Outside our room sat a *yiayia* dressed head-to-toe in black, someone's granny or superannuated nanny. Her function seemed to be to hand out three minuscule pieces of lavatory paper and to receive them back, when used, in a bucket beside her. She also issued a lighted candle to anyone entering the water closet, a closed cupboard which stood assertively in the middle of the hall, the water consisting of a jug which was passed unnervingly through the unlocked door when she thought the time was right.

In our room, which smelt of beeswax and elderly carpets, the shutters were closed tight, seemingly impenetrable until we noticed the occasional headlights pricking the dark and recognized the rise and fall of the shouts from the rioting prisoners that echoed round the walls. I opened my penknife and made sure it was ready to hand, beside the bedside candle. We got into bed, swallowed two sleeping pills each, lay precariously and hoped for the morning.

It had not, I thought, been the most propitious introduction to Nina of a country and people of whom I was already much in thrall. I could hear myself saying that she ought to see the clarity of sea and sky, feel the joy of swimming in liquid silk, the enchantment of the spring air, the certainty of summer. But it was close to Christmas and the nights were cold. We had been turned back by fog somewhere between Xanthi and Alexandropoulos, a wintry rain had spoilt Larisa and as for piling Pelion upon Ossa, both had been hidden in heavy cloud. I felt as I did when bringing a best friend home to meet my mother and father and it was clear that he, the other child, failed to match my earlier description of him: I had to explain, excuse, almost apologize. And then there was the food. It was mostly unappetizing, largely because we were skint and could not afford the more interesting choices, and invariably lukewarm. Finally, there was this lavatory, enough to frighten anyone given to a nice sensitivity in these matters to consequential months of unease.

*

In the light of the new day, crisp and clear, with the shutters flung open and the everyday noises of a town waking up and getting to work, our night fears, and the open penknife, seemed absurd. We had in fact slept soundly and the prisoners perhaps too: certainly the noise and presumably the riot had abated. After a ewer of warm water and a floral basin had come and gone we packed what little we had unpacked and thought about leaving. As I moved towards the door, in came a tray and the lady of the house. We were gestured towards the table where the three of us sat down. She welcomed us with a "*kalos orisate*" and gave us each a tumbler of brandy, a spoonful of rose jam, a larger dollop of grapes in honey and two glasses of water. Presumably she had either been out or had already gone to bed when we arrived. Where were we from? How many children? Then I think she asked where were we going and we variously said Athens and London. She wished us a good journey, shook my hand, embraced Nina and went. We had finished everything except the water. Not just because we had not eaten anything the night before, but also because it was an unexpected delight.

Downstairs Dimitri was waiting, cap on, car gleaming, flag flying. He had paid, he said, we could pay him back later. It was something under a pound. As he swept us off to see the pass at Thermopylae in daylight before getting on with the serious business of getting back to Athens, he turned round, gave us one of his most comprehending smiles and said, in Greek, something along the lines of "you see, I was right". Then he repeated, in German, that a home was better and grinned with a shared sense of satisfaction. Nina chimed in, surprising herself as much as me, "I like these people. I could live here."

Pleased beyond measure, I said, "When I retire."

And we both contemplated that unimaginably far-off time as Dimitri drove us fast, the immediate future already obtruding (he was looking at his watch), towards Athens.

Twenty-five years later, when I retired from the BBC after a fairly hectic time as managing director of the World Service, and after decades of visiting and exploring, it was clear where I wanted to go: Greece had become our second country. We had never had a weekend cottage or another house, and now I thought was the time, a new life clearly beginning at 60, to call in Nina's offer. We would have a place in Greece. Hotels were comfortable enough for holidays but Dimitri's unforgotten *ein Heim ist besser* rang true. It was important anyway to have a stake, however small, in the country and among the people we had come to love. The only problem I foresaw, and that a pleasing one, was choice.

Of course, I knew that Greeks did not like to sell the family house, that their way with wills was formidable and their habit with taxes disregarding, but we had time and energy and friends. And then we happened on Number 19 Kapodistriou.

I

There may not have been precisely twenty-seven heirs throughout but the figure lodges in the mind. Certainly if Uncle Vangeli had not been whisked into hospital for an emergency amputation of the leg on which, as he loudly protested, he had been standing perfectly well for eighty-three years, they, the twenty-seven, would never have agreed to sell their house in Nauplion. They had not, to be sure, agreed beforehand not to sell it: they had not even discussed it. The combination however of an insistent buyer and warning bells from the hospital launched the family into crisis management.

The shiver of doubt that Uncle Vangeli might not weather the operation was enough to alert and alarm the existing beneficiaries, his co-heirs. If he were to die, another eight assorted cousins would share the estate and, worse still, would have to be consulted. The telephone wires, cables and satellites

hummed throughout the Greek diaspora – Toronto, Montreal, Vancouver, Pittsburgh, San Francisco, New York, Melbourne, Sydney, Leeds, London – and local calls fanned out into the rest of the Peloponnese. Within weeks the house was sold to Nikos and within months a third of it, the top floor, to us. On the face of it, this second transaction seemed simple enough: only one vendor, or to be precise two, Nikos and his younger brother, Andreas, selling to the two of us, Nina and me.

The last resident in the somewhat crumbling house in Kapodistriou, a narrow street in the old town of Nauplion, was an elderly lady called Eurydice. She appears to have been quiet, well-liked and solitary. The neighbours thought she was also a touch dotty, eccentric verging on the loony. The oddness mostly seems to have consisted of monologues from the balcony overlooking the street. "*Ti na kano*," she would cry, "What to do? What can I do? Will no one save me from the bombs?" As the Second World War had finished over forty years ago and Nauplion, although its inhabitants had suffered harshly, had seen few bombs, the old lady's piteous pleas were assumed to be evidence of senility mixed with war neurosis. To the end she was muttering about bombs, bombs in the roof, would no one save her. So Eurydice died and her twenty-seven relations, including the shortly to be monopode Uncle Vangelis, inherited the house.

She might, of course, have taken the other route much favoured by old Greek ladies: that of leaving the house to the Church. This, at first blush, would seem an admirable and sensible course for the pious: in fact, it almost invariably means that the Church does nothing and the house falls down. Why it is that old women in Greece are more religious than old men? Why it is that they seem to spend the last quarter of their lives wearing black? Why it is that in what remains a largely sexist, patriarchal society, the matriarch rules? These are mysteries akin to the dark underside of Greek life summed up so often by Greeks themselves with the words "Greece is not in Europe". They do not mean by that their not-quite-readiness to assume the full rigours of membership of the EC. It has more to do with the evil eye, the wise woman, the soothsayer, the fortune-teller and the seer. And perhaps with the *papas*, the priest. Binding spells and nereids may be patently pre-Christian but the ceremonies and the superstitions surrounding birth and death, the surprising dangers of the post-parturition forty days, for example, are closely interwoven: no seams where the pagan leaves off and the Orthodox Church takes over.

As we were soon to be reminded, Greece's is still essentially a cash economy. Ordinary cheques are not accepted and even the bimonthly electricity bill which has to be paid on the due date – usually it arrives the day before – has to be paid in cash, and it combines the actual electricity thought to have been consumed as well as the TV licence (whether or not you have a TV set, thus at a blow doing away with all the nonsense of detector vans and people thinking they have the right to choose not to pay for public service broadcasting) and the local and municipal, or mayor's, tax. Banks themselves are viewed with cautious ambivalence; this is not altogether surprising in the light of the Koskotas-Bank of Crete scandal. With high inflation, deposit accounts, yielding a decent dividend and until recently free of income tax, are popular; current and cheque accounts are not. For any significant purchase, you pay cash and take a reticule to hold the drachmas.

House buying is significant enough to require, at the proper times, large, stalwart reticules stuffed with notes. I dare say gold would be even better but we never seem to have collected sovereigns or thalers or krugerrands. Paying for a house is one thing, finding one for sale is quite another, and arguably more difficult. Ah ha, you say, what then are all those signs along the highway saying *poleitai, POLEITAI*? Does that not mean FOR SALE? Usually followed by an 01 Athens telephone number? Yes, indeed. But these are mostly barren lots of land, sometimes with a collapsed shed giving dubious evidence of habitation. Houses and apartments, other than in Athens and the Piraeus, where there are columns of advertisements in the newspapers, are learnt about by word of mouth, osmosis or death notices.

We thought we might start with the police station. I had

been reading some pamphlet enlarging on the helpful activities of the tourist police. If you're at a loss, ran the burden of the advice, if you think a taverna has overcharged you, or if you haven't found a place to stay, go to the tourist police. And so we did.

It was not strictly true that we were looking for a place to spend the night: indeed we were booked in at the Xenia Palace Hotel, high above the town in Acronauplion. But, on the other hand, we were looking for somewhere to stay, to rent or buy, admittedly for rather longer periods. It was this distinction rather than any simple linguistic misunderstanding that bedevilled our attempts at dialogue. The tourist policeman spoke some English but also what sounded like more German.

"You want rooms?" he said.

"No, thank you," I said. "We're looking for a house."

"Rooms," he said rather louder. "*Zimmer*."

"A house. To rent or buy."

"To bai?" he said rather as though it were Dubai and just as unlikely. "*Sygnome*. Excuse me." And off he went to get a colleague.

I confess that the improbability of expecting the police, even the tourist police, to have a list of available and desirable properties was assuming hideous proportions. You would not, after all, I said to myself, think the police station in Upper Street would take kindly to the notion of keeping ready to hand a list of Islington des. res. for the benefit of weird foreigners. A typical British assumption of superiority, I thought, as I tried to put together some basic building-bricks of Greek.

Once, in Morocco, we had driven some distance to Rabat and found ourselves surrounded by the Friday crowd waiting for King Hassan to ride to the mosque on his white horse. We parked the car, intending to find a café and a lavatory, but by then the crowd was pressing forward towards the Palace and we were engulfed and swept along. Rapid reconnaissance, as ready intelligence would have suggested, yielded no public conveniences. The square was cut off by police and soldiers. Excitement was mounting among the crowd, panic likewise for us. I ran across to a side entrance to the Palace, outside which an elegant gentleman in an exquisitely tailored grey silk suit and sunglasses was standing somewhat proprietorially. I asked for his help and explained our predicament in French. He rather nonplussed me by asking if we were American. He then, by way of explanation, said the WC was in the ancient mode, and called a turnkey who had large clusters of antique, oversize keys at his belt. As I thanked him warmly, he said with a half-smile that he did not suppose that he would have found a WC quite so easily outside Buckingham Palace. Touché. Why should we always imagine that when abroad we merit special treatment? At home we would be shocked at the idea of for-eigners being given privileges denied to the ordinary British citizen. What cheek, what presumption! To ask to use one of the loos at Buck House! I recognized my helpful Moroccan official later. He was Chief of Intelligence and Security and later still was to be executed because of his involvement in one of the many attempts to assassinate the king.

There was, I suppose, some small justification in imposing on the Nauplion police: we had been told there were no estate agents. The second police officer was not able to do much more for us although he understood, and was surprised by, our request. The best he could manage, after reflection and con-versation with other unseen but audible officials, was to suggest that we went to the *kafeneion* next to the bus station and asked for Spiro, who, he thought, had a house to sell.

There were two, perhaps three, places where buses stopped but only one ticket office, outside which the hourly buses to and from Athens began and ended their journeys. There were three almost adjacent shops where you could get drinks or coffee, but which of them was to be considered a *kafeneion*? Traditionally the *kafeneion* is a male preserve, the men sitting around for hours settling the affairs of the world in general and the politi-cal and economic future of Greece in particular while the more serious play cards, or backgammon, or chess, gambling solemnly and often heavily. The only one that had *kafeneion* painted on its rather opaque window had a complement of four slow-sipping elderly gentlemen, none of whom answered to the challenge of "*Kyrie Spiro?*" Not a blink, not a shifting of the head.

The second, on inspection, was not a *kafeneion* but a dark, narrow, snacks, ices, ouzo and beer fast-consumption facility. There were two girls, tourists with backpacks and sunburn, and three Greek men. Two of them answered to the name of Spiro. "Are you," I painfully enunciated my Greek and addressed the younger, more alert Spiro, "the Kyrios Spiro who wishes to sell his house, *to spiti tou?*" He lifted his eyes momentarily to the roof in that splendidly economical gesture of negation and mouthed a guttural "*Oxi.*" I turned to the other Spiro. "And you, sir?" He shook his head in assent and jumped to his feet – an exaggeration, he stumbled to his feet. He was quite old, sixty-five to seventy-five, and although it was a fairly hot day he was wearing a dark three-piece, buttoning up the waistcoat as he walked towards the street, gesturing us to wait.

We sat and ordered some coffee. We finished the coffee and sat some more. Just as I was about to pay the bill he reappeared with an older and scruffier person, his father, perhaps. More likely an uncle, on consideration. "And this," said three-piece suit with a flourish (I revised him down to sixty) "is the Kyrios Spiro who wishes to sell his house." He and Uncle Spiro both sat down, and more coffee was ordered. Time idled away. Hours seemed to pass. I ventured to ask where the house was, and Spiro the house-seller gestured vaguely towards the great prominence of Palamidi with its marvellous Venetian fortress. Could we perhaps go and see it? Yes, of course, but he was waiting for the key, or for his son, or both. Perhaps it was the key of his son. Lassitude came with two small (but large enough) bottles of ouzo, the equivalent of two trebles. Nina would not drink her share, I suspect because she did not want to swallow any water or ice, a continuing conundrum. I had mine neat. Suddenly we all stood up. Nothing had happened, no one had come; no son, no key, no explanation. Three-piece paid for the drinks and coffees and the older Spiro went out into the blinding sunlight and set off up the hill at a fair lick, climbing towards Acronauplion, but not, thankfully, up the more mountainous, and unbuilt on, save for the castle, Palamidi.

The higher we climbed, the steeper the incline and the faster went the dusty black boots ahead of us, like the hooves of a skittish old goat leaping up the mountainside. Right, past what must have been some sort of market; left, up a flight of uneven, marble steps (a *scala* in Greek). Right, up another precipitous *scala*. Left, more steps, steeper still. Up another flight, without pause. Then, suddenly, halt: we had arrived.

We were breathless, with exertion as much as excitement. Spiro blew his nose, without benefit of handkerchief, and grinned. "*Na to*," he said. "Here it is!" At first blush it was difficult to make out what "it" was. It was not, patently, a house. The plot was rather small and somewhat vertiginous. A horizontal of cement and concrete, with some straggling vegetation, may or may not have covered a room in which a gnome might have stood head high. We were never to find out: the key was lost. Then, part of the rock itself, there was a vertical face of some fifteen feet and then on top of that what looked like a not very commodious outside privy. Although quite high up, the view was negligible because the sea and the main part of the old town was round the corner and invisible.

Spiro continued to grin and hop from foot to foot with excitement, a diminutive, elderly but spirited satyr. His face was not so much ugly as odd. The two halves, right and left, seemed to have nothing to do with each other. When he looked in the mirror he must always have seen himself as no one else did, completely reversed. His asymmetrical smile lingered on. He pointed out that at the lower level there was water and electricity. "How much?" I asked, trying to impose some semblance of reality. "One-two million drachmas." He cavorted round the horizontal space conjuring up visions of building, floor upon floor. "*Polla domatia*. Many, many rooms." Large gestures now suggested a minor palace, ballrooms, swimming-pools. I looked at the outside privy again. It clearly had no water, no drains and no room for a cesspit so presumably it was not a privy. We climbed up to it. It was a minuscule shack. "A butt and ben," said Nina knowledgeably.

"*S'aresei?* It pleases you? You like it, eh? Look." He paced the lower terrace, gesturing with his hands to indicate two, three, four floors. "Hundreds of square metres. Very good. Electrics. Water. A very good price."

"How much did you say it was?"

"Where do you come from, eh? *Nea Yorki?* Melbourne? Munich?"

"London."

"*Po, po, po.* Very cheap for you. Three-four million drachmas."

"Thank you," I said and added dishonestly, "we'll think about it." It was still hot and dusty though the sun was going down. A small part-poodle bitch with heavily distended teats barked and chased us unconvincingly as we stumbled down the steps towards the street. Spiro skipped down alongside us.

"*Pamftino.* Cheap as can be. Should really be seven-eight million. For you everything at five-six million. Everything. Dirt cheap."

We decided to phone Plato, our oldest friend in Greece. Not without some tinge of Athenian hauteur, he said, "I told you it might be difficult to buy a house in Greece." Earlier, in Athens, when we had revealed our plan he had raised his eyebrows in a way that contrived to suggest we were embarking on a piece of naïve folly but he was too polite to say so. Our Athenian lawyer was later to call us and the enterprise "adventurous", but she meant the same thing. "Try the bars," Plato said. "Or rather, go to the best bar in town and ask Phaidon. Tell him you're a friend of mine."

There was no doubt that Phaidon's was the best bar in Nauplion. It had been the first to stay open late, till four a.m.; it had been the first to serve proper meals as well as snacks throughout the evening; to cater for Greeks and foreigners, locals and visitors; to welcome Naupliot families as well as solitary tourists, male or female. It was a serious drinking bar – beer from Pilsen, single malts – but also a splendid place for children, for whom Phaidon made elaborate fruit-juice cocktails with exciting trimmings. It was fun, it was decent but it was also a fine place, both parties being willing, for liaison and sexual by-play, opening moves, hetero or homo. Phaidon presided over all this from the horseshoe bar, hard-working, swift and neat, polyglot, apparently with eyes and ears giving him 360-degree surveillance, keeping three or four conversations, in as many languages, going at the same time while supervising the waiters and greeting newcomers. It was, it is, a nightly *tour de force*.

At first it had been quite a small operation but Phaidon had built it up by painstaking meticulous effort and the subtlety of his personal style: courteous, sensitive, wise and discreet. Behind the charm and serenity of the efficient host, schooled in the hotels and restaurants of Germany, France, Britain and North America, lies a reserved, perhaps rather cautious man, wary of giving too much of himself away. Once committed to friendship, he makes a very good friend. He has made a considerable success of the bar-restaurant which is now the size of a large eating-house inside with as many tables outside for summer use. He also knows everything that is going on in Nauplion. For example, houses for sale.

"Houses?" he said. "No, I don't think so. Not at the moment." He turned away to mix a sangria for some young Dutch folk. "But," he said, looking at us from the other side of the bar and switching from Dutch to English, "there may be the pharmacist's house." He handed over the jug to a waiter who led the Dutch group to a table outside. "The old pharmacist died a couple of days ago. I don't think the family have decided what to do with the house." A thinning of the lips, a very Greek but slight shrug with smile, along the lines of Lord, what fools these mortals be. "But it's worth a try. I'll phone one of the cousins in Mycenae." He looked at his watch and went away to refill an ouzo and a whisky.

Five minutes later he returned. "No, the cousin was out. But I spoke to his wife." Another Greek facial shrug, meaning we can't win them all, better luck next time, eh? "And the family have decided to keep the house. Not sell it." He poured us some more drinks, all on the house. "I'll ask around and see what I can find."

II

When viewed dispassionately on a bad day Nauplion is a rather
scruffy little port, used infrequently by cargo ships, mostly
Russian, taking aboard fruit and potatoes, comparatively rarely
by yachts (it is said because of high mooring and docking fees)
and only occasionally by cruise ships, the largest of which have
to lie off. On a good day it is the loveliest town in Greece.
Walking up and down and around the old town enjoying the
views of advancing and receding layers of mountains is a never-
ending delight. In some weather, hot and misty, none are
visible and Nauplion seems to stand at the edge of a vast sea. At
other times the shoreline of the bay is well-marked and the first
row of hills clear, with to the north the Frankish (roughly
equivalent to Crusader or Norman) castle of Argos improbably
perched on a slope, as though it were at any moment, when
unobserved, going to slip down a couple of hundred feet. On a

clear winter's day the mountains, a few fringed with snow, stand in rank upon rank marching to the horizon.

The jumble of Byzantine-tiled roofs, houses of several generations but somehow of a piece, one-time mosques and domed orthodox churches, the narrow streets bisected at right angles by lanes and marble stairs climbing up the side of the hill on which the town is built – all this makes Nauplion memorable. But it is the fine Venetian buildings, the delicate decorations on the preserved but crumbling Turkish fountains, the astonishing marble-floored *plateia* with bank, pharmacy, restaurants, cafés, foreign-language newspaper and bookshop, and its Venetian lion of St Mark, much-patted and used as a resident goalkeeper by children who otherwise speed by on bicycles and whatever kind of skates are in vogue, that eat into the heart. Over the years, having spent nights and the odd weekend there, we found ourselves drawn back again and again.

For the last few years Nauplion has had the benefit of a lively and energetic mayor (a member of *Nea Demokratia* or New Democracy for those who care about Greek party politics and in the Community we all should) who plants trees and enriches parks. The town displays a distinguished looking high court house, the first primary school in Greece, the first public library and was, indeed, the first capital of independent Greece. Nauplion, rightly and properly, is a heritage area. We did not want to abandon it and our search but the weather was becoming fearsomely hot and lethargy was adding to our disappointment.

Perhaps sensing our increasingly crestfallen spirits and our evident frustration at there being no way, apparently, short of selective assassination, of making property available for sale, Phaidon, ever a perceptive man, threw us a bone.

"Well, there's always Nikos' house," he said. "It needs doing up." This last was added less as deprecation than for the sake of accuracy and to make sure that everything was on all fours. There had been doubt too, in the accompanying shrug and half-smile and this, added to a certain reluctance to put forward the suggestion – I could only assume Nikos' house had been lying there in wait for us all along – must constitute, I supposed, some kind of warning. In all events, we had nothing to lose. We would just look.

Where was Nikos to be found? Who he? Which and what his house?

It's difficult now to believe that there was a time when we didn't know Nikos Nondas. Of course we must have met him, or at least seen him at the bar, a tall, dark and remarkably handsome man in his mid-thirties with a sunny smile and a fine roving eye for the girls. I often felt, sitting with him in the *plateia*, that he had some special in-built telepathic receptor. He would stop in mid-sentence, rotate his eyes, head, neck and shoulders so that all were focusing on some passing beauty – it was always a foreign, not a Greek girl and he seemed to know this before looking – and then would swing back, eyes remote, unfocussed, to the unfinished sentence and matter in hand. This would make for protracted meetings, much interrupted if the tourist flow were good. Of course, this was long before he became engaged, let alone married, to Célestine and the father of a beautiful blue-eyed blonde-haired belle Hélène; before he rejoiced in the joint responsibilities of fatherhood and entre-preneurial business.

There were lots of ways of approaching the house that might be for sale. The old town is fairly densely packed and covers an easily walkable area. Most of the cross-streets seem to run par-allel to each other, as do some of the intersecting narrower alleys which turn themselves into stairs or *scala* as they climb up the hill. The higher you climb the more you realize that the orientation has radically changed: the plan is not really rec-tangular and you are not facing the direction you expected. Nothing is quite where you thought it was.

We decided on the simplest set of directions.

"You start from the square, the *plateia*," Phaidon said, "with Noufara behind you." Noufara was the Greek-Italian restau-rant, notable for its rigatoni with four-cheeses sauce. The *plateia* was, not very originally (although being Nauplion perhaps this *was* the original), called *Syntagma*, Constitution Square. "You go up to the next street, that's *Staiko Staikopoulou*. You turn left past Vassili's" – a taverna with good stuffed tomatoes, cheese pies and rabbit stew – "and you pass tavernas on the left and on the right. Past the Pink Panther ice-cream place and then you see a cleaner's on the right and a baker's on the left and a *scala* on the right going up. That's *Kokkinou*, Red Street. I suppose it's really the street of the red steps, or red marble." He was called away by a waiter to deal with some complication. "Well, you go up the steps – you know it might be the *scala* of the Red King – to the next street and the house is at the corner on the left. Or," he said, looking at our faces, "since it's hot weather" (the temperature had reached forty degrees during the afternoon) "don't go up the stairs. Keep along *Staikopoulou* till you see a road going up to the right and that takes you into St Spyridon's Square. You'll see the church on your right and the narrow street going past it. Take that street, go past the bullet holes showing where Kapodistrias was assassinated in 1831. You know about Kapodistrias?"

"Yes, first president of Greece."

"First *governor of the Greeks*." Phaidon, like most Greeks, was a didact at heart. "Anyway, second house past the church *Agiou Spyridiou* on the right and there you are."

The next morning we walked down from the Xenia Palace, looking speculatively and carefully at the splendid array of houses, the assortment of multi-coloured Byzantine-tiled roofs, the varying steepnesses of the runs of marble steps. Nikos' house was, clearly, in the Old Town, and that was where we wished to be. But what shape, size, pretensions? At least we had no preconceptions based on estate agents' hype. There were of course no estate agents to hype. Would it be a hovel like Spiro's shack or a small stone-built cottage, two-up, two-down, as it were, dominated by larger, taller houses? Or, improbably, would it be like one of these rather grand, if worn, three-storeyed houses with tall, wooden-shuttered windows and balconies of marble and ornate wrought-iron? What sort of view would it have? Would the sea be visible, or the mountains, or the castle of Palamidi? Would it have one of these shady, secretive court-yards? Or better still a secret garden? Or an arch of bougainvillaea springing across the street to the house opposite? Perhaps with painted wooden ceilings like the ones glimpsed as we walked past while the shutters were being closed?

Our eyes firmly fixed at balcony level, deciding whether we preferred the geometric wrought-iron or the designs of lions, griffons or winged horses, we were very nearly knocked down by a demented motor-scooter accelerating against the admittedly not very heavy one-way traffic with which pedestrians share the narrow street of Staikopoulou. It was a necessary reminder; pedal- and motorcyclists in Greece drive as though traffic instructions do not apply to them. Indeed, perhaps they don't. And motorbikes revel in noise: silencers are cissy.

Up a short, steepish slope the little square of St Spyridon was tranquil and charming: a large, shady tree and the heavy scent of honeysuckle, a little white church, a sixteenth-century Turkish fountain, a *scala*, according to the notice, leading to the Catholic church, a place of worship not often to be found in Greek towns, neighbours calling to each other across the *plateia* from their balconies, a few neatly parked cars, a handful of children playing quietly, an elderly, white-bearded priest – all was serenity, order and harmony.

"*Kalimera*," we said to each in turn. "*Kalimera sas*," they replied, friendly and smiling. We walked up and turned right at the church into a narrow lane, all white light and coloured shade. Montmartre. Vence. Naples. To the left there must have been houses climbing up the hill, but all that was visible were the houses in the street itself, ochres and cream and dusty pink, crumbling at the edges and contrasting with the sharp white lines of the church opposite with its bell-rope casually looped round an iron curlicue on a windowframe. There were the bullet scars protected by glass, and a marble plaque to explain the significance. On the left stood a couple of smaller houses, the second one a touch derelict. Another, rather beautiful Turkish fountain in decorated stone, the inscription in elegant Arabic script, then a patch of wasteland and out of the weeds and self-sown straggly flowers a Turkish dome; a mosque perhaps or, from the outside concave curve of the front wall, perhaps a hammam. Padlocked, deserted and derelict. Why? Preservation, conservation, rejection? Behind it a garden with trailing geraniums and a cascade of roses led up to more houses and then, much higher still, to the fortifications of Acronauplion. Opposite this there was another old Nauplion house with a balcony bright with flowering plants and neat lines of washing.

All this careful slow, closely observed cataloguing, closely observed from balconies and behind lace curtains as much as by us, had to come to an end. We could postpone the confrontation no longer. For one thing there had, for some time, been a rhythmic and increasingly loud banging. For another we had, you might say, arrived. I am not sure now whether excitement or apprehension was uppermost; trepidation, perhaps.

Nikos sprang out from the house as though there was no front door. There was no front door. He was carrying what looked like a sledgehammer.

"Mr Austen," he said, "Mrs Nina. Phaidon told me you will come by to see my house." Nikos had recently retired from the sea, at the age of thirty-seven. He had been a chief engineer in tankers and had decided to take his pension money and invest it and himself in another occupation. He had chosen to buy an old house and do it up. His English was idiomatic and fluent, if occasionally fractured and eccentric. Nikos had no trouble in making himself understood. "You see," he said, smiling engagingly, "much, much restorating. Much, much," he gestured expansively and then coughed. "Also much, much dust." He took out a packet of cigarettes, offered them around. We refused, muttering that we had given up. "Yes," he lit up and coughed again, "many people give up. Not so much in Greece. Me, I like to smoke."

Nikos' house, it was true to say, needed rather a lot of doing up. It was not so much rundown as tumbledown. It was still standing, but without much assurance of solidity. There was the impression of gaps, holes in the fabric which might open up at any minute and run like ladders in a nylon stocking. The substance itself was insubstantial. And yet it occupied its dominant corner position with an air of rightness and certainty.

We stood back to look at the house as a whole, but the street was too narrow. We climbed up the next flight of the *scala* and looked down. We walked down the steps towards Staikopoulou and looked up. It was impossible to get it in one frame: it was too large and too tall. We returned to the front and I peered and peeked and tentatively tested the remaining floorboards. As Nikos talked on, I began to see the place for what it had been.

It was a high three-storeyed building of handsome proportions, probably nineteenth-century, possibly eighteenth, but with much earlier foundations. It might have been a rich merchant's house, in the Venetian style, with four large storerooms on the ground floor and two living floors above, each with six windows and a French-windowed balcony overlooking the narrow street, another five windows and a balcony at the top looking out towards the harbour, and two windows, on each floor, at the side giving on to the marble *scala* going down to the next street. There was also, I could see, a cellar, made somewhat larger by exploratory and not very expert excavation work and some wobbly remains of floors and ceilings within.

Nikos arranged an assault course of rickety ladders and near-horizontal planks. Climbing, and balancing, gingerly – there was a decided list and tilt which made the rungs of the topmost ladder which were still intact slant alarmingly – I reached the top floor, that is my eyes were level with what had been the top balcony. I could see a pattern of tiled roofs, the dome of a one-time mosque, balconies spilling with flowering plants and green bushes, masts in the harbour, two spots, hinting at blue, which might be the sea, and, craning dangerously around, almost a semicircle of mountains.

"Good view," said Nikos. I was not sure whether he was asking or telling me. "Better higher up." I declined the invitation and climbed slowly and carefully down.

"A nice old painted wooden ceiling," I said. "You'll want to keep that." Nikos gestured dismissively. "Yes, yes, but look." I looked. There were boards everywhere else hanging down or fallen down and glimpses of rafters above.

It was charming, picturesque; a lovely old house, ripe for restoration. Just what we were looking for – well, almost. I was enchanted.

*

"It must be the heat," said Nina. She looked rather pale herself. "You must be drugged insensible with it. That and the retsina last night." Nina had a theory, taken over from our doctor son, Robert, that overdoses of retsina were responsible for damage to kidneys, livers and lights, provoked gravel and gout and probably led to Alzheimer's. I don't suppose that Robert really thought this but he had said something as a joke and Nina almost believed him. Anyway it was a weighty stick to flourish at a dazed husband.

"Dazed. That's what you are," she said. "Bemused. Crazed."

"Enchanted," I said.

"All right; enchanted. But in the worst sense. Got at by the little people."

We were sitting having an ouzo at the Blue Chairs, the only café on the south side of the square and much frequented by disputatious members of Pasok and silent readers of yesterday's *Guardian*.

"I admit," I said fairly, "it's little more than a shell. But it's in a marvellous position and *au fond* it's a fine house."

"*Au fond*," said Nina scathingly, "it's unstable." She resisted the temptation to add "like you". A look was enough. "Didn't you see Nikos' excavations, rootling away at the foundations?"

"Oh that," I said. "I expect he knows what he's doing."

"You do, do you?" said Nina. "I don't suppose he's ever worked on a house before."

"He's an engineer, isn't he?"

"Ship's," she said scornfully. "Marine not civil."

Now here's a rum thing. Nina, who read Philosophy, Politics and Economics at Oxford and writes novels, lays claim to engineering nous on the basis of heredity. "As an engineer's daughter," she will say, and immediately acquire a spurious expertise. But her father, like Nikos, had been a chief engineer at sea; a ship's engineer, admittedly of a grand kind – Commodore Chief Engineer of the P&O in its post-war heyday. So, I said quietly to myself, what's suddenly so wrong with marine engineers?

"I thought," I said aloud, "marine engineers could turn their hands to just about anything."

There was no reply.

"All that will be looked into by surveyors and people," I said loftily.

"What surveyors?" she said, glancing critically round the *plateia*. The pharmacist paused to greet an elderly acquaintance. The large restaurateur tried to entice a group of Italian students to the awning-covered tables owned by his taverna – Greek cuisine a speciality. Various people were arguing loudly either about football teams or Mr Andreas Papandreou.

"We'll see our lawyer right away," I said. "She'll know what to do."

I had said almost exactly the same thing to Nikos.

"Why go to Athens for a lawyer?" he said. "I don't like lawyers. Lawyers eat money. You can use mine."

I tried to explain: it took a lot of explaining. Maybe this was our first conflict of cultures, I thought, but maybe it wasn't. It would be better for all of us, I said. We would be better protected and so would he. Our lawyer would, in a manner of speaking, stand surety for us, guarantee our good intentions and therefore his money if negotiations were to go ahead. We were babes in arms when it came to Greek property law, and so on.

"But why?" Nikos said, a heartfelt plea. "Why two lawyers eating everything? Don't you trust me?"

"Yes, of course," I said prosily. "One must always trust people until that trust is betrayed. But it is only prudent and sensible for everyone's sake . . ."

"Prosy old fool," Nina muttered an encouraging aside.

"Sensible, safe. *Po, po, po,*" said Nikos. "Friends are safe. You trust me is sensible. You ask anyone. Phaidon. Anyone." He took breath and changed tack. "Lots of others are interested. Some French people. A German professor. A Greek family from Athens. You must be quick and make up your mind. I like you Mr Austen and Mrs Nina but this is business too for me."

He had explained his plans; probably three or four apartments on the top two floors, some shops on the ground floor and a bakery with an entrance on the *scala*.

I had said that we might be interested in the top floor; without prejudice, of course. Nina thought I was fair, barking mad. I admitted to myself that my vision of the house had about as much validity as one of those would-be archaeological descriptions, a Bronze Age palace, for example, conjured up out of a rubble of stones and the remains of one pillar; it was a highly imaginative reconstruction.

III

Nikos had given us a month. He would hold the house, in deference to our interest, for a calendar month and after that all deals were off; it would be up for grabs and, we were given to understand, the competition would be fierce. I cannot pretend that I fully believed this; on the other hand, I did not wish to gamble on disbelieving it.

Our Athenian lawyer was delighted to hear from us. Nauplion, eh? The Old Town! *Poly oraio.* Athina, an extremely pretty, lively woman in her forties, warm-hearted, voluble, efficient and enthusiastic, had one dominant eccentricity: a certain waywardness with her English tenses. It was rather as though she were a spirit moving freely in time leaving the rest of us place, time and date-bound and inevitably lost. Her enthusiasm wavered a bit when I hinted at the state of the house. "Why," she said over a rather indistinct and noisy telephone line, "didn't you find a house ready to go in? There will be thousands. In lovely places; islands like Mykonos. My sister had a house there and I too one day have built a little house there. But not this year. Perhaps next. Why you want an old house, falling down? Why? Why?"

I placated her partly by explaining that at our age the mainland was more sensible. I enlarged; it would seem perverse, particularly now that we were in our sixties, when hospitals and newspapers (for the obituary columns) loom large, to renounce the town, the city, the *polis*. In any case we hadn't yet made up – Nina interjected a loud "No *indeed*" off-mike – our minds, and that we were, even now, going to explore Evia, the Pelion, even Skiathos where we had heard an Austrian countess had a villa for sale.

"Yes, yes," she said, "very nice places. Very beautiful. Lots of houses. Ready-made, new."

We would be in touch, I said, after our little tour. No reasonable stone would be left unturned, no bill of particulars unexamined. We were, after all, sane, responsible, mature people, always taking proper note of our advisers' advice .

Evia was fine; well-wooded, some dramatic mountainous scenery, some charming, rather old-fashioned resorts catering for Greeks of a certain age, all rather reminiscent of Switzerland, a Switzerland on the sea.

The Pelion was lovely; much-treed, the dense forests climbing the slopes providing a credible home for centaurs and satyrs, or for bears and wolves, glorious mountainous scenery, rich orchards, dramatic views of the Sporades, fine traditional houses of a distinctive type with outside timbers supporting, at an angle, the overhang of the roof, and new Tyrolean-style villas. It was a bit reminiscent of Austria, an Austria on the sea.

Skiathos was a holiday island with marvellous sandy beaches and a less than enthralling interior. We had been to Skiathos before, in the early seventies, just after I had spent ten years with Greece and Turkey as important parts of my BBC World Service parish. A friend who was a senior Greek civil servant arranged for the Greek government to pay our holiday hotel bill. I found myself in the disagreeable position of turning down what was clearly a generous offer. As he saw it, as no doubt any Greek would have seen it, it was an insult: I was accusing him of trying to bribe me. In return for a hotel bill, I was saying, I would be in the debt of the Greek government and feel obliged to broadcast favourable comments. It was nonsense of course. It was just that I, being in the BBC, was a public servant and was constrained to behave like one. It was a classic misunderstanding, a conflict of cultures and manners. My friend was affronted and hurt. For ten years we barely spoke to each other and then he agreed to come to the small party for my sixtieth birthday we were holding in Athens. I was delighted; it would be a chance to make up. Three days before the party he fell down dead of a sudden and massive coronary.

If we were to look at islands, Skiathos had much to recommend it, not least a well-spoken-for house for sale. It also had a pharmacist who gave Nina some antibiotics for a minor infection. In the middle of the night she woke up, her face swollen to balloon proportions. We summoned the duty doctor at about three in the morning and he came put-putting up on his scooter. He sat on the bed, pumped Nina full of cortisone intravenously, smoked cigarettes and told us his life's story as he waited with us to see the swelling go down. He had specialized, he said, lighting another cigarette, as a chest and lung surgeon but all Greek doctors early in their careers are assigned to a rural village or to an island. He had drawn Skiathos and he spent most of the summer months looking after tourists who had eaten or sunned themselves unwisely. He was waiting for a suitable appointment in Athens – or Salonika at a pinch, but he was Athenian – and such appointments were rare. In the meantime his daughters were dug in at school in Skiathos and were less easily transferable.

"Difficulties," he said, clicking his tongue. "Problems."

Nina's problems were meanwhile diminishing. In the two hours he had spent with us, Miss Piggy had given way to a slightly plumper than usual version of the famous novelist's face I love to live with. Reading a recent interview in the *Observer* which spoke of its "improbable beauty", I thought how much more improbable had been this bloated distortion.

Like a character out of ITMA, the doctor said, "I go. I come back," and added that he was, not surprisingly, very tired.

He was still tired and still eager to sit on the bed and smoke a cigarette or two when he returned at lunchtime. As indeed he was when he reappeared in the late evening. He found Nina gratifyingly normal, fit, cured. He warned against ever using this particular antibiotic again and suggested she tell our GP about it when we returned home. Nina threw the bottle away and we both immediately forgot its proper name.

I asked him how much we owed him, rightly impressed by his prompt and efficient service. He wanted to know if we were insured.

"Insurances are trouble," he said. "I make this out to four home visits on two days. Then no problem."

His bill was inadequately small but he refused to take anything more; just a glass of the emergency, duty-free whisky.

"It is good to talk," he said and then, enunciating a profound truth, "In islands you have sea all round you." With winds, storms and high seas, he explained, you were cut off; the airport closed. Even surgical crises could not make helicopters fly in impassable weather.

"Problems, " he said and enumerated another, shuddering. "Winter; just all the same people."

The next day we tracked down the man who had the countess's key. He was also the mayor and, one rather gathered, the local big-shot entrepreneur.

"Is she selling?" he said, swivelling round to glare at me, tense in the back seat, as he drove us round hairpin bends, the sea a few hundred feet below.

"I don't know," I said. " Perhaps she's going to let it."

"A *very* nice family," he said as though ours couldn't conceivably be. "They've come many, many years. The children were small." He paused suspiciously. "You know them?"

It seemed too complicated to explain that we were friends of friends of theirs .

"Yes," I lied.

"They well? When they coming?"

Luckily, with a swoop round one last bend and a screeching of brakes, we had arrived.

"I leave you here," he gestured largely, embracing mountain behind, sea in front, the world his and the countess's oyster. "I pick you up in thirty-forty minutes. Down there," he pointed to some precipitous steps cut in the rock, "private *plage*."

It was not really, of course: in Greece the coast belongs to the state. But it was difficult enough to get down to from the house and from elsewhere virtually impossible. It was a lovely holiday house for a large family with children. It would have been marvellous to have had it when our children were growing up. That's what it was: a Greek island version of the seaside holiday house at Frinton or Studlands Bay with lots of British ex-pats and a surprising number of South Africans for neighbours.

By now we had fully understood the limitation of islands. "No," said Nina firmly. "And not just because of emergencies. As the good doctor put it: just all the same people."

It had been marginally cooler on the island, if anything in what was one of the worst heatwaves this century could be considered cooler with the thermometer still hovering around thirty-eight degrees. In Athens it was forty, baking hot, and the taxis were on strike. Just walking the two blocks from Syntagma to our hotel with two light cases was a Herculean effort, energy seeping away with every dragging step. The air was heavy and offensive with fumes and particles of pollution. The *nephos* was a solid lid, tightly containing the smog within the mountain-circled bowl of the city. Many people died; the rest wheezed, gasped, drooped and complained. We tried to sleep with the sour, stale taste of the air-conditioning in our mouths.

The next morning we set off for Nauplion in Athina's car. It was a two- to three-hour drive from Athens, almost due south. She had brought along with her a consulting engineer of some eminence and considerable experience both of constructing and restoring buildings in Athens. Pericles was a neat, slim, quiet-spoken, smiling man of great charm. Rising fifty, he exuded calm assurance. His English was good and his use of words and tenses precise. Athina drove, as she did everything, with considerable, and idiosyncratic, verve. Pericles took over, as he said, because he knew some shorter cuts for getting through the Athenian traffic. By the Corinth Canal and the entrance to the Peloponnese the skies were beginning to clear, the suffocating sulphurous yellow giving way to pipe-clay white cirrus cloud and the bright, bright blue in streaks beyond.

The long, broad and fertile Argive plain was hot and some-times steamy but the orange trees marched on, unpolluted, towards the sea.

"They planted too many," said Pericles. "Of course, it's an easier crop. Not much work at all except the picking, and that's done by gypsies and foreign students. And the irrigating. The Community paid for the irrigation and now they are having to pay the farmers to destroy their fruit. There are too many oranges in the Community and not much of an export market except Russia and Eastern Europe. And they're short of cur-rency. There are some barter deals but not very profitable."

Pericles had spent a year of his time in the army in Nauplion and loved the place. Athina agreed with us that it was a gem, one of the few surviving towns in Greece worth preserving. I think all of us felt a lift of the spirits as the great castle of Palamidi emerged clearly, if rather somnolently, from the heat-haze.

We parked between the mayor's office and the harbour. It was still hot but appreciably less so than in Athens and the afternoon breeze had sprung up, making strolling quite agree-able. We were late for our appointment with Nikos .

Athina said, "No matter. We're in Greece. Time is different." She should know, I thought. Pericles chimed in with agree-ment, "No; it doesn't matter. People cannot expect that when you're driving down from Athens the timing will be exact."

He led us nonetheless at a clipping pace across the *plateia* and then, at my suggestion, up one of the gentler approaches to Kapodistriou.

"Nauplion is very, very good," said Athina. "*Poly, Poly oraio.* Very beautiful. Very old. Very historical. Important for us Greeks; the beginning of modern Greece. That's the church, isn't it, where Kapodistrias is shot and the balls are in the wall."

"*Agiou Spyridiou*," I said.

"He was stabbed," said Pericles.

"Stabbed *and* shot," I said.

"Those Maniots were a violent lot," said Nina.

"The brothers . . ." I stumbled after the name.

"Mavromichalis," said Pericles.

"Two brothers," added Athina. "The others are dead before."

We had reached Kokkinou. We all looked up the *scala* and exclaimed how lovely and picturesque and romantic it looked.

"And here," I said, persuading them to redirect and refocus, "is Number Nineteen."

The whole world seemed to go still. You could have heard a lizard move. Or rather you could have done had not Nikos and his brother Andreas bounded out of two separate openings and called out great cries of delight at Mrs Nina's and Mr Austen's return. Welcome too to our friends, relatives and professional advisers. Nikos looked defiantly at Pericles. Andreas, a younger, darker, jokier version of his brother, a deck officer ("like captain but not captain") with the lack of diffidence that characterized him had made a beeline for Athina who was obviously Pericles' decidedly dishy wife or girlfriend, just along for the ride. I managed to introduce them hastily before Andreas got handbagged. But I saw it was taking them some time to sort out who was really who or, more important, what.

Taking another look at Athina, something altogether different was amiss; not the fierce, powerful lady lawyer I had expected but under her tan a very pale and almost tentative person. She had peered through one of the openings and blanched. We were not often to see her taken aback or indecisive, indeed nothing is more foreign to her nature. On reflection, she was not being indecisive now. She was just wondering how best to dissuade these wayward foreigners from making even greater fools of themselves. She was not, I know, debating whether to leave us unprotected, although well she might. She was a high-powered marine lawyer employed as senior legal adviser by a famous shipowner. She had a few private clients and we had been wished on to her, so to speak, by close and dear friends who were on her privileged list.

For their sake, and increasingly for ours, she was fiercely protective.

"Look," she said, urgently, conspiratorially, "there are other houses. Near here. With walls. Modern bathrooms. You would walk in. All ready. We went this afternoon?"

"Yes, all right," I said. "But I like it. I like being in the middle of the town. And I love the house itself. It's very handsome, isn't it?" If I was hoping for a reassuring nod from Athina, I was not going to get it: she was glaring in a disbelieving way at a rhombus of revealed and crumbling fabric. "I know it's old and much in need of repair," I continued firmly, "but that can be put to rights." In retrospect I am amazed at my confidence. "The walls can be restored, rebuilt if needs be. Modern bathrooms can be put in . . ."

"Look," Athina whispered insistently. I was tempted to take her literally, to poke my head inside and see whether Pericles, who had ducked through one of the openings, had made some really calamitous discovery, but I fixed my eyes on hers. "Look," she repeated. "We won't know these people. We will not know what they can do. We have said nothing. We leave, see other houses and later we have talked. But now, nothing." She put her finger to her lips.

Andreas had shifted his attention and not inconsiderable charm to Nina who was questioning him about the extent, and indeed the need, the rationale, for the excavating programme which had produced a significantly larger hole in the cellar. It looked to me like the beginnings of Nauplion's first ice-rink: the brothers Nondas were nothing if not enterprising, enterprising and innovative – some might say daring.

It seemed time to make a move. It was also a quarter past three. "What about some lunch?" I said. "No, no," shouted Nikos, his voice coming as it were from the top floor, if there had been any floor left. "You are our guests. You like fish? We go and eat fish."

It had been a *politesse* and he had neither waited for nor expected a reply. Everyone likes fish. Except a handful of us whose relationship with fish is a mite more complicated. In my case it is nothing as simple as aversion or revulsion. I like the look of fish in sea or river. I can even look at them dead on marble slabs without a sense of disgust. I love shellfish (crustacea, testacea, molluscs, whatever) but it's the finny, scaly ones that bother me or, more precisely, have bothered me on and off for much of my life – and mostly on. I know, I hear myself bleating, I'm the wrong way round: most people are worried about shellfish but for me it's fish without shells.

At private school, an eager seven-year-old boarder, I tried to persuade the headmaster's wife that fish-eating was against my religion. I had tried this ploy earlier, and equally unsuccessfully, at my pre-prep school with rice pudding. The result was the same: the dreadful dish was re-presented. I persevered, under duress ate it, and vomited. It was decided that I had something, then very fashionable, called "acidosis" and I was dosed with hearty helpings of Glucose D and Virol and was still told to eat up my fish and rice pudding .

I suppose we all know early on that we need to be tough, inventive and resilient to survive; certainly that was true in the English boarding schools of the thirties. I learnt to regurgitate the repulsive lumps into handkerchieves, or lavatories if they were convenient, after lengthy and judicious chewing, meanwhile carrying on the other segment of my party piece, a running dialogue. "O Matron." We were much into the vocative, we classical chaps at Seafield Preparatory School for the sons of gentlemen at Cooden Beach, Bexhill-on-Sea. "O Matron. Matron, you don't mean *all* of it, do you? I think I want to go to the lavatory. May I be excused? . . . Oh, Matron . . . If I just finish another mouthful . . . Really, Matron, I'm going to burst . . ."

"Yes," I said to Nikos, "fish would be lovely."

IV

There were, of course, plenty of other houses, Athina said as we drove along the road towards Epidavros, but she had decided that one more was enough for the day. This was a marvellous property belonging to the client of a friend of hers who was looking for a quick sale. It was, she had been told, in excellent condition and was "very luxe".

I said, grumbling, that it was not very close to Nauplion. We had already travelled some twenty-five kilometres. The countryside was magnificent and the views were spectacular but wasn't it perhaps the tiniest bit remote? Athina, a city girl by election and conditioning, pooh-poohed the notion. At that moment Pericles wrenched the wheel to the left and braked. We had almost missed the half-concealed turning. He steered us along a minor serpentine road. In fact we were climbing, winding along an escarpment which consisted of a series of linked S-bends with sheer drops and dramatic panoramas, marred only by the collection of slow-moving, uphill, and dangerously careering, downhill, marble lorries and the rather more than occasional rubbish dump. Nina was looking pale and pained. "Why?" I could see her mouthing. "Why am I always on the precipice side?"

It cannot, of course, be true, unless she changes her seat on the return journey, which would argue that she was daft rather than vertiginous. Nonetheless, like buttered toast landing sticky-side down, it does seem that more of the time she is defying mathematical logic and sitting on the precipice side. The only sensible explanation, apart from sheer, wilful cussedness, is that neither she nor anyone else takes any notice when she is on the protected side .

We were into the village almost before we were aware of it. There was a handwritten card saying "Welcome" in Greek, German and English, about an equal number of Pasok and Nea Demokratia flags and posters, looking messy rather than colourfully competitive, a crossroads, a new and rather large church and a small *plateia* with one unhealthy-looking plane tree. It was decidedly bleak. It is not uncommon to find a Greek village which at first sight, and from the outside, lacks charm and is short on visible *joie de vivre*. But this one was both bleak and sullen. The men sitting outside the *kafeneion* regarded us closely and without any change of expression. They had decided, one was given to understand, to opt out of the Greek conventions of hospitality. They could hardly have become bored with the constant press of visitors.

Pericles wound down his window and addressed one of the lugubrious elders and was rewarded with a gesture, a hand with cigarette in it pointing across to the other side of the square. We got out and walked across to the tree. Under it, at a small table, sat three men talking loudly and boisterously and laughing. Seeing us approach, one of them, a tall thin man with a parrot's beak of a nose and clusters of improbable white curls on his head, got up and greeted us in English.

"I wasn't at all sure when you'd get here," he said. "So I plonked myself down with an ouzo and read the paper. Then of course I got to talking politics with the locals. It's our national pastime, you know."

I found myself mumbling an apology for keeping him waiting.

"Don't think a bit of it," he said with a large, flapping gesture. "I didn't really notice the time. I knew I couldn't miss you. Few cars come along that road after sunset; indeed very few strange cars come to the village at all. Anyway, I'm jolly glad you've arrived. I'll tell you what; I'll just jump in my old jalopy and lead the way."

As he got to his shining, and by no means old, Alfa Romeo, he invited Nina and me to drive with him. Nina sat safely in the back and I occupied the death seat. He drove steadily and at a reasonable pace but the road out of the village was, as he put it, a bit on the bumpy side and he was given to watching his passengers rather than looking out for the holes which were deep and numerous. After one particularly drastic thump, which I was convinced had dislocated my neck, he shouted out, "Stand by to go about," and we turned sharply left on to a rocky lane that ascended steeply. He continued at the same steady, relentless and by now bone-breaking speed.

"I say," I said, catching his style, "do you own this house we're going to see?"

"Oh no. No. Not that. Not at all my kind of place. Belongs to a cousin."

"Why is he selling?"

He turned and gave me a disconcertingly cool appraisal, his grey eyes keen and piercing, as though I had asked quite another, and improper, question. Had the owner, I wondered, also defrauded the Bank of Crete? His eyes, piercing or not, had left the road for too long. With a great clatter the car hit a dwarf menhir, Nina's head hit the roof and my front teeth bounced back from the dashboard, off the much-prized and polished wooden veneer, only slightly loosened. Our driver apologized fulsomely.

"Oh dear, oh dear," he said, "I'm dreadfully sorry about that. It shows what happens as soon as one ceases to concentrate. Are you hurt?"

"No," I said abruptly before he had a chance to slew round and examine Nina. I could see a miniature Stonehenge ahead.

He navigated it gently. "You see it's all this Greek diaspora thing," he said, resuming the conversation as though there had been no interruption. "I was brought up in Alexandria where the family had been for . . . oh . . . centuries, perhaps millennia . . ." His hand started to wave and flutter, to represent aeons passing, I supposed.

"Yes, yes, " I said.

"During the War my aunt Frosso – such a frivolous diminutive for the splendid Euphrosyne, I always think . . ."

"Yes, yes," I said, a nervously chirruping chorus.

"Frosso married a Canadian soldier. He was really some sort of Scanwegian. A lumberjack, I should think. They went to Winnipeg and made quite a lot of money, I understand, manufacturing prefabricated log cabins. And Luke, that's the son, expanded into pre-stressed concrete house sections, computers and radio stations and that sort of thing. Sold out a few years back, came to Greece and built a house. Now he's gone back to Canada; left a note saying something about having to look after his interests." He smiled, the ripples reaching up to his eyebrows. "Perhaps he's gone broke."

We had by now climbed well above the village, which was hidden behind a hill or two. There were no other houses within sight. There were just the darkening folds of land and the purple mountains catching the last of the sunset. The evening star and Venus were already visible and the sky, pulse-beat by pulse-beat, was turning itself into its midnight-blue hemispherical map of the heavens, bejewelled and magical.

Slightly spoiling the effect were a row of tall metal posts on our left, canted sharply outwards for the top two feet or so. It was not exactly Colditz but there was enough tightly strung wire to deter the casual burglar. On reflection, there would be nothing casual about a visit to this two-thirds up the mountain retreat.

"Listen to that silence," Nina said, exaggerating, as is her wont. Our deutero-host had turned off the engine, as had Pericles in Athina's car, but a donkey was braying a mile or two away, a nightingale was warming up and an owl trying out its hoot; soon the night noises would be deafening.

"How do we get in?" I asked.

"Let's see the house now, *Kyrie* Androusaki," said Athina a touch impatiently, straining to see the time on her watch. It had all taken much longer than any of us had expected.

"What's your name?" asked Nina, grasping as ever after bedrock essentials.

"Aristotle Androusakis," said Aristotle Androusakis. "Ari." He juggled with an outsize ring of keys, a torch and a remote control device which glowed red every time he pressed it. Nothing seemed to happen. We all moved a few yards further along. Still nothing. Ari strode ahead. Suddenly there was an explosion of activity. A dementia of *son et lumière*. Blinding lights flashed, illuminating us and the cars, a section of the fence revealed itself as a gate and swung slowly back and a siren started shrieking. Ari marched firmly to some kind of control box on the gate jamb. The siren stopped. The flashing lights went off. In their place a series of illuminated giant toadstools, tasteful in red spots on beige, traced a drive up to the house which was now floodlit. As was a considerable fountain which was splashing and arcing. M. Hulot was winning. Everything was under control.

We got back into the cars and drove up to the house past orderly lines of orange trees. There was a circular sweep round the fountain, where we parked, and a ramp with a low rustic stone wall leading to a paved terrace. The house itself was stuccoed and painted what looked in the floodlights to be ochre. The upper storey (it was really just a central gable) was clapboard and the roof, at both levels, was timber-clad and steeply pitched as though the architect had improbably expected heavy falls of snow. It was, no doubt about it, a well-found house.

Ari unlocked the front door and turned on lights. Pericles admired the thickness of the walls, Athina the solid yet well-oiled way the door shut with a clunk, like a well-bred car, and Nina the black marble floor, although she had the sense to admit that it wasn't very practical.

"Oh no," said Athina. "Marble, you have seen, is very easy, very practical."

We hadn't and we didn't: it was the beginning of a long, unresolved, highly emotional debate. Marble.

"You just wash it. And perhaps dry it although it dries on its own. But it has maybe then been streaky."

Yes, indeed, streaky and smudged, and cruelly marked with indelible hoofmarks recording every fly's stopover. And no maybe about it either, just absolute, relentless certainty. But that daunting knowledge came later. At the time I was drawn to other things, like the electrics.

The sitting-room had rust-red roughcast walls, the ubiquitous black marble floor and flokati rugs. It had dimmer-switches, upper and downer lights, two large pieces of sculpture, contemporary hankering after classical, in bronze-seeming fibreglass lit from behind, and quadraphonic speakers.

Quadraphonics had a brief and improbable spurt of interest for those seriously addicted to technical gadgetry before the searchlight moved on to binaural and circumambient sound or DAT or whatever. The downside, to use the jargon, was the set-up itself – four separate feeds of differentiated sound to four separate speakers – and the need for a special array of microphones at the source, whether live or recorded. The effect could be impressive; aircraft roaring across overhead (you could tell the direction) or being in the middle of the promenaders at the Last Night of the Proms, with every shout, sneeze, incomprehensible message or splutter not only precisely audible but precisely located. The general feeling was that it was a clever idea but the gadgetry was not neat enough, that it required special recordings not to mention specially tailored transmissions, and in brief who needed it? But the final death-blow was the revelation that it mattered where you sat or stood, precisely, within centimetres.

I went towards the centre of the room and rolled back two of the rugs. Ari and Athina looked at me in some amazement but there, sure enough, slightly to one side of the geometric centre was a red cross on the black marble. There the absent owner must have plonked his chair whenever he wanted (approximately) three-dimensional sound, or rather placed it carefully, finely adjusting his position when the music or the sound effects started up. I suppose he must have got hold of two or three of the experimental tapes or discs: not many were in circulation. All the works – tuners, amplifiers, tapedecks, disc-players – had been removed: only the speakers high on the walls remained, woofless, tweeterless, looking down at the revealed red cross. It all seemed very rum, very unlikely half-way up an Argive mountain.

The kitchen was marvellously equipped, everything elec-tronic that could be, and almost everything that couldn't, being old-fashioned electric, with a handful of mechanical devices, like the barman's levered corkscrew fitted beside the sink. Just next to the back-door, built half-in, half-out, was a traditional *fournos*, a brick, stone and clay oven. Properly outside, con-structed out of a convenient rock, was a deep shelf used as a barbecue with a spit large enough to take a whole sheep – the Greeks call it a *souvla*, while the hand-held version is a *souvlaki* which in turn embraces the meat grilled on the skewer. The mechanism for turning the spit had been removed.

An ornate spiral staircase led us up to two bedrooms and a bathroom. Ari pointed out that the bedrooms were so arranged that someone in bedroom A could not see someone entering or leaving bedroom B, and vice versa, a nicety not likely to be on the list of priorities of your average householder. I think the same principle applied to getting in and out of the bathroom, which, apart from a lingering scent of chypre, was remarkable for a half-sunken oval jacuzzi bath without its working and whirling parts, and walls clad in bronze-tinted mirrors. You could see several versions of yourself whatever you were doing and an extension meant that you could answer the telephone at the same time, or rather you could have done had the handset still been there.

Bedroom A was clearly the master bedroom; it was bigger than the other one, it had a larger bed – a very large bed which Ari said had been a waterbed but the water mattress had been removed – pictures and hangings on the wall and a large dormer window with a spectacular view of hills, plain and sea. There were also dark wooden boards and a scatter of kelims. The framed pictures, the only ones in the house, were pen-and-wash, slightly misty treatments of mythological subjects: a Pan with all his equipment on show and pipes at the ready, a centaur galloping through the woods, chasing a small, gender-less figure in wispy garments, a beautiful Actaeon arrested in flight and about to be savaged by hounds – they, or the bushes and trees through which he had run, had already stripped him naked. Concealed ceiling lights diffused a pink glow while a black iron standard lamp rested on a replica of the Boy riding a Dolphin. There was a decent walk-in cupboard and hereabouts the chypre gave way to musk, Musk for Men.

The second bedroom was simpler, with earth-red walls, bare boards and one blue bath-mat next to the rather narrow single bed which was covered with a fluffy blue chenille bedspread. A newish teddy bear, arms rigidly to his side, lay face down on the bed, generally conjuring up the notion of abandoning hope for all who entered here, especially teddy bears. There were two small spotlights which seemed to focus on the pillow.

"A bit difficult for reading in bed," said Nina, thus breaking a silence which was threatening to become embarrassing. Athina joined in. "I didn't know, *Kyrie* Androusaki," she said, picking up the teddy bear and releasing a cloud of dust and a burst of musk, "that *Kyrios* Loukas has a little boy."

Ari winced.

"I should think he's had a good few," I said *sotto voce* to Nina but not *sotto* enough. "Too few?" said Athina. "What's too few? Pericles shall add window, room, door; whatever pleased you. But now we can go. It is late when we came to Athens."

Pericles agreed. We thought it time to go, too. We had a quick look at the olive trees mounting up the slope behind the house and then, with Ari locking doors and turning off lights, we got into the cars and exited the premises with more lockings and electronic beeps.

Ari said he would drive us back to the Xenia Palace Hotel in Nauplion. I promised to phone Athina and Pericles the next day. "Think," said Athina, tapping her forehead significantly. "All ready to go in."

"Not on your life," I whispered forcefully to Nina, before we returned to Ari's Alfa. "The place reeks of Sybaritic sodomy."

"Yes," he sighed, acute of hearing. "I thought you'd say something like that."

V

Mulling it over that night as we sat drinking cool, tall whisky-waters on the terrace, high above the harbour and the town, I wondered at the strong and strange attraction that Greece, and indeed Nauplion, seemed to hold for both of us. At least I assumed, from Nina's contemplative silence, that we were both held in some sort of common thrall.

A belief in reincarnation would come in handy, I thought; no need for involved and unconvincing explanations. I am returning to Sparta, you would say, where I was a helot in 350 BC (of course we didn't know it was BC then or even what C meant); a Mycenaean charioteer in Agamemnon's retinue (all those disgraceful family goings on, with Cassandra, as part of the loot, crying *Woe, Woe, Woe*); the stage-manager falling asleep, looking after the book in Euripides' *Medea* (I've never felt the same about Euripides since meeting a real life Mr

Euripides who called himself, in the approved contemporary pronunciation, Evry-pee-these); or whoever in whatever period you care to mention.

As it is, I am not Greek, Nina is not Greek, and I doubt, looking at the snail's pace at which our lessons in Greek progress, that either of us ever were Greek. Mind you, assuming the existence of some hyper-memory leaping across the boundaries of previous lives, the chances are that mine would be as inefficient and incomplete as the current twentieth-century model: an earthbound, jumbled, lumber-room of a mind that passes for a memory store.

So why Greece? Why Nauplion? Why Kapodistrias Street? And, as Nina had twice remarked, why should we swing from one urban cheek-by-jowl in Islington to another in the Peloponnese? All that bustling, thriving, shouting world of balconies, narrow streets, heat, cement dust, near-feral cats, bestarred nights, boisterous children and cooking smells from a handful of nearby tavernas overlaying the heady scents of flowering shrubs and blossoms and, when the wind is in the wrong quarter and the dredger has been at work, being overwhelmed by the stench from the harbour and the drains.

This had not been the plan. Islands and olive groves, a donkey, some vines, some orange trees marvellously in flower and in fruit at the same time, an unspoilt beach, incorruptible sea and uncluttered landscape. A retirement home with a difference. Infinite heart's ease with the wine-dark Aegean as back-drop and Homer (in translation) as companion.

In the sixties, when I first came to know Greece reasonably well, Nauplion was a good place to spend a weekend, to escape from the heat, dust and stress of Athens. Later it became the jumping-off point for our holiday exploring of the Peloponnese. Over the years it had grown into a favourite place to spend a few days, a base to return to. Now every time we came back, it felt like coming home.

"Well," said Nina, "I suppose we've given up the donkey and the olive grove. It was a bit daft at our time of life anyway."

This, I thought, was acceptance and handsomely done, without any show of reluctance.

"Mind you," she said, following her parallel track, "I shall regret the vine-shaded terrace we never had." There was a pause for me to look regretful. "Oh," she went on, "don't worry; I dare say we were destined, condemned, to be slum-dwellers."

Nina is given to hyperbole. In her idiosyncratic and often perverse usage, Nauplion is a slum and Islington is a slum. Goodmayes, a respectable and no doubt desirable residential corner of Ilford, where she was brought up, is the East End, and might as well be a collection of slums in the East India Dock Road of the late nineteenth-century.

It hardly seemed the right moment to deliver a homily on accuracy or, for that matter, fairness.

"Anyway," she said brightly, seeing that I had failed to rise to the dangled bait, "it's your idea; get on with it." This was to become a leitmotif, variously referred to as "your project", "Austen's retirement fruit", whatever that was assumed to mean, and, when things were not going well, "your great idea".

The phrase had reverberations. The Greeks' Great Idea, *i Megali Idea*, was the ambition of incorporating into the modern Greek state Cyprus, Crete and those parts of Asia Minor which had been traditionally and predominantly Greek in Ottoman times. It was a reaching-back to the dream of a latter-day Byzantium and as its basis it sought the restoration of Greek power within the boundaries of the Byzantine Empire. Crete was achieved, but not Cyprus and not, after a bloody and doomed fight in 1922, what were regarded as the lost lands in Turkey. As for the impossible dream-city of Constantinople, which Greeks still refer to as *i Polis*, the City, it remains undeniably and irredeemably the Turkish Istanbul.

The Great Idea was revived during the seven-year dictatorship of the Colonels in the late sixties and early seventies. All conscripts, as I recall, were confronted virtually daily with a map which showed, in different colours and ever-widening arcs, the Greek national boundaries at Independence in 1829, the subsequent gains of Crete in 1908, of Thessaloniki (Salonika), Ioannina, southern Epiros and much of Macedonia in the Balkan Wars of 1912 and 1913, and the post-First World War grants by the victorious allies, with whom Venizelos' army had fought, of the whole of Thrace. Then wider still, and in the immediate future as shown to these young soldiers, a vast arc embracing the Greater Hellenic Dream, advancing even, I think, to take in Alexandria and, naturally, the whole of Asia Minor. Always a dangerous notion, it was disastrous folly as the basis for a political or military strategy for the 1970s. Even in its more confined form the Great Idea led Greece into the Greek–Turkish War of 1922 and into calamity. The result was the burning of Smyrna (İzmir) and the destruction of its Greek population, the defeat of the Greek army in Asia Minor, the return of eastern Thrace to Turkey via the Treaty of Lausanne and the exchange of populations which meant an impover-ished Greece trying to resettle some one-and-a-half million refugees.

It was just such dangerous underlying thinking that led the military junta in July 1974, then under the control of Ioannidis and looking for some popular victory, to intervene in Cyprus. The plan had been to kill Archbishop Makarios, seen by them and the Americans as pro-Communist, and replace him with an ex-EOKA hit-man, Nikos Sampson, whose anti-communist credentials would be recognized even by the CIA. Presumably the next intention was to incorporate Cyprus with Greece (referred to as *enosis* or union) and ensure the continuity of the junta. In the event they failed to kill President Makarios, who escaped to the British base; they provoked Turkey, or some might say they enabled Turkey, to invade Cyprus and thus brought about an unhappily long-lived impasse in that tragic island, and they did much to wreck the Greek economy by their military expenditure. This farce managed too to bring about the end of their corrupt, cruel and unconstitutional regime and led to the trial and imprisonment of the Colonels. Greece was free of dictatorship: Cyprus paid the price.

One of the discredited Colonels' lesser Great Ideas was the Xenia Palace Hotel at Nauplion. It was, I suppose, to have been a contemporary parthenon built on the heights of the first modern capital of the Greeks. Certainly a great deal of money and work went into the project. Fittingly, it was finished after the dictatorship's demise. Built on a marvellous site, almost at the summit of Acronauplion, looking down on the assorted tiled roofs and domes of the old town and out to sea past the tiny fortress island of Bourtzi to the mountains far beyond the north side of the bay, it has a certain pre-eminence to it.

Conceived as a Grand Hotel, the finishings of wood and marble are pleasantly impressive as are the generally empty public rooms; the plumbing veers between the merely eccentric and the farcically flooding; the food is unambiguously undistinguished; the service is sparse in the other public rooms, and if hotels were to be graded by their bars, the Xenia Palace would be off the page. It falls into the category of "a man could die of thirst . . .", man in this case being deemed to be a universal, a generic, not a gender distinction; *anthropos* in the Greek rather than *andras*. But the bedrooms are large and comfortable, the balconies are spacious and all have glorious views, and the bathrooms, despite the little vagaries of the water systems, are grand in plan and rich in marble. The room-maids and the desk staff are agreeable and helpful. There is a resident plumber not only always on call but often, of necessity, at work. The swimming-pool is of a decent size and open to the breeze, highly necessary in the hot weather (although to be fair the sea is not far away), and it is usually, but not altogether always, filled.

We had always enjoyed its eccentricities and on this occasion, a temporary home-from-home while we explored the Naupliot housing market, it was a marked relief from the aggressive heat outside. It was not perhaps that the Xenia Palace's air-conditioning, ageing and audibly creaking, functioned so efficiently: it was more that the walls were thick and kept out the worst of the heat while the height above sea level meant that the balconies caught any breeze that was stirring.

There was no whisper of air when I got up the following morning and walked out on to the balcony. A heat-haze had already blotted out the mountains and the shore on the other side of the bay. The sea seemed to merge into misty sky at some mysteriously infinite point. It was going to be very hot. It was, I corrected myself, already very hot and, no doubt, getting hotter by the minute. The rooms faced north and there was no sun on the balcony. Everywhere else – sea, trees, roofs, horizon – there seemed to be an elusive sparkle, caught out of the corner of the eye and occasionally bursting into dazzling splinters of refracted sunlight. It was a scorcher.

"What's the weather like?" a sleep-sodden croak drifted out to the balcony. Stunned by the question – what was the weather like in Greece in late July? – I paused. A clearing of the throat, the voice higher-pitched, louder this time: "That is you, isn't it?"

"Yes," I said, unfairly pinned down.

"What sort of day is it then?"

"Hot."

"It feels like earthquake weather to me. All hazy and shimmering and still. Anything-could-happen-weather."

Nina stepped out of bed, shrieked and slid, rather elegantly, towards the bathroom door where she plopped down into what, looking from the glare of the outside into the shade of the room, seemed to be an elephant's puddle.

We had made some earlier calls on the duty plumber's time but these had been matters of fine tuning; the lavatory cistern that went on filling and emptying all night, the upward jet of the bidet that got jammed in the on and hot position, and no one could accuse the Xenia Palace of having tepid water. This time it was altogether more cataclysmic, urgent and mystifying: the water was apparently bubbling up from no visible source. We phoned for the plumber, dressed hurriedly and splashed out into the corridor, carrying our shoes .

It somehow seemed an appropriate day for making decisions and perhaps for starting back to London. We had been away for nearly three months. There was nothing much more we could usefully do. Children and grandchildren beckoned or, if not beckoned, lurked. So did work. Friends waited. We had missed parties galore; the Lord's test match; the toad mating, usually a rather unedifying gang-bang; most of the roses and all the Pimms and cucumber sandwiches. Suddenly England looked green and pleasant; Islington an attractive place of shade and cool, a good home to return to. And Greece, as all our new Naupliot acquaintances constantly reminded us, was suffering a heatwave of record-breaking dimensions.

The brothers Nondas were sipping iced coffee at the Blue Chairs, the café on the shaded side of the *plateia*. They waved us over, sat us down and ordered two more frappés. It was agreeably cool, relatively speaking, in the shade. Even Nina, abandoning her health and hygiene precepts, sucked the ice in the frappé until it melted.

"Mr Austen, Mrs Nina," said Nikos. "You should go back to England. In Europe it is better in July-August. In Greece it is very hot. Now even for us Greeks it is very hot. Many, many people die in Athens."

"Yes," I said, " it must be awful, particularly for the very old; with the *nephos* in Athens not lifting or dispersing . . ."

"Not only the *very* old." Nikos looked warily at us.

I thought I had better reassure him. "We've decided to go ahead."

"Full steam ahead," laughed Andreas.

"You buy the house, then?" asked Nikos.

"A third of it," I said. "The top floor."

"Good," said Andreas. "Very good."

We shook hands all round. Nikos said, "I think you'll be very good neighbours."

"Will you both live in the house?"

"No, I will," said Nikos. "I make a *garconnière* on the floor below. Andreas has an apartment with his wife in Athens."

"What about the rest of the house?" I asked.

"Another apartment on the same floor as mine," said Nikos. "Many people, foreigners and Athenians, are interested. Shopping on the street floor and the baker wants a *fournos* going from the *scala* into the basement."

This all sounded highly improbable; for one thing there were no other shops in the street and for another it hardly looked as though there would be enough room for the baker's ovens. But I did not then know Nikos, or Andreas, well enough to judge. Nor had I fully gauged the extent of the cellar excavations.

There would be time enough, I thought, to check or object. Meantime we could imagine the smell of newly-baked bread.

"That will be nice," said Nina.

We wrote out in some detail names and addresses and telephone numbers – ours in London, while Nikos said Phaidon's bar would always find him – and announced that we would see *Kyria* Athina in Athens within a day or two. Nikos said that for the moment he would be staying with his mother in Nea Kios, a few kilometres away, but he was in Nauplion every day and they would be getting on with the house. It was not altogether clear what he thought he meant by this but again I reckoned it would be better to let Athina and Pericles deal with it, if they could be persuaded to agree to do so. However there was the matter of planning consents, or whatever, for the restoration of the house. I had heard (or so I thought, it being in Greek) Pericles speak to the brothers about building licences in Nauplion.

"What happens about planning licences for the Old Town?" I asked.

"Plannings. *Po, Po, Po*", Andreas snorted and flapped his hand dismissively.

"You mean permissions?" said Nikos. "Permissions for restorating the house?"

"Yes. Isn't Nauplion a preservation area?"

"*Po, Po, Po,*" repeated Andreas.

"Much talk," said Nikos, "much wastings of time. Paper. Officials. Meetings. Bureaucrats. Lawyers. Engineers. Much, much time but not difficult, I think. No problem."

"No problem," echoed Andreas.

"It will be a very good house; very well restorated. I see to it myself. And you will have it how you want it." Nikos was pledging his word with due solemnity and sincerity. Within the limits imposed by my own ignorance of the circumstances and scant acquaintance of the brothers Nondas, I found myself thinking of him as a man of his word, a trustworthy man; I believed him. I said we would rely on him.

VI

In Athens it was hotter still, and when it was a bad day for the *nephos* – and it was just such a day – the sulphurous smell and gritty taste of the pollution somehow enhanced the heat. The piercing blue that was the sky in the Peloponnese gave way here in Attica to a dark yellow smog. It was not at all agreeable even if you were able to breathe. If, as the local radio stations and ET 1 and 2, the national television networks, were saying was true of half the population over fifty you had breathing difficulties, then you puffed your way to the nearest overcrowded hospital. The Great Wheeze Continues: Not Many Die. Not *very* many. Just a few hundred.

It has become fashionable in Western Europe, and no doubt in North America, to say "Ugh!" whenever Athens is mentioned. The sad decision over the centennial Olympic Games may have owed almost as much to this perception of Athens as to the financial benefits of holding them in Florida, that well-known cherisher of the Olympic flame.

Athens is, it must be admitted, a fancied runner in the least lovely city stakes. Its approaches, wastelands of ribbon misdevelopment, cement and car dumps, made conspicuously hideous by over-bright neon lights and the untidy structures of hundreds of advertizing hoardings, assault the unwary with dismay. The effect has the sickening impact of an unexpected affront. Then suddenly the Acropolis is in view and the perfection of the Parthenon stills the churning. How could a people whose parents grew up in the shadow of that marvel, whose remote ancestors even, so it is claimed universally by Greeks, built it and hundreds more of a like but lesser genius, how could they have created, and now inhabit, the inchoate, ugly, noisy, polluted conurbation that is the Athens of the nineties?

A third of Greece lives in Athens and the nearby Piraeus, something over three million inhabitants, perhaps nearer four million. The urban population has grown fast and continues to grow not as a consequence of any great biological explosion of philoprogenitive Athenians, however much they love children, and their mothers, but by the flow of non-metropolitan Greeks seeking a better life and by the large influx of refugees, notably those from Asia Minor in and after 1922.

When Nauplion became the first capital of newly independent Greece, Athens was little more than an extended village, with huddles of one-storeyed stone cots grouped round the slopes of the Acropolis. Flocks of sheep and goats roamed the hills and plain. Even when the nineteen-year old King Otho – the son of Ludwig I of Bavaria – moved his capital to Athens in 1834 it was a small town. By the 1850s the population was said to be 20,000. There were still no railways, hardly any proper roads and transport was not very different from the villages elsewhere in rural Greece; donkeys and mules and horses carried the pack goods. There was considerable poverty and therefore, at that time paradoxically, an emigration took place to the wealthier settlements in Ottoman hands, in Asia Minor particularly.

In 1960 Athens seemed to me, and probably was, not only in

rosy recollection, less sprawling, more encompassable; a town
for walking in, for exploring, for enjoying; for climbing up to a
monastery or scaling the Acropolis by way of the jumble of
picturesque one-room houses on the slopes. It was, though, the
poverty and the ever-increasing number of incomers in the
fifties and sixties and the consequent lack of housing that led to
the unlovely stretches of cement and concrete that disfigure the
city today. In the thirty years to 1981 the population of Athens
rose by roughly a million and·a half, mostly from the rush from
the countryside to the city. Old houses were knocked down,
and with no planning restrictions in force to impose some aesthetic order, or to replant some of the trees and recreate the
open spaces between the houses, apartment blocks went up,
quickly and as cheaply as possible, cheek-by-jowl. Various gov-
ernments were no doubt partly to blame for what happened,
but the desire for cheap housing and for house-owners to cash
in fast meant that a city of low houses was replaced by the
Athens of cement blocks of flats that we see today, a city of
woefully little green, sadly deficient in lungs.

Kolonaki is one such lung that partly survives. It is a square
that has given its name to an area, a class, a cast of mind, and
in all its roles it seems to have shifted down-market. The cafés,
which used to be political, élitist, chic and fairly busy at appropriate times of day, are now very crowded all the time. They are
comparatively apolitical and, certainly during the summer,
patronized by the rather less elegant tourists. The *jeunesse doreé*
of Greek society, by now very young and international in
clothes and manners, still hang out at their favourite café of the
season, but the square itself and the shops that surround most of
it are full of non-Kolonaki Greeks apparently preoccupied with
shoe bargains.

It was the latter rather than any former glories that took us
on this extravagantly hot day along Skoufa to Kolonaki. We
had been visiting Athina in her office and had decided to climb
the final few feet to find some evening sandals for Nina. At
Athina's she had seemed hot and subdued, quietly drinking
orange juice while Athina warned us of the perils of taking
anything (I think she was referring to house-buying but it could

have been society at large, life itself) at face value. We arranged, whatever her doubts, that she would act for us and alert us if and when any actions, decisions or funds were required. We left, wrung out.

It had been quite a long and uphill walk but Voukarestiou was a pedestrian precinct and anyway the taxis were still on strike. They were being made to conform to the rule about odd and even numberplates being allowed in central Athens only on odd or even dates and, not surprisingly, they thought it stupid. Hence, to express their contempt of the Government, no taxis. It did not seem to bother Mr Papandreou and the other ministers much as they swept through relatively uncluttered streets – the removal of the taxis certainly had that effect – in their official limousines; but it bothered us and many other foot-soldiers.

To be fair, Mr Papandreou had more pressing calls on his attention, such as inflation, now at twenty-five per cent the highest in the European Community, and, despite a wounding automatic wage indexation tied to the cost of living, daily strikes, protests and demonstrations. It was the Greek summer of discontent.

Musing thus while Nina tried on shoes, I suddenly noticed that she had gone very pale, an almost linen white against the browns and bronzes of the faces around her. I got her to her feet and out into the street. When Nina is persuaded to leave a shoeshop mid-purchase without complaining, something is wrong. Something was. In the glaring heat, as we walked down the hill towards Syntagma, she said she felt shivery and sick and lifeless. In the G.B. – the Grande Bretagne, the oldest and still the grandest hotel in Athens – where the air-conditioning was functioning effectively, making it a cool oasis in the cement jungle, she felt no better. Indeed, she could not tell the difference; for her there was no air-conditioning, no cool. Alarmed, and made somewhat less lethargic by the relative briskness of the atmosphere, I got us on an early flight to London the next morning. That would mean a taxi – they were running a booked-in-advance service to the airport – in the comparative cool of the early morning and for the rest of the time we would be air-conditioned.

Nina was unable to eat, could barely drink and refused the salt that she clearly needed to redress the balance. I cancelled our appointment with Pericles the following morning. He wished us luck with our venture, said he needed to know a lot more about the plans for restoring the house and what, if anything, had been approved. He would be in touch as soon as he had something to report. I thanked him with as much enthusiasm as I could muster but the heart seemed to have gone out of our great Greek adventure.

Nina summed it up in her usual neat way after our doctor in Islington had confirmed that she had suffered grave heat exhaustion and probably a heat-stroke, and could have died, nay, *would* have died had we stayed in the heat any longer: that was a fine bloody idea of mine, wasn't it.

"Well," as my favourite sage of the seventies, Tosco Fyvel, used to say, dragging out the single syllable for two full beats, "yes. And no."

Later the newspapers announced that in that July of 1987 over a thousand deaths in Athens were directly attributed to the combination of sustained high temperatures and pollution.

VII

After the fag-end of an admittedly rather good English summer and the onset of autumn, Nina was less apprehensive and less anti-Aegean. This is not to say that she had been expressing any great positive aspirations, let alone approbations, but she had stopped her censorious muttering whenever Greece was mentioned. It was not that she had anything against Greece or the Greeks: it was merely, as she put it, that she could not take the Great Heat. All this had abated with her thankfully almost instantaneous recovery (salt, glucose, water), the passing of time, the seasonal lowering of temperature and the increasing awareness of the state of Islington pavements (dirty and befouled by dogs), which was just as well since events in Nauplion had not stood still.

"Must you come," read the telegram dated 15 September, or what passes for a telegram these days, delivered with the morning post, "to sign contract. All prepared. Athina." There had been an earlier telephone call and a letter. Plans had been drawn up and agreed, a price settled and, so we understood, building begun.

High-speed decision-taking saw us into the air before we had time or breath to ponder and debate. By then there was the twinge of excitement, of daring the unknown. One, or both of us, managed a "Do we know what we're letting ourselves in for?" to which the answer was clearly no. "Is it wise?" said Nina, almost tentatively, as though it were an indecent thing to say. "No," I responded bravely but forbore to ask what, I suspect, was uppermost in our minds; were we sure it was really what we wanted to do? Courage, *mon vieux*, I said to myself in what I fancied was a thick Marseillaise accent, Raimu as Marius in part one of the Fanny trilogy. A man who is unwilling to risk his savings on an affair of the heart is as uncertain of his affections as he is unsure of his finances – de Rochefoucault, or Johnson, or William Keegan. This whiled away the journey, until I found myself saying out loud, presciently, in the role of a jolly, Micawberish person, "Well, we haven't signed anything yet ."

Nor, according to the distracted and somewhat dejected Athina who met us in Athens, was there/would there be/had there been anything to sign. "Your journey is not necessary," she said, pained at the trouble and expense to which we had been put.

It was a bit difficult to extricate, such was Athina's despondency on our behalf and such the confusion of her tenses, what had happened or was to happen and, indeed, when.

"Let's go to Nauplion anyway," I said firmly. "Now that we're here, we might just as well go and see for ourselves."

"But why, why," said Athina returning to form, "when there is no house? Excuse me, when there *will be* no house. Why?"

Mind-reeling, and boggling. Shades of Professor Ryle. The real question is, was there ever a house? Or was it all in the mind? But what is the mind, where is the mind? When we laugh, where is the laugh? Is it in the throat, the belly, the face, the eyes?

"Look," I said, grasping after reality and adopting one of Athina's favourite injunctions. "Look, this is all very confusing. We have only just arrived and I think we haven't quite taken in what's happened. Can you come with us to Nauplion and explain on the way? If you have the time, that is."

"Yes, yes. We take my car. Must we take also Pericles." It was not clear whether this was a question or an obligation. It seemed sensible, however, if he was available. "But," she went on, somewhat peremptorily, "why you want Air?"

It was the first mention of Air, and not by a hundredfold the last. Athina managed to invest it with heavy almost mystical meaning but it was a chameleon word, at one moment to be discarded as a sleight of hand, a mere conjuring trick, and at the next to be of prime importance, a glorious element, or else a sinister piece of black magic.

Air, Fire, Water. Very potent juju. The very air we breathe. Adam was formed of the dust of the earth but the God of Genesis 2:7 breathed life into him. Air is fundamental to life, to us, physically and symbolically. "Give me air, Hardy" is much more probable than "Kiss me" unless Nelson was prophetically calling for the Kiss of Life. Air, I thought, was a bit of a stunner suddenly to be launched by Athina, just like that. The only other person I could think of who always started the word, as it were, with an audible capital was Nina's mother, Judy. Her most notable performances were played in department stores where she would cry, "Air, Air", flap her arms and make for the nearest exit. But she would also fling open windows with the same cry and on tops of hills in howling gales would take deep breaths and, satisfied, exhale an "Ah", followed by another invocatory, "Air, Air".

In the event there was no more of Air for the moment. We left Athens early the following morning, with the windows down (it was a decently warm autumn) in Pericles' somewhat larger car, and as the road to Corinth quickly unfolded so, more slowly, did the story of the house.

It was a simple tale of ordinary Naupliot folk. The brothers Nondas, as their explorations advanced, reached the roof. They found, hidden between the roof beams and the eaves, two hand-grenades. In fact, old Eurydice, whose death had endowed the twenty-seven heirs, had been neither dotty nor fanciful in restlessly crying out for help against the bombs in the roof. The trouble was that no one had believed her or taken her fear as grounded, or roofed, in reality. But she was dead and the grenades were all too likely to be live.

Presumably they had been put there by someone in the Resistance who never found an opportunity to use them. They were of Italian manufacture so it seems likely that they had been captured, lifted or stolen from the Italians before the Germans invaded Greece in 1941. The Greeks, having sent a resounding "*Oxi*" to an ultimatum on 28 October 1940, routed the Italian force in Epiros and the Albanian border area. The grenades would have been made in 1940 or earlier and their use-by-date was long since passed. They were known to be unstable and indeed there was a canard, unknown to Nikos and Andreas, that they often went off as the pin was pulled, and occasionally before. The brothers sensibly decided to call in the bomb-disposal squad. The Greek army experts arrived, dealt with the hand-grenades and then thought, if two, why not three or four. They began to search and lifted the roof to do so more thoroughly. Unfortunately the still extant fabric of the house was being held together by the roof.

The consequences were dramatic: no more bombs were found but not much house remained. It happened just about the time we were taking off from Heathrow. I imagine it, as it must have been, in rather slow motion, the upper walls surrounding the top floors crumbling away. That, of course, already gives a false picture because by then there were no internal top floors to surround. By the time we saw it the process was complete and no doubt some tidying up had been done. There was only evidence, and that not exactly substantial, of a structure at ground level and up to about ten feet high. Above that there was emptiness and sky; what Athina, I reckoned, would call Air. It seemed that the upper-storey walls were constructed of wood and plaster, rendered inside and out, a sort of lath and plaster, or wattle and daub, using branches of trees. The walls had held together over the decades even when there were cracks and crevices vulnerable to rain and wind, but the lifting of the roof, possibly in partnership with the excavating below and the removing of wooden ceilings, had weakened the cohesion irreparably and the house of cards had come tumbling down.

It was neither an edifying nor a comforting sight. I thought perhaps that as the night got darker it might acquire a romantic, picturesque quality. To this end I half-closed my eyes and thought of it as a ruin. It did not need much imagination: it was a ruin, an unromantic ruin, eyes open or closed.

We stood for a minute or two in varying degrees of dumbfounded shock, the bubbles above our cartoon heads large with shriek marks and words like catastrophe. The silence was broken by a replay of an earlier scene with Nikos and Andreas popping out of a shrunken stage-set. They were, as always, genuinely pleased to see us and beautifully polite, but there was much shrugging of shoulders and pushing up of lower lips.

"What to do, Mr Austen, Mrs Nina? Eh?" said Andreas.

Nikos approached it differently, forward with the positive thinking. "We go to meet our engineer, Kosmas Papadopoulos," he said. "We perhaps should all meet together," and led Pericles down the *scala*.

As we walked down to the *plateia*, Nina said, her hand on my arm, consolingly, "It's an awful shame, love, but it's nobody's fault. Perhaps it's all for the best. It's a sign, a message: we were meant not to have the house."

"Oh rubbish," I said, and then for no very good reason other than I liked the sound of it I broke into Greek. "*Ba! Then nomizo.*"

"What's all that about?" asked Nina, who is even slower than I am at picking up other languages, particularly Greek.

"Bah! I don't think so."

"Well, I do."

Athina had been tapping my other arm during this inspired dialogue and now she could hold back no longer. "I think," she said sternly, "we do not have to meet this engineering man. We need to eat," she looked at me, "and drink. So we go with Nikos for now. Yes?"

"Yes," I said.

Kosmas Papadopoulos, when we met him at Noufara, turned out to be young and bearded, with twinkling eyes and no English – or French or German for that matter. He was, as Nikos told us, of the Left. He was also not very experienced, least of all in the question of restoring or rebuilding old houses.

"But that hardly matters," said Nina, "since we're not going to rebuild . . ." Her voice tailed off as she looked at me. "Oh no," she said, with rather more force, "no, you can't really be thinking of . . ."

But I was.

Pericles was hugger-mugger with Kosmas looking at plans and calculating something, perhaps stresses and strains, or why the house fell down. Andreas had gone inside to the bar, with luck to order some drinks. Nikos was watching the two bent over their papers and Athina was watching me.

"You see," she said, Nanny addressing a stupidly recalcitrant child. "No house." She gestured largely towards the castle. "No top, no side, no house." She smiled, perhaps with a trace of pity: the logic was irrefutable. "Now must we go eat. Where? Savouras, I think."

She turned and spoke in Greek to Pericles and Nikos. Ouzo arrived with nuts and olives, as well as ice and water. Nina said she'd rather have a Fanta. Everybody else poured their ouza and waited, looking hungrily, thirstily, lustfully at their glasses. At last the Fanta arrived in its frostily bedewed bottle and we began the round of "*Yeia sas*", "*Stin iyeia sas*", and the clinking of glasses.

"You know why we do this?" Athina said to Nina and me. "We will have all three things at the same time. We will look at the wine." She touched her eyelids. "Taste the wine," she touched her lips. "Smell the wine," she twitched her nostrils. "But is missing something," she touched her ear. "We make noise, like music," and she clinked her glass against mine, thus starting off another round of toasts. "Look, we Greeks think of everything. Smell, taste, see and," another clink, starting another round of toasts, "hear."

What Athina and the other Greeks seemed not to have

thought of, at least for some half-hour, was eating. Food. It had been a long day, a very long day, and a long two days since we left Islington. Much had happened. Feed a trauma, starve a cold. Osmosis or psychokinesis, or somesuch other Greek-derived word, did the trick and within minutes we were at Savouras ordering *garides* (large prawns) for all of us and *barbounia* (red mullet) for everyone but me. The draught retsina came in litre containers and we started toasting each other and the company at large. No one mentioned the house, though before he left to return to his wife in Tolo, I saw Kosmas hand over a sheaf of papers to Pericles.

VIII

The next morning, after breakfast, Pericles phoned our room to say that he was going down to the house to meet Kosmas. Could we have an early lunch with him and Athina before they drove back to Athens? That seemed sensible enough. There was time to tackle Athina and to have a discussion with Nina.

"I think we should have a completely open mind," I said, a touch disingenuously. "Listen to what Pericles says and advises."

"Yes, darling," said an unexpectedly meek Nina; and then, wistfully, "I suppose there really isn't time to have a swim?"

Well, I muttered to myself, what can you do with a woman who at moments like this thinks about sea-bathing, and I went to find Athina.

"Athina," I said, "I have a favour to ask of you. Please." She waved a gracious hand.

"Would you mind terribly if we didn't go to a fish place but went to an ordinary taverna instead?"

She had not been expecting this. She waved another gracious hand. "*Then birazee.*" This roughly translates as "it doesn't matter" and is as common as "no problem" which in turn, I assume, is a simplified translation of the Greek "*Then einai problema*", there is no problem, or the very common "*Then exo problema*", I have no problem. One thing is certain: problem is a Greek word.

"Oh," I said as Nina approached, "Nina and I think we should all keep an open mind till we hear what Pericles says."

Pericles was concise and judicious. "It will still all depend on the planning permissions. If Nikos and Kosmas get a licence to rebuild in the modern technology, it will be easier and safer."

It was the first we had heard of modern technology. I decided to let it pass for the moment. "Do you think this is what they wanted all along?" I asked.

"Probably," said Pericles. "But the planning committee is a difficulty. I think they will say they must rebuild in the traditional way. And that is not easy. We shall see."

"There's one thing for sure," I said. "Nothing will be done without money being invested. I think we ought to enter into some sort of contract to buy part of the property. Then we can plonk down a deposit to show them we're serious about taking part in the rebuilding."

"As long as it's for the whole of the top floor," Nina said slightly unexpectedly but encouragingly.

"Bah," this was Athina exploding. "What are you wanting? There is no top floor. There is no house. No house, no buying. No house, no contract. Isn't it?"

Luckily the waiter appeared. We were eating at Noufara. Athina ordered an ouzo; she usually did before meals. Nina called for a gin and tonic, a drink she rarely touches. Pericles and I had beer. We waited, fairly silently, for our drinks.

They came and we clinked glasses and gave our orders for food. For Athina swordfish; she said it pleased her. For Nina shrimps and bacon on skewers, souvlakia, because, she informed us, she fancied it. Pericles said he felt like a steak and had one and I chose rigatoni with four cheeses because I liked it but said nothing for fear of Nina attacking me for having a) pasta, b) beer and c) both together.

"Look," said Athina, despatching her swordfish with certainty and speed, "perhaps we found another house in Nauplion. A house," she added with an audible yearning, "with bathrooms. And walls. And floors. And roofs."

"Athina," Pericles said gently, "there are not many houses for sale in the Old Town. And if Mrs Nina and Mr Austen want a house in Nauplion, this one is possible. It can, I really think so, be well built, well restored. We can make into a very nice home the top floor, the whole top floor." He smiled gallantly at Nina and returned to his steak which he had neatly divided into bite-size segments.

"*Poios?*" Athina dragged the word out magnificently, *Peee-oss*. "And who does all this? Who rebuilded? Who was making apartments?"

"I think. *Pistevo* . . ." he paused.

"You believe . . ." I dived in, it being a word I knew and anyway I had not opened my mouth, except to eat, for hours.

"I believe," he said and I returned to my rigatoni, deciding to leave a strand or two, I suppose for Mr Manners, "I really believe that we can work together. We can see that Kosmas and the two brothers do a good job. Athina can draw up a strict contract."

"Of course," said Athina.

"And all the details of materials and methods, I can put down. We can make sure they build it well, properly, nicely. It could be good. I think I see how to make it very good. We can make a lovely open apartment. There will not be another one like it in Nauplion. Perhaps not in Greece."

"No, I don't suppose so," I said, a touch ambivalently, not really wanting to dim his enthusiasm. But I had. Or perhaps Pericles had caught Athina's eye.

"It is, of course, a risk," he said quietly.

"Yes," interjected Athina, a shrug heavy with meaning.

Pericles continued undeterred. "I don't know all about the planning licences in Nauplion, to start with, and we would need to know too about the quality of the local craftsmen. And Athina will tell you about the legal problems."

"Yes. Now," said Athina.

"In a moment. I am only saying that I think technically, as an engineering operation, it could be done. And that I could plan it and oversee it. But whether it would cost too much, whether it would be worth it to you . . ."

"Look," said Athina, at last getting her hands on the reins. "Must we get back to the facts. There is no house. There is Air. Will you buy Air?" She turned to me but did not leave me time to reply. "Mr Pericles is very clever but we do not know if Kosmas was clever. We do not know that Nikos and Andreas build houses. We know only that they will be at sea."

"Were at sea," I said automatically, and then wondered if she had meant what she said. Athina had occasional idiomatic insights.

"Never mind. What must we do now? I am in Athens with a judge tomorrow. You think to tell me what you want to do after the law."

"The law court," said Pericles.

"After I am in the court, you telephone, say what you want to have been done. If you want, I make ready the contract. Very exact, very tight."

"Very strict," said Pericles.

"Never mind," said Athina. "But I have not advise. I think if you do this, perhaps you have been very courageous. But I do not recommend."

"For courageous read stark, staring bonkers," said Nina later as we lay down for what seemed like a well-deserved siesta.

It was the hours of tranquillity when even Greek children are kept inside and quiet in partial deference to the semi-defunct law which says, virtually, that neither manservant nor maidservant nor the dog within the gates nor the donkey without shall disturb the snoozing burghers of Greece between the hours of two and five. In fact, it is a grave solecism to phone anyone before six at the earliest and it is safer to wait till seven. Anyway it was Sunday.

Athina and Pericles had driven back to Athens hoping to beat the rest of the Athenians returning from their weekend jaunts. We fell asleep, in my case thinking about Air. Was it limited, was it, indeed, defined in law? Never mind.

In the evening we met Nikos at Phaidon's bar. He had brought us a copy of Kosmas' revised plans so that we could discuss them with Pericles. On the Monday evening we tracked Athina down and telephoned her at home. She had had a strenuous day in court.

"Oh yes; I have won. You see you have a very good lawyer." She laughed. "And what you decide?"

I told her.

"So you buy Air." She sighed down the telephone line; it vibrated with regret. "*Ti na kanoume?* What to do? Never mind; I come down to Nauplion tomorrow. The afternoon."

IX

Athina arrived, shortly before nine p.m., looking happy and rather beautiful, with an outsize gold wristwatch and a handbag large enough to be the prop in *The Importance of Being Earnest.* She was bubbling.

"We have a good contract," she said enthusiastically.

Was it, I wondered, the same contract that we were going to sign before the house fell down? Had she had to do a lot of extra work, amending it?

"Never mind. We shall have a good contract before. Now it has been a better contract. More strict, more detail, more penalty, how do you say, clowses."

"Clawses," said Nina exaggeratedly, an eager helper at the private elocution class.

"Clowses," said Athina. "I find it difficult. Closses."

"Think of claws," said Nina.

"What is that?"

"Claws? What birds have. Or lobsters," said Nina, getting into her stride.

Athina looked at me in some bewilderment. "Lobsters?"

"O *astakos*," I said, teacher's pet.

"Show-off," said Nina.

"I *astaki*," said Athina, pedantically putting it in the plural. "And how," she continued, a mixture of reproof and bewilderment, "have *astaki* to be in the contract?"

"It was claws," said Nina. "Talons."

"Talents?" asked Athina. "Like clever?"

"No," I said hastily, "like nails", but seeing the carpentry trap ahead, I rushed on, "like nails on hands or feet. I think the Greek is *i nixhi*."

"Ah," said Athina, a great light dawning, "*oi nixhes zoon*. The nails of animals."

"Yes, yes," I said, not allowing myself to be led further astray. "We were talking about how to pronounce clauses and Nina was saying it was like the sound in claws, the claws of animals. But never mind." It was catching . "You were saying something about penalty clauses. Penalty clauses for what?"

"For not doing. Not for not getting the permissions. But for not doing after. By the due date, on time, prompt execution." Athina rolled out her legal English with relish.

"Any failing, we take the oranges. Prompt execution. *Grigora!*" She made a swift, chopping motion.

Quickly, indeed. Off with his head. A very prompt execution. But oranges? I saw them, crates piled high on the docks. How many crates for a million drax? How much vitamin C? What on earth could we do with them?

"Ah," I said, quick off the mark as ever, "you mean orange groves."

"Fields. Where you have orange trees."

Or rather where the brothers Nondas had orange trees. I imagined them, miles of them, running alongside a village road, deep in the rich soil of the Argive plain. Then reality obtruded. Athina was used to attaching ships whose owners had failed to pay or otherwise honour a contract; the brothers Nondas had an orange grove, so why not attach that, if they failed in any particular of the contract? This was no flight of fancy, just a sensible assessment of what assets could be seized.

"Look," said Athina, "Greek people need to be chased. Constraint? Is that right?"

"Constrained," said Nina.

"Yes. To do what is to do. Then we watch them all the time. Not you. I watched them." The -ed was stressed emphatically. "Mr Pericles watched them."

This sounded a recipe for bankruptcy: Nina's and mine. Admittedly, the Greek system, as Athina had explained, worked on a unified profession with no separation between advocacy and conveyancing, say. Either way Athina would be the equivalent of a distinguished QC or the senior partner of a well-known city practice. How could she find the time to check on what was going on in Nauplion? And how could we afford it, if she could?

"But would you have the time?" I said.

"Time. *Po, po, po.* Always very busy but I find time."

"And Pericles?"

"When must he come, he came."

"Will come," said Nina.

"When must he will come," said Athina firmly, "he came."

"But he must be very busy, too," I said. And, implicitly, expensive.

"He is very busy, very important. But –" Athina paused for syntactical guidance – "will he come."

It was a statement of certainty. I was not sure whether to feel very pleased, as I was, or financially anxious.

"I do not like this buying of Air." She shook her head. "But we have a good contract."

"And," I added, "we also have a famous lawyer and a distinguished architect." Athina smiled winningly.

As long, of course, I said to myself, as we have enough money. The same thought occurred as we sat down to a heaped plate of *karavides*, the delectable small crayfish: could I pay the bill? Just. Perhaps the same would be true of the house.

*

Breakfasting on our balcony at the Xenia Palace, looking at the mountains, the sea, the tiny, fortified island of Bourtzi, Nina spoke out. "I suppose you know what you're doing. Or rather what *we're* doing. Tell me." This was a serious challenge. "Just how much are we letting ourselves in for?"

It was a good question. Even a timely one. Athina was at that moment arranging what I understood was a pre-contract meeting in front of a *symbolaiographos*, a notary public. In Greece all contracts are argued and presented before these officials who are there to protect the state and the public interest and to see fair play between the contracting parties, including for example making sure that non-Greek-speaking participants have the final draft made clear to them, often by having the whole document translated, before any agreement is registered.

"We'll know more," I said, "when Pericles gives us a detailed costing for the rebuilding. All we're doing now – I think – is paying for our share of the freehold."

"Think!" said Nina. "*Think?* Why don't you *know?* Here you are gambling away our savings."

"My lump sum," I said quietly but tellingly, "as we pensioners call it."

"*Our* savings," Nina resumed. "What *we* were putting away for *our* children and *our* grandchildren."

"Oh come," I said. "We both agreed the price in July or whenever it was. It's just the same now. Be reasonable."

"Reasonable? The same? There's nothing left to buy."

"There's Air," I said placatingly.

"I don't see why we should pay the same now."

"Because we're buying the same thing: a third of the freehold."

"A third of an imaginary house," she said. "And *you'll* spend tens of thousands more of *our* money trying to rebuild it."

"What do you want to do then? Abandon the whole thing? It might be kind to let Athina know before she sets up this meeting."

"No, no," said Nina, "you go ahead. It's your scheme, your great idea."

Athina telephoned before I had time to react suitably. She

wanted to have a final word before we went to the notary.

We met her in the *plateia*. She was raring to go. We must leave it all to her. She would explain. Later.

"First must we speak to Mr Pericles." She dashed us to the *periptero* just off the square and took charge of one of the telephones. But even for Athina the Athens exchange was elusive. Every time she dialled the 01 prefix, the engaged signal purred with self-satisfaction. After some five minutes an enraged lady lawyer finally got through to Pericles' office. He was out.

"Never mind," she said, briskly cutting her losses and paying for the telephone call. "We know what he will say. He likes the house. House, ha!" She relished the interjection, paused momentarily and then rushed on. "He says the plans will be OK but he makes changes in the top floor. You remember? Out the pillars."

Kosmas' original plans included thirteen supporting pillars of reinforced concrete running from the foundations up to the roof. Pericles said most of these were unnecessary on the top floor. With four, he could support the roof and allow us a large open space for living in, sitting in, entertaining, eating, cooking and washing up. The outside had to conform, had to look exactly the same as the old house, but there was no reason to reproduce the former scheme of small rooms with ceilings. The original, painted wooden ceilings had, in any case, disappeared or come apart in somebody's hands, as I had feared. The plan now was to have a wooden roof, tiled on the outside, and a concrete top to the bedrooms and bathrooms. The water-tank would be in the attic on top of the main bathroom.

We knew as much as was good enough for us. So I said yes, I remembered. Reassured, Athina led us along one of Nauplion's narrow streets, somewhat improbably, and often impossibly, open to traffic in both directions.

"I don't know where here," said Athina, "but somewhere must be Nikos." She looked around her as though he would do one of his materializing tricks. But no; no Nikos. I peered into one of the still narrower side streets and there, materializing fast out of a doorway, half-way down, was Andreas.

Inside what was a not very large office – a lady stenographer sat in the minute semi-vestibule – were the notary at his desk, Nikos to his left, together with a man in a dark suit, his jacket slung over the back of his chair, his shirt collar open and tie dangling. I thought he must be Nikos' lawyer. He had a nice smile of welcome. The notary got up to meet us and shook hands. Andreas bounded in. A few other assorted characters, unexplained, not introduced, came in and took chairs. Various people got up and shook hands with other people across the room. Everyone smoked.

Athina took up her place on the other side of the *symbolaiographos*. Nina and I were made moderately comfortable at the window, near the brothers Nondas and their lawyer who offered Nina a cigarette which she actually took and puffed away at, as if there was not already enough carcinogenic fumes to lay low a prize-fighter. When I reproached Nina later with this unbecoming behaviour, she said that I knew she only took other people's cigarettes, that she smoked once in a blue moon, that it was a sociable thing to do in the circumstances and that anyway despite the amount of cigarette-smoking Greece had the lowest figure for lung cancer in Europe. So there. Meanwhile, the room was very hot and smoke-filled. I coughed once for form's sake and then found myself wheezing and spluttering in earnest.

"Take a hold of yourself for heaven's sake," hissed Nina as I struggled for breath. "Stop making an exhibition of yourself." She smiled at her neighbour.

"I expect it's psychosomatic," I whispered asthmatically. "It's the suspense getting to me."

The notary was of a like mind. He called the meeting to order; greeted everyone; said to us in English that he was sorry he didn't speak English well but someone would explain everything to us before an agreement was finalized, and then he raced away in Greek. The draft contract was waved about. Everyone started speaking – very fast – at once. Nina looked somnolent amongst the noise. I wondered how she managed it. My eyelids began to close. I shook my head abruptly to find that we were being offered cold drinks. I smiled affirmatively, grateful that in Greek body language a shake of the head was not a negative: a reverse nod, up and pause, with perhaps the eyes rolling dramatically heavenwards, signifies a no.

"Look. I tell you later." Athina came over to pat our hands. "Some problem, perhaps."

She was away, striding back to her chair, looking the only cool person in the room, before we could ask what she meant. As she picked up her papers the hubbub began again; not a gentle susurrus gradually winding up to a firm exchange of views and peaking at rare moments of extreme disagreement, but maximum volume from the beginning. It was not perhaps that they were all shouting at each other, just that it sounded like it, rather in the same way that to our English ears an ordinary conversation in the street more often than not sounded like an argument. No doubt this was just what all those Achaeans parked on the beach below Troy sounded like.

I listened attentively again but could make nothing out except that it seemed more and more like a real argument. Earlier it had been like a traditional jazz recording, the various voices alternating between ensemble choruses and individual assertions, harmonic, contrapuntal, dissonant but all within a convention, returning to some sort of choral unity. Now there was one clamorous soprano sax rising again and again, in the same phrase, not playing the game, refusing to let the others in.

It was, of course, Athina. "*Sygnome*," she was saying, "*syg-no-me*." A simple three-syllable word, the stress on the middle syllable. How many ways, I wondered, could you say it? Our lawyer seemed to ring a whole belfry of changes without really exerting herself. They ranged from the polite, "Excuse me", through the fairly assertive, "I *beg* your pardon", to the downright aggrieved, "*Do* you mind". *Sygnome* seemed a thoroughly useful word.

But what on earth was it all about? If a discussion about a pre-contract was like this, the real thing must be pretty daunting. Perhaps Nikos had been right when he said it was silly, time-wasting and expensive to use two lawyers. With one lawyer you could have a discussion; with two it was bound to be a theatrical performance; with three . . .? I paused to count the suits. Including the notary public, there were probably five. The whole thing was getting out of hand.

"What," I said out loud, "is . . ." but Athina cut me off with an imperious raising of the hand and a look. "*Sygnome.*" She was off again addressing the *symbolaiographos.*

Nina dug me, fairly gently, in the ribs nearest to her. "It's just like being a child again," she whispered. "Don't interrupt! Don't ask questions! We'll explain later. Keep quiet now! If you're good, you can have an ice-lolly."

On Nina's other side Andreas lent forward and said in a stage whisper, "Nikos talks of the recording studio."

"Recording studio?" I whispered equally stagily. "What recording studio? Has everybody gone mad?"

The Nondas' young lawyer smiled apologetically, conspiratorially, at Nina. Athina again raised her hand admonitorily; children should be seen and not heard. "*Sygnome.*"

Mind you, I muttered largely to myself, if we're on to recording studios and heaven knows what else, it's just as well we've got a separate and, by all accounts, shrewd lawyer. Recording studios, indeed; whatever else?

What came next were two recognizable words, taverna and *mpouat* which is approximately how Modern Greek accommodates the French *boite*, having no B-sound in its alphabet (where B is pronounced V) and indeed no W, but in any case meaning nightclub.

"Boggle," said Nina with her instinctive feel for the niceties of the English language. "Boggle, boggle, boggle."

While our imaginations roamed riotously free, another word came bobbing across the linguistic divide: *fournos*, a bakery. This made rather more sense since Nikos had told us that one of the local bakers might be interested in the much-excavated cellar. There had also been talk of shops on the ground floor, although this seemed unlikely to take off as Kapodistriou, however much visited by Greek and foreign visitors looking for the glass-covered bullet hole recording the assassination of the first Governor of the Greeks, was not a shopping street.

Abruptly, before we noticed it, the quality of the sound had changed. Everyone, or almost everyone, was smiling. Two or three of the unknowns were still looking dyspeptic. Perhaps they preferred the cut-and-thrust of the previous two hours, or perhaps they were hungry.

The notary public was addressing us. "Good," he said, "Mrs Sideropoulou will explain." Who she? We glanced at the stenographer. She kept her eyes firmly on the telephone which she looked as though she was about to hit. Athina was collecting her papers and then opening and rummaging through her handbag as though to make sure she still had the sacks of doubloons or whatever it was she carried in it.

Nina said to Andreas, "Who is Mrs Siddy-something?"

He looked amazed. "*Kyria* Athina. Your lady lawyer." He used the Greek "*i dikigorina sas*", the equivalent of your lawyeress, a form not used in polite society; properly *dikigoros* embraces both genders. It was one of the few times I saw Nikos really angry. He told his younger brother never to say that again and then, in so far as I understood him, he added that there was a *dikigoros* all right. Hard. There was more than a hint of admiration in his voice.

As indeed there should have been. When Athina explained it all patiently to us, we began to understand. The main argument ranged round the Air – who would have thought it? – but not what we might have thought of as Air. It was the space above what would have been the ceilings, the Air between the ceilings and the roof, in other words the attic. Nikos had argued that this was not part of the top floor. What if, he had wanted to know, he decided to build a recording studio there? And he might do just that. He had the right to do that.

"Bah," said Athina, recounting the debate. "I tell him the Air is ours."

Then there was the matter of the nightclub in the basement, and the taverna. Athina had written in clauses banning noise, smell and public entertainment, and had insisted they remain. They remained. The bakery and the shops were left unbanned. "But I do not think they happened." As it turned out, they did not happen.

Athina returned to Athens. She had a lot of work waiting for her. We arranged to meet her at her other office in Piraeas in a couple of days' time. There would be lots of details to work out.

That evening we had dinner with Nikos at The Boatyard. We were joined by Phaidon's American wife. Laura was young, just touching thirty, good-looking, tall, athletic; a West Coast girl. We celebrated our agreement. This was the beginning, was it not, the real beginning. So in a sense it was. Nikos and we were now committed, short of an actual signing. Phaidon came over and offered us congratulatory drinks.

I said I thought it would be a lovely house and for us a marvellous apartment.

"Yes, I think so." This was Phaidon. I thought he was being diplomatically cautious, or even perhaps a touch doubtful. He had, after all, been the marriage-broker. I realised later that when Phaidon said, "Yes, I think so", he meant it.

Laura said she hoped we would be happy in Nauplion. Nikos hoped our partnership would be very good. He looked forward to working with Mr Pericles. He did not mention, we noticed, Athina. Phaidon brought out photographs of his and Laura's two small daughters and one of their wedding, with Nikos as best man. We drank too much. Nikos started to explain about "the permissions". I thought I understood.

The next morning I had a very confused idea of a hierarchy of planning authorities (Nauplion, Sparta, Athens) and a concatenation of committees (archaeological, heritage, architectural, engineering) all no doubt disagreeing. I gave up.

"Why didn't you ask him about the recording studio?" said Nina brightly as we drove back to Athens in a rather small and not very lively rented car. "That would have been more interesting. And the nightclub. Did he really mean it seriously?"

I was concentrating on my driving. I thought I would go to Piraeas direct, rather than go in to Athens and out again, and I was looking for a turning.

"Why do you never answer me?"

"Because I'm looking for the turning to Piraeas."

"That's a mistake," said Nina.

Of course I lost the way. It took us hours. We stopped at an eating place high over the sea, Piraeas in sight.

"What an attractive place," said Nina, forgoing her right to complain further about what she persisted in calling my detour. "Look at all the white pebbles on the terrace."

I looked closely – I had my glasses on: the white pebbles were cigarette stubs. And the kitchen was closed – for the season. We could have a drink. We had two very gassy lemonades and arrived at Athina's office just in time.

"Must we hurry," she said, looking at her watch and picking up a file.

She took us down and along to another office. Another *symbolaiographos*. This time it was just the four of us. And a Bible. We swore out an affidavit to allow her to sign for us. We had already arranged a joint account. So that all seemed taken care of, for the moment.

We returned to her office and admired the view while she telephoned a shipowner or two, and then were swept off to a fish lunch. Athina took us to a family taverna on the harbourside at *Mikrolimano*, Little Harbour, known in earlier days, when Turkish coffee was still Turkish and not Greek, as *Turkolimano*.

She had not exactly taken us there; she had put Nina in her car and I had tried to follow. It was not the easiest of journeys. Athina drove dashingly through the traffic of hungry Piraeans making for their food. I lost her frequently and I did not know precisely where we were going. Mostly she stopped and waited for me but towards the end she swooped on to her target and by the time I had found her car and parked mine, some furlongs away, she and Nina were happily seated, drinking, and chatting.

"It's all quite clear," said Nina when I joined them. "We now put some more money into Athina's bank. We've done the equivalent of putting down a deposit but when Athina signs for us, the next instalment must be handed over."

"Next we make the detail of building with Mr Pericles. More still strict contract. With stage paying. Each stage we pay. I write down and send you the line-out."

"The outline," said Nina.

"Yes," said Athina. "Must you now see Mr Pericles. Then we do the bathrooms. Before you go back to London. When you go?"

"Saturday," I said, "and we can't change the flight."

"Never mind. We have time."

"It's Wednesday," said Nina.

"*I tetarti*. You know the Greek days? Like numbers in the beginning, *i devtera, i triti, i tetarti, i pembti*. Second, third, fifth, fourth." Nina corrected her. "*I paraskevi*, the preparating." I froze Nina with a basilisk glare. "*To savvato*, the Sabbath and *i kyriaki*, God's day. You know already?"

"I do," I said. "I'm not so sure about Nina."

"Must you learn. Now," she said, all solicitation, turning to Nina.

"No, not now," I said peremptorily in order to prevent a repeating of the days of the week. "Look. *I astaki*." And we ate the lobsters instead, with messy enjoyment.

X

"It only gives us two days," said Nina when we had checked into the Electra Palace Hotel, between the Plaka and Syntagma.

"It's ludicrous," I said, thinking of something quite else, "the way we forgot, pretended we hadn't ever heard of Athina's surname. Sideropoulou. All right, it's not that easy to remember. But still."

"She asked us to call her Athina," said Nina, aggrieved. "*She* said her name was difficult. I didn't. But it is."

"Take it syllable by syllable," I said kindly. "Sid. E. Ro. Poo. Loss."

"I thought you said Loo, before." Nina takes delight in back-to-childhood tactics; the unspoken So there, caught you out.

"The name *is* Sideropoulos. But because Athina's surname is that of the wife of Mr Sideropoulos . . ."

"Widow," said Nina.

"Same thing. Wife or widow, the -os goes into an -ou, the genitive case. Athina *of* Mr Sideropoulos."

"What a sexist language. No wonder I can't get on with it."

"Anyway," I said dishonourably, "we were talking about how much we had to do . . ."

Flying back to London on the Saturday, it seemed that we had managed, egged on by the tireless Athina, to do virtually everything we had to do except, to take first things first, the bathrooms. I had persuaded her that fittings could wait till later. What could not wait were decisions on basics. Like marble.

Pericles' office was large, bright, airy and, by the time we had been there five minutes, full of dozens of samples of marble. They differed in colour, in quality, in durability, in veining, in patterning, in grain, in finish. They came from the north of Greece, from Ioanina, from the centre, from Attica, notably the glorious white Pendeli marble of which the Parthenon is built, and from the Peloponnese.

Pericles explained, indicated, showed us the oblongs from different angles and in different lights, and then said that the choice was ours. It wasn't, of course; we could barely tell one glorious slab from another.

"*Loipon,*" a splendidly useful, all-purpose word, pronounced lee-PON and meaning then or, often, well then, "let us think about the roof. The wood will be what colour? I think a natural mid-brown. Like this." And we were suddenly surrounded with wood samples. "You must think of this big wooden roof. Then of a floor to go with it."

I did: acres of cool marble reflecting the warm brown of the heavy timbers. Not so much an apartment; a palace.

"Surely –" this was Nina fighting the prudent, careful corner – "you would want wood to go with wood."

"Oh no. No." Pericles shuddered and then smiled, indulgently. "No, Mrs Nina. That would be much too much. The total floor area is 138 square metres. The roof is larger because it is peaked. Pitched?" He made a cathedral of his hands. "All of wood, floor and roof? It would be very heavy. Dull. No life in it. No contrast. No counter – what is it in music when you sing another song at the same time?"

"Counterpoint," I suggested.

"And," he said turning to Nina, "in Greece we have little wood. And we have lots of marble. So wood, of course hard wood, is very expensive." It was the gentlest of put-downs. "But you can have wood in the bedrooms. Marble is too cold there."

He pointed us towards some Ioanina marble of considerable life and variety, grey with hints of reddish brown, and towards a hard wood and a polished sealed finish for the parquet floors in the bedrooms.

Then it was back to architectural features and details. Which bedroom would we want for ourselves? We didn't have to decide there and then but he would need to know fairly soon in order to plan for the door into the *en suite* bathroom. Where would the kitchen area be? He thought here, pointing to the plans. We nodded our heads. And the second bathroom, just shower, basin and WC, here? Yes? Yes.

"What about books?" said Nina.

"Books?" Pericles was momentarily nonplussed. "Ah. The library."

"Just a few bookshelves," said Nina.

"Quite a few," I added, recalling that having somewhere to put our overflow of books was a very positive justification in Nina's eyes for a second house.

"Not very many?" he asked in clarification. "But anyway, you can decide later. This now is more important, I think." He looked at each of us in turn. "Look at the plans." He handed us a copy of the latest version. "We have now this space. Over the stairs that lead up to your apartment and over the bedrooms and bathrooms. We can use this." He was excited. "We can use it for anything you like."

Anything we liked? Recording studios. Nightclubs. We were back to Nikos' dreams. Orgies, perhaps? Theatricals?

Nina asked if we could fit another bed in and he looked disappointed.

"I try to make windows," he said, sketching a dormer. "One on each side."

"Could we perhaps work there?" I asked.

"Maybe. You understand we have no permission. We will see."

It was all heady stuff. To people like us who knew architects only socially, if at all, and who had never tried, had never even thought of designing, let alone building, a house, this was a world of different, rich imaginings; exciting and somehow unsettling. Add to this The Memorandum of Agreement which it turned out was what we had been discussing in front of the notary public in Nauplion and which went into, for example, our third part, as Athina put it, translating loosely, of the common parts, and it explains our lively dreams as we flew over Europe.

Just before we landed, Nina said, "You know for the money you're spending, we could go out to Nauplion whenever we felt like it and stay for as long as we liked at the Xenia Palace. We could have a suite reserved for us."

Well, yes, I supposed we could. We could spend our capital. We would have nothing to show for it. All that. Anyway the contract was well on the way to being signed. But not quite yet, of course, to be honest. I said nothing.

As we moved rather dozily through London airport, Nina had another thought. "For this sort of money we could have bought a château in the Loire. In good condition." She paused for effect.

"And another thing," she said. "I forgot to ask about a broom cupboard."

A *broom* cupboard? Just so.

XI

The remainder of that autumn, the winter and part of the spring were taken up with other preoccupations. In the interstices of what seemed an introduction to the jet-set, except we were mostly flying uncomfortably in tourist or economy or whatever they call steerage these days, we kept in touch with Athens and Nauplion. I used some more of the lump sum and sent money to Athina. A revised contract was drawn up, to include the attic. A licence for the continuation – ha! – of the building works had been issued by the Nauplion authorities. "Congratulations!" wrote Athina. "We expect the works to begin in the near future."

First Nina had to see her publishers in New York. I went along for the ride. It was October 1987. I was playing tennis (real, that is or, as the Americans say, court tennis; in old-style Oxford jargon, realers not lawners) at the New York Racquets and Tennis Club with two stockbrokers and one banker when the market crashed so catastrophically. I was in good company. A dozen or so stalwart and stoic gentlemen of some maturity, almost all mother-naked, walking around the large, comfortable dressing room, looking at the fortunes collapsing with the speed of sound as they read the tapes. Barely anyone said anything, except thank you. They munched and they drank, abstemiously.

There were no such reservations back on Riverside Drive. Why, this was the nub of it, had I put so much of my lump sum in equities? Or, to put it another way, why hadn't I sold them before we left London? If not earlier? Everybody knew equities were a high-risk gamble. What price Greece now, eh?

In fact, the price in Greece remained the same. When Athina's letter caught up with us it became clear that the preliminary contract of sale had been signed a week earlier and a deposit, a seventh of the agreed price, had been paid to the brothers Nondas. I wrote back expressing our thanks and pleasure but asking, in view of what I politely called the fragile nature of the market, for plenty of warning about dates and amounts of further payments.

We returned to London for the Booker. Nina did not win it. There was much discussion with friends about this, and about the Greek Adventure. As to the latter, some were frankly admiring but "rather you than me, my dears". Some were downright condemnatory, however politely expressed. "Is it altogether wise, old thing? I mean is this *exactly* the time to buy into the er, Greek, er, economy?" A few were encouraging, notably Phyllis James, who said, "If you want it, go after it. Don't leave it until it's too late", and then quietly asked if we needed any help. Our children looked quizzical rather than doubtful, said little and got on with their lives.

Meanwhile, miraculously but slightly disconcertingly, the work in Nauplion seemed to gallop ahead. When the floor to our apartment was up, the final contract was due to be signed and a larger sum of drachmas handed over As Athina pointed out, there were also the fees to the notary public, to the members of the Nauplion bar (oh ho, that's who they were) who assisted and an as yet unresolved sum of property tax due to the government. No light matter this; it threatened at one point, on the provisional tax assessment, to be as much as a hundred per cent of the stated purchase price. So, as Athina's letter contrived to suggest, the money in hand in our joint account was no longer enough. More shares were sold, this time at fairly low bottom.

Just before Christmas a cheery telegram arrived from Nikos saying, "Concrete terrace your floor completed Merry Xmas." I made sure we paid Athina's and Pericles' fees to date. Just after Christmas I set off to advise the Governor of Puerto Rico on reviving public broadcasting in the island. He liked my plan. Others clearly did not. Nothing came of it. They took something over a year to settle my expenses.

Photographs arrived from Pericles. We were a little surprised to see that the brick walls were going up on the top floor first, rather than starting at the bottom. We flew off to join my father who had returned temporarily to South Africa, his birthplace, to celebrate his ninetieth birthday.

We got back to London to find that the contract for the Sale of Horizontal Property, to wit an apartment . . . had finally been signed. The delay, it turned out, was not of our making: it was a matter of someone else's tax debt. And, what was more, Athina had reduced the tax assessment by nearly ninety per cent and had paid it. All was neatly tied up, shipshape and Bristol fashion and we were, in equal undivided shares, the owners of what was still, as Nina reminded me, partly Air.

Pericles had written to say that there was no need for us to go out to Greece earlier than mid-April, as we had planned, since he would follow all the work and check and verify each payment stage. Later despatches kept us *au courant*. All the walls were up. Our external walls were insulated. The wooden roof was constructed. It was insulated. The outer tiles were on. The plumbing installations had started.

"Your flat," wrote Pericles, "becomes very nice, particularly the attic and the appearance of the wooden roof are very impressive. We had many discussions held with Nondas Bros trying to convince them to use suitable thick and treated woods." I bet. "Finally, the work effected was very good."

Having had a week or two to turn around after South Africa, we set off for Nauplion via Bologna, which Nina wanted to visit for the annual Children's Book Fair. We had a marvellous Easter lunch at Imola with Dorothy Briley, George Fenn and Bill Tarbutt and came out late and very full to meet the cold air and find a parking ticket on our car. On Easter Sunday? In Imola?

We had the Orthodox Easter, a week later, on board the *Mediterranean Sea* sailing from Ancona to Patras. You could tell it was the Orthodox Easter because when we left our cabin in the morning to stroll round the deck all the stewards were on their hands and knees with hot irons and brown paper. They were trying to remove the candle-wax that had dripped on the carpet. The Greeks attending the midnight *Xristos Anesti*, Christ is Risen, ceremony had taken their lighted candles back to their cabins. It is important to keep the light going till you have crossed the threshold into your house, room or, in this case, cabin, to ensure a good year.

The Greek year really begins with Easter. This is the main religious and popular festival, understandably – in theological terms it clearly is the central Christian event. Christmas is a lesser feast except where western fashions dominate. Almost all Greeks go home for Easter, back to the village, small town, or island where their parents and grandparents grew up. The passengers on board had clearly not been able quite to make it but they would drive fast the following day to spend the rest of the holiday with their extended families.

We docked the next morning something before seven o'clock after two nights and one splendidly relaxed day on board. It was a holiday week in Greece, so we decided to drive to Monemvasia and spend a couple of nights there before going on, or rather back, to Nauplion, by which time we thought things would have settled down after Easter. While most of the cars raced east towards Corinth and Athens, and a few shot west and south to Kalamata, we took a minor and gloriously mountainous road over the centre of the Peloponnese to Sparta.

I think we saw one bus, two tractors, three cars and four donkeys in the two and a half hours before we joined the main road. The air was quite still, the sun very bright, the sky a paint-box blue and the wild flowers making changing patterns of colour along the edges of the road, in the pastures and under the olive trees.

The scents were powerful enough to confuse the other senses. The sense of smell is a mole, burrowing away at some deep, unvisited level, an ancient pre-civilization part of our being. Evocative, sometimes painfully so when prodding back to half-remembered, half-suppressed, childhood events, affairs, people, it also unexpectedly alters moods and provokes unordered, disproportionate emotions. Whatever the explanation, a fine, hot spring day in the Peloponnese does wonders for recharging the olfactory memory bank. The scents shriek at you as you drive over the hills and round the feet of the mountains.

By the time we arrived at Monemvasia the sun was setting and the great elephant hump of the rock was a purple shape, fading into darkness. We stopped at the first hotel we could find. It was new and on the mainland, looking out at the ruins of the fortified Byzantine city.

Monemvasia – the one gate, the only entrance – was the last part of the Peloponnese to fall to the Turks. It was a formidable, natural military redoubt, Greece's Gibraltar. The visible fortifications at the top are Venetian, sixteenth-century and mostly in ruins. Elsewhere, both in the upper and the lower town, the ruins are Byzantine, going back to the sixth century AD, and then Ottoman and Venetian the better part of a millennium later. It is one of the most romantic places in the world.

The Peloponnese, with a bit of imagination, looks like a hand with the little finger missing. The thumb is the Argolid; the ring finger is the Pylos-Methoni-Koroni peninsula, west of Kalamata; the middle finger is the Mani; and the forefinger is the south-eastern tip of Greece ending at Cape Maleas and dominated by Monemvasia.

In Greece history matters; it is ever-present. To understand modern Greeks you need to roam back over the centuries.

Marathon, Salamis, the Peloponnesian War are a year or two back, the Fall of Constantinople last week. A friend walking in the mountains of Crete met a shepherdess who recounted as a matter of fact the story of Demeter and Persephone – "There was this girl, daughter of an important person, a queen, who was walking in these meadows . . ." as though it had happened a few years before, when her grandfather was a young man.

Take Monemvasia. The city was founded by the Lacedaemonians somewhere between 560 and 583 AD. Lacedaemonia, the chief city of Sparta, was abandoned and a diaspora set in motion from most of Sparta to Sicily, to Mount Parnon and to this steep, inaccessible and hitherto uninhabited rock. It was either in anticipation of attacks by Avars and Slavs or as a consequence of them: probably the first since there is no firm evidence of Slav attacks until 587–8. The Lacedaemonians and the Byzantine Empire to which they belonged needed a city able to be properly fortified and a defensible harbour to go with it, with easy access to Constantinople. These issues may appear academic and remote; but not so to today's Greeks. The question of Slav penetration of the Peloponnese, albeit in the sixth century, is a fighting matter of fierce dispute and intense racial pride.

Twenty-five, or more, years ago the housekeeper at the Athenee Palace Hotel – alas no more; for years it was closed, and boarded up, over a protracted legal battle and now it is Barclays Bank – accosted Nina in the corridors and said how glad she was to have us staying there. "The English and the Greeks," she said, "are the only racially pure people." Oh dear, oh dear. Leaving aside Nina's Scottish, Irish and Italian ancestors and my Russian Jewish forbears, leaving aside Nazi over- and undertones, the idea of ethnic or genetic homogeneity in societies which have lived through centuries of movements of population, of immigration, emigration and re-migration, let alone invasion and occupation, is bogus and dangerous romantic twaddle. The disastrous break-up of Yugoslavia shows that tribalism alone, or rather tribalism reinforced by religion, is calamitous enough without the further horrors engendered by notions of ethnic or racial purity.

It had become something of a fashion amongst nineteenth-century travellers to Greece, even the philhellenes, perhaps *particularly* the philhellenes, to confess with pain and confusion that they could see no trace of the glories of ancient Hellas in the faces and bodies of the contemporary Greeks they encountered. "Another Athens shall arise," sang Shelley, having in mind some soaring recreation of a city peopled with Socrates and Sophocles, and Sappho down the road apiece. This was precisely what the travellers were looking for and could not find: even a classically straight Greek nose was as elusive as a centaur. Enter the scholars to put things right, or mostly wrong, notably the German J.P. Fallmereyer who published, at Tübingen, between 1830 and 1845, books supporting his theory that the Greek population of the Peloponnese had been displaced by invading Slavs in 587–588 AD. He claimed he had proof that Patras, Argos and Corinth had been abandoned and Monemvasia founded as a consequence of the depredations of the marauding Slavs. Ergo: the latter-day inhabitants of southern Greece were not the descendants of the Hellenes but of Slavs. And this is why they did not look like living replicas of the statues of fifth-century BC Greece which is what European travellers expected them to be.

Not surprisingly these and other similar theories, such as that the Slav (notably Albanian) settlers covered most of Greece and that it was *their* descendants who fought and won the War of Independence, aroused fury amongst contemporary Greeks and others determined to trace an uninterrupted bloodline between antiquity and the present. Considerable dissension, bitter controversy, these are weasel phrases to describe the historians' and others' wrangling. While scholars try to answer the slavification question in proper detail, politicians, priests and people angrily resent any suggestion of miscegenation, of dilution of the pure genetic strain leading back through Christian Byzantium to Homer and beyond. Understandably.

The rather meagre facts suggest not only that Monemvasia was founded before the Slavs attacked the Peloponnese in force but also, from archaeological evidence, that Corinth was never abandoned in the sixth century nor indeed during the first half of the seventh. There had been a run of severe and destructive earthquakes but each time there had been rebuilding and reconstruction, arguing continuity. The diaspora, the flight from Patras, Corinth and Argos, probably took place in the late seventh century. By the time St Willibald visited Monemvasia in the 730s, the first stop on his pilgrimage from Sicily to the Holy Land by way of Ephesus, the city had already established itself as a major mercantile centre, a main port on the road to the imperial capital, Constantinople. The Irish saint unexpectedly however stirs troubled water by describing Monemvasia as being *in Sclavinica terra*.

Later in the eighth century a disastrous plague swept through the Byzantine empire. It came from Sicily and Calabria and was passed on via Monemvasia to Constantinople around 747. It left large parts of Greece uninhabited, which naturally encouraged the incoming of more Slavs. The Byzantine emperors saw no particular reason to put off potential taxpayers, even if they were barbarians. The country seems to have become known as Sclavinia sometime thereafter. These were the dark, not well-recorded centuries. By the tenth century the existence of a warlike barbarous community on the other side of the Aegean had begun to bother the imperial power. Military action, seen as pacification, was followed, or accompanied, by Christianization. The Slavs in Greece became fully paid up members of Byzantine society.

The histories of Nauplion and Monemvasia overlap. Monemvasia replaced Corinth as the most important port in the Peloponnese and developed wide trading connections, despite the growing power of the Arabs and their ships conquering Crete and Sicily and attacking mainland Greece much as their brothers had attacked western Europe, pushing through Spain and into France.

The next wave of attackers to dent the Byzantine Empire were the Turks in the east. They had captured Palestine and mopped up eastern Anatolia. But the immediate threat came from the West: first the Normans and then the Crusaders (or, as the Greeks know them, the Franks). King Roger (of Sicily), as Norman as Duke William, plundered parts of mainland Greece in 1146 and the following year his ships failed to take Monemvasia. Towards the end of the century the Byzantine Emperor called in Venice to help oust another major Norman incursion. It was an error of calamitous proportion. It not only opened up the empire to Venetian trading ships, it also gave Venice the opportunity of becoming the dominant force in the Levant. The Fourth Crusade was the bleak, disgraceful and, for the Byzantines, catastrophic outcome.

In the rather appallingly insular version of history that we were taught at school, with its attendant stereotypes and prejudices, I don't think I ever heard of this first sack of Constantinople in 1204. In my early days at the BBC, in the middle to late fifties, I remember becoming obsessed by the baleful ignorance that was the legacy of nationalist, self-centred and self-interested history teaching at school. I put up a scheme for a radio documentary series – I think it was called 'Six Nations In Search Of Their History' – to look at the way children in France, Germany, Belgium, Holland, Italy and Britain were taught about the same events, such as the two World Wars, the French Revolution, the Battle of Waterloo, the European grab for land in Africa. (John Sherwood went on to make the programmes and they won an Italia Prize.) If such enormous differences existed in the perception of an often common past, and they did, and these were being perpetuated by nation-centred teaching, the chances of any of our children understanding events within, let alone beyond, the tidy confines of western Europe were minimal. Still, there was hope; the European Community would begin to break down more than economic barriers. Or so we thought. And the north-south, rich-poor divide was bridgeable. Or so we hoped.

Ethnocentricity is perfectly understandable, on occasions is psychologically necessary for survival, but it can rather distort reality. "Khrushchev Meets Eisenhower" blasted the *Cyprus Mail* in a notable banner headline announcing the first meeting of the Titans in 1959, "Cyprus Discussed". Well, yes; perhaps. But like that? At the height of the Cold War?

At the very beginning of the thirteenth century, as most of us I suspect did not learn at school, the Fourth Crusade established all sorts of undesirable records: greed, wanton destruction, Christian killing Christian – not that in any proper scales killing fellow-Christians outweighs killing Muslims, it just seems especially repugnant, like incest or fratricide. Begun as a religious war to recapture the Holy Places by means of a Venetian fleet, when the money ran out and the Venetians determined to recoup what was owing to them, the Crusade turned into a murderous, greedy and unprovoked attack on eastern Christendom.

In 1204 Constantinople was besieged, sacked, plundered and burnt, "thereby" wrote Timothy Boatswain in his and Colin Nicholson's excellent and brief compendium, *A Traveller's History of Greece*, "staining for ever the good name of the West in eastern Christian eyes. Constantinople had eluded capture by any enemy since its consecration by Constantine in AD 330 and it was the one city of antiquity that had not been sacked, thus bridging the divide between the ancient and medieval world. It was full of treasures from the ancient world (from precious works of art to the countless manuscripts of ancient authors); the rapacious crusaders breached Constantinople's previously impregnable walls and proceeded to burn down much of the city. What treasures remained were carried off and became dispersed around Europe."

The Fourth Crusade was an act of irredeemable criminal folly. It destroyed the bulwark that safeguarded Western civilization and changed the balance of the world. It laid the seeds for centuries of discord in the Balkans and it moved the centre of our culture away from its eastern Mediterranean cradle. It irremediably weakened the Byzantine empire, it created a chasm between western and eastern Christendom and it destroyed many of the cultural bonds, grounded in works of art and literature, that linked pagan Athens with pagan Rome and imperial Rome with Byzantium and Christian Constantinople.

The battle between Latin and Greek was taken to Greece itself, which for decades was divided into Frankish dukedoms. These are remembered in the crusader castles whose ruins on the mountainous skyline delight travellers in the Peloponnese, then called, and for centuries ahead, the Morea.

Monemvasia fared moderately well in this period while large

chunks of the empire were being carved up. The Venetians, for example, for their disgraceful part in the iniquitous crusade – the Doge told his troops after the city fell that they could spend the next three days pillaging, and they used them to good effect and to the glorification of Venice's churches and palaces – received three-eighths of the conquered lands. For a while Corinth, Nauplion, Argos and Monemvasia seem to have kept out of the hands of the Franks who had been allotted the Morea and were largely self-governing. Eventually the cities fell to force or persuasion, but Monemvasia held out for some years under siege. It too surrendered finally, probably in 1252 – a Latin bishop was elected in 1253 – and, in surrendering, arranged terms which enabled those who wished to emigrate to take their ships and settle in Pegai in Asia Minor, and for those who stayed to retain many of their previous privileges.

The stay-at-home Monemvasiots seem not to have suffered too much or for too long. After the battle of Pelagonia in 1259, Mystras, Maina and Monemvasia were returned to Byzantine Greek control, although the rest of the Morea remained under Frankish rule.

Constantinople itself was regained in 1261, but this was the last fling of the Byzantine Empire which, after a golden Indian summer, petered out in intrigue, corruption and incompetence over the first half of the fifteenth century. Constantinople fell, as most fifth-formers used to know, if only as a date for general knowledge quizzes, fighting gallantly to the last, to the Ottoman Turks led by Sultan Mehmet II on 29 May 1453. The West had failed to respond to pleas for help while the cannons of the Turks had hammered at the walls for nearly two months. It is no wonder that eastern Christendom, after the western church's behaviour in the Fourth Crusade and during the siege of Constantinople, felt a righteous anger and an intense antagonism towards the historical other half of Christianity. This has not appreciably diminished since then. The enmity between Catholic and Orthodox is everywhere apparent, not least in the Balkans.

Monemvasia was one of the parts of Byzantium that kept the culture of the empire alive for a while. It was largely autonomous, completely so after the fall of Mystras in 1460, but it realised that it could not hold out alone against the Turks. The Monemvasiots turned first to a Catalan mercenary, then to the papacy and then, neither protectorate working, finally and reluctantly to their much larger and stronger mercantile rival, Venice.

To Venice, Monemvasia was a plum, a rich military and commercial addition to their other Greek coastal possessions. Napoli di Malvasia (Monemvasia) joined Napoli di Romania (Nauplion) as Venetian bastions of the Aegean. For the better part of a century they flourished, as the remains of buildings of stone and marble, and carvings of the lion of St Mark, show today; but the Serene Republic's power was waning as the Ottomans' waxed. Jostling first for primacy in the eastern Mediterranean and then increasingly fighting defensively to retain what she occupied, Venice was effectively at war with Turkey for two and a half centuries, a war that was predominantly fought on Greek soil and in the seas surrounding it. The second Turko-Venetian war and the treaty that followed it in 1503 left the whole of the Peloponnese, with the exception of the two Napolis, Nauplion and Monemvasia, in Ottoman hands.

Twenty years later, with Suleyman the Magnificent, came the most ambitious and fiercest Ottoman drive. By 1529, with much of the Balkans and Central Europe behind them, the Turks were at the gates of Vienna. Rhodes had fallen and, after the battle of Preveza in 1534 when the Turks destroyed the Venetian fleet, Venice gave up its last hold on the Greek mainland. Nauplion and Monemvasia were in Turkish hands, the latter surrendering on 2 October 1540.

Although Greece was, to use the conventionally emotive term, under the Turkish yoke for approximately three centuries, with local interruptions, the onward sweep of the Turks met significant setbacks. The weather was intemperate and Suleyman's troops failed to take Vienna. The weather changed again at Lepanto, off the Gulf of Corinth, to aid Don John of Austria's Christian League victory in 1571. More than a century later, in 1683, the Turks again failed to take Vienna and in the fifth

Turko-Venetian war the Venetians re-occupied the Peloponnese, returning to Nauplion in 1686 and to Monemvasia the following year. It was during this war that the Venetians, firing on what was to them little more than an unimportant village on the way to Evia, destroyed part of the Parthenon when one of their cannonballs blew up a Turkish magazine storing gunpowder in the ruins.

The Venetians failed to hold their gains in the rest of Greece and were unable to withstand a revived Turkish army and fleet that attacked the Peloponnese in 1715. The Turks besieged Nauplion, which fell after a few weeks of intense bombardment, and the Venetian *podesta* surrendered Monemvasia for money. With Crete, Cyprus, the Peloponnese and virtually every other major naval strongpoint in Turkish hands, Venice was finished as a marine power. Greece itself became a sparsely inhabited backwater and Monemvasia declined and dwindled to near-extinction.

Looking at the rock now it is difficult to believe that in its heyday it had a population of something over 40,000. When we first walked through the massive entrance, carved through the rock, and emerged into the lower town, it was to find almost empty streets and a city largely peopled with cats, spiders and occasional black-garbed old ladies. Everywhere there were giant spider's webs shimmering undisturbed. In the twenty-odd years since then there have been changes: more, and smarter, shops; better hotels and tavernas; an impressive amount of mostly appropriate restoration and rebuilding, and greatly increased tourist traffic. Essentially, it remains the same romantic ruin, but with a touch of prosperity. Now you only see the spider's webs in the wilds of the almost totally ruined upper town, a glorious expanse of wild flowers, lizards, butterflies, Byzantine foundations, Venetian cisterns and fortifications, and an Agia Sophia, sometimes known as the Hodigitria.

"Perhaps," Nina said as we breathlessly approached the church, the morning after we arrived, "we should have chosen Monemvasia. It was always our first love." I gulped, whether with shock or responding emotion. "No. I don't mean that," she added hastily, crossing her fingers. "It's just that it's such a marvellous place."

"And marvellously isolated, marvellously far from airports, hospitals, libraries, people . . ."

"Yes, I know, dear." Nina always uses that particular endearment as a cold put-down. "And, no doubt, from the English newspapers."

In studied and purposeful silence I inspected the octagonal church. Perched, vertiginously, on the cliff's edge, it crowns the site and is a synopsis of Monemvasia. Built in 1150 during the town's great Byzantine expansion, the Hodigitria is of a plan taken from Constantinople. The loggia in front is fifteenth-century Venetian. The interior frescos were whitewashed and a *mihrab* added, pointing to Mecca, when the church became a mosque. It was later re-dedicated to St Sophia. It has been, and is still, in the process of being carefully restored.

That afternoon the weather was a delight, a bright hot sun in a cloudless sky warming the April breeze, but during the night the temperature fell. The sky was leaden, the fitful rain cold, the rock menacing and the hotel had no heating. I tried to carry on with my dilettante research projects. To start with, names. Is it Monemv*a*sia, or Monemvas*i*a, which I first heard and prefer. I asked the locals. It was difficult to get them to understand what I wanted.

"I say what you want. What you want?"

After considerable discomfort the score was two of one and three of the other. In fact, both forms are found in early documents, as are Monov*a*sia, Monovas*i*a and, a turn-up for the books, Monovati. I learnt this arcane information from *Byzantine Monemvasia. The Sources* by Dr Haris Kalligas, who, with her architect husband, has been responsible for the regeneration of Monemvasia, however pronounced.

She points out that back in the twelfth century Monemvasia grew in power for the same reasons that led to Venice's advance: administrative independence, naval power, mercantile privileges. She quotes the monk Isidore describing Monemvasia in the twelfth century as "the sea-ruler of almost all the seas within the pillars of Hercules".

A singularly well-educated fifteenth-century monk who had studied in Constantinople, Isidore was on close terms with the Emperor Manuel. He worked in Mystras and Monemvasia, assisting the Metropolitan, meticulously collecting manuscripts and historical information, and eventually became Metropolitan of Kiev. Like the European philhellenes 400 years later, Isidore had expectations based on the classics. He too was taken aback. Landing in the Peloponnese, he went to Oitylon and was astounded, he wrote to the Emperor, at the uncivilized customs of the inhabitants. Influenced by Homer he expected to find a Greek population: instead he found Slavs.

Surprisingly, in his letters from Monemvasia he only seems to have mentioned wine once, in an attempt to get the taxes decreased for some people farming on the mainland who had lost their grape harvest. But if wood, iron, ship-building and the provision of seamen, ships, safe harbours and warehouses made the Monemvasiots rich and powerful, it was the wine that made then famous throughout Europe.

The first time, it must have been in the early 1970s, we explored as far as Monemvasia we were tired after a long, gruelling drive; the road had been rough and sporting. Why, Nina asked, had we come so far and driven so fast on such an appalling surface with so many giddy drops over the side? She had looked unimpressed at the seascape and what she clearly thought was a boring old piece of rock. By the second day she was photographing it at dawn, at sunset and at high noon. We stopped at the unprepossessing D-class hotel facing the rock and entered with some hesitation, which was not warranted. If the accommodation was a touch Spartan, the lobsters were magnificent and the cooking simple but, with many herbs, delicious. Bold as ever we asked if we might try the local wine. A carafe of a deep rose-red wine was brought. It seemed rather decent. We ordered another one, and I suspect yet another. We noticed the other diners looking at us askance but we smiled back. It all went down remarkably well, smoothly. Until, of course, we tried to stand up.

Malmsey was first grown in the vineyards around Monemvasia, from which its name was derived. By the thirteenth century it was one of the wines specially selected for imperial banquets and shortly thereafter became the most popular festive wine at the courts of Europe. Other wines at other times have played a similar role – champagne, cognac, port and madeira. Later the Monemvasia vines were also cultivated in Crete and other Greek islands. Now there is no Malmsey produced in Monemvasia but, as the hotelier alleged, the vines still grew in Crete and this is where his brew came from, a direct descendent of the original great delicacy.

This time there was no Malmsey, no heating and, on the following morning, no hotel. The owner decided to pack up, return to Athens with his family and wait for June before opening up again. We thought we might as well head north for Nauplion. Crossing the pass between Tripolis and Miloi on the old Tripolis-Argos road, we stopped for a coffee.

"Oh look," I said to Nina, before we got out of the car, "look at the blossom blowing across that herd of goats over there."

I looked again. It was snow.

XII

Number 19 had undergone a total transformation: it was in fact a new house, occupying the same site. All the external dimensions of the original were copied, including non-rectangular corners and other variations, but all was now built in brick and concrete, the new technology. Inside it was strangely empty and somehow more noticeably unfinished. The stairs were free-standing, sharp-edged, a semi-spiral, mounting steeply, eerie and isolated until we reached our floor which was, in a manner of speaking, complete.

The floor existed, not yet surfaced. A vast wooden pitched roof of large timbers supporting planks which in turn were roofed on the outside with Byzantine tiles drew the eye. There were three wooden posts on top of the concrete ceiling of the bedrooms while over the open living area there was an arrangement like a medieval crown-post. It stood on top of a considerable transverse beam which ran the full width of the house, just over 8 metres, say 27 feet. The crown-post, about six feet tall, stood under the apex of the sloping roof and, together with the three other posts, supported a longitudinal beam, the spine as it were, which ran the remainder of the length of the house and in turn supported the rest of the roof till it abutted on the house next door. The crown-post sprouted five angled arms or props, like leaves on a stem.

It all seemed much larger than we expected, agreeably so. It had shrunk, in retrospect, and anyway our memories were of incomplete views of a house near to or in the process of collapse. Neither of us were used to or gifted in the reading of plans. And it was all in metres. I am too old to gauge things metrically without first estimating in yards or feet, along the lines of cricket pitches, dashes and sprints and my own height. Nina never liked sports and, I suspect, is not too hot on poles and perches either.

"It's bigger and higher and much more impressive," said Nina, "and lovely and airy. And *light*." Which it was. "But I don't think I want to climb up that ladder to the attic. I'm sure," she said tentatively, "it will be marvellous when it's finished. And don't you go near those French windows. They're very scary."

The two sets of French windows actually gave on to the two balconies, one on each side of the house. But the doors and windows were not there yet. Nor were the balconies. To be precise the supports and the ironwork balustrades were in place but not the floorboards. To lean out was a touch frightening. We seemed very high above the street.

"A sheer drop." Nina shuddered.

"Yes," I said turning round. It was a drop of two floors and nearer three at the back where the *scala* descended sharply. Nikos and Kosmas the engineer ran up the stairs. They must have been doing something in the cellar. We exchanged embraces and Happy Easters.

"I think the wooden ceiling is magnificent, stunning." I pointed to the crown-post . *"Para poli oraio. Katapliktiko!"*

Katapliktiko is one of those excellent polysyllabic Greek

words which have a rhythm of their own. It means amazing, breathtaking. Kosmas demurred. He was clearly pleased but he wanted me to know that the design had been Pericles'.

"But you and Nikos did a splendid job executing the plan."

"We learned," Nikos stressed the second syllable, "from *Kyrios* Pericles." He added, not exactly reproachfully, "He was very strict about the woods."

I climbed up Nikos' ladder. It still wobbled a bit, seemed very tall and had two or three rungs which tested one's faith. They had built two dormers. From one, I looked out over the roofs towards the harbour, the sea and the mountains.

"Look. Sea. Mountains. There is the radar and there Argos Castle." This was Andreas on an upbeat. He had appeared from nowhere.

"There is troubles. The permissions are no good for the windows." Nikos, downbeat. He too had followed me up the ladder.

"But I thought," I said lamely, "Athina said the dormer windows had been approved?"

Nikos said, "Ha!"

Andreas said, "Bah!"

And Kosmas muttered something about Nauplion-Tripoli-Sparta-Athens which sounded like a bus route.

"Do you think we *will* get permission?"

"I don't take the permissions yet. They talk. They decide not."

"They decide not to give the permission?"

"No. They not decide. But work stops."

"Why does work stop?" I said, taken aback.

"Because no permissions," said Nikos reasonably enough.

"All work? Even inside the house?"

"Outside no good," said Andreas. "Inside they not know."

I decided to take some photographs, in case the dormers had to be removed, to show the views we might have seen. Not having thought of the dormers originally, we were now horrified at the prospect of their vanishing. With them, the attic was a working space, an extra place for a bed, a play area and a room for bookcases, shelves and whatever else, as well as for the water-tank for which it was intended. Without them, darkness, gloom and disappointment. Like children whose parents had half-promised them a treat ("Who knows? If you're good, we might even . . .") which cannot be fulfilled, we were immoderately cast down.

Nina said, "It would have been better not to have had it dangled in front of us. Let alone *seen* it before it's snatched away. We would have been satisfied with the rest." She gestured almost dismissively at the wooden ceiling, which still looked magnificent.

Nikos, sensitive to moods if not always to meaning, intervened. "Many more meetings. Talk, talk, talk. Here in Nauplion. Then in Tripolis. Everywhere. In Athens perhaps. But you like?" He also gestured at the beams and rafters.

Yes, yes, we said. We liked it very much. Too much. That's why we're upset about the dormers.

"Too much? What too much?" This was Andreas.

I shifted ground in preference to over-elaborate explanation. "Too much talking. Too many meetings."

Unfair perhaps. Greece came to protecting its more recent heritage rather late. A great many buildings dating from the newly independent nation of the 1830s and '40s were torn down in Athens. Some too were destroyed in Nauplion and replaced with unsuitable not to say ugly and commonplace structures. Since then various planning laws have come into effect and a healthy process of conservation and regeneration is now well underway. The Plaka in Athens is a notable example. Nauplion is becoming one. This means, quite rightly, that all new building, rebuilding and restoration is under strict planning scrutiny.

It also means a system of stops and starts, of intricate interlocking committees, of subtle Byzantine hierarchies and of bewildering delays. Take, for example, the system in our part of the Peloponnese. First of all there is the archaeological committee. If there is any reason to believe there might be bronze age, iron age, even classical remains on or around the property, nothing can be touched until the responsible inspectors have had a look or, if thought desirable, a dig. There is a long queue for the archaeologists – months, sometimes years. Then there are the Byzantologists who stretch themselves to take in Frankish and Venetian and probably Turkish remains.

After you have cleared those hurdles you have to face the planning sub-committees and authorities. The proposed plans go, for example, to a group of structural engineers and to a group of architects. Both have to approve the scheme. But the architects have their little ways and the engineers their rather different assessments. If the architects ask for some modification which the engineers feel is impracticable, the argument can go on for months. The architects have the final shout at this stage. Next the recommendations, when agreed, go to the *demos* of Nauplion, then, if approved, to the planning authority for the Peloponnese, and then to the ministry in Athens for a penultimate overview before being returned to Nauplion. At any point, almost anyone can object. If an objection is upheld, the process is repeated on appeal. All right and proper and admirable, in principle at any rate.

The process can be very long-winded and somewhat confusing. The two sub-committees often disagree. The various planning authorities likewise. As the brothers Nondas described it: many meetings, much talk, no permissions. And permissions it was. No mistake there, properly plural.

Nikos, perhaps because of his years at sea or just through temperament, viewed bureaucracy with distaste and bureaucrats, particularly if female, with a mixture of contempt and distrust. They were never there. Work was done incomprehensibly slowly. They kept you waiting while they nattered. They could never take decisions. By which he probably meant favourable decisions but would extend it, if challenged, to any. You always had to work through layers of underlings before you could get to see anyone capable of sensible discussion.

I thought, when I first heard the litany, that he was suffering from some particular piece of bumbledom presumably effected by a particular harpy. But no: it was a general complaint and not eased by the fact that he appeared to have been at school with almost every official in town.

We went to OTE, the telephone organization. Nikos thought

it would be a good idea to put our name down for a telephone. After waiting for some minutes for the assistant who took bookings to finish copying information from dockets into a ledger, Nikos shouted to some man at the back who was a friend of his. He came over. I was introduced. We shook hands. Nikos explained. The friend shrugged his shoulders, gestured towards the assistant and went on to discuss football, politics, the state of the economy.

Eventually the young woman looked up from her ledger and said the equivalent of, "Yes. What do you want?" Unoriginally I said, "A telephone." She was not much given to smiling. She asked for my passport, looked at the photograph and at me and decided that I did look like the brutal staring-eyed thug that glared at her from its blue-bound fastness. As passport photos go it was a dilly. It would have looked more at home outside a French police station with words like *ASSASSIN* or *VIOLEUR* underneath it. Undeterred, she wrote down the number and copied my surname. Nikos was listening with half an ear.

"She asks your father's name."

"My father's? Why on earth? It's the same as mine: Kark. Kappa. Alpha," I said to her, "Ro. Kappa."

"No, no," said Nikos in some exasperation, "his other name."

Other name? I reeled at the thought. His cover. His *nom de guerre*. What did they know that I didn't?

"First name."

"His or mine?"

"Yours first. His after."

Austen was not too bad. There had been a time when Austin cars were known in Greece. It came out as Ostyn. Norman was another matter.

"Nouma," said the OTE official.

"Noma," said Nikos, astonished. He thought he had once known an Australian girl called Noma. Was it Norma, or Mona, or perhaps, indeed, Noma?

"Norman," I said, "like the castles."

It was no good. The Greeks call the Normans Franks, and anyway I was speaking in English. I tried to spell it in Greek but it went down firmly, and not inappropriately, as Nomen.

It is confusing. For us, I mean; not for the Greeks. They have their baptismal name. They have their family name. And in between they put their father's name, like the Russian patronymic. It means that they assume any second or middle name is a father's name. Of course if they ask for your father's name you then find yourself becoming some stranger with a different set of initials.

We moved on to addresses. Was the house mine? Well was it? We had not yet taken delivery, as it were.

"Yes," said Nikos.

I signed a form. A docket was placed in a filing basket.

"How long will it take?" I seemed to remember that Mr Papandreou had promised everyone a telephone within five years of taking office.

Nikos passed on the question to his friend who paused and stroked his chin.

"What to say? Five, ten years?"

"Years?" I squeaked.

He, the friend, walked over to a filing cabinet and crashed all three drawers open. They were very full.

"Up to 1979," he said and pointed to other filing cabinets presumably equally full and perhaps going up to who knows when; 1984 perhaps.

"That's what the girl is doing," said Nikos. "Progressing them. Perhaps they find some are dead." He laughed. "They're the only people not wanting a telephone."

We walked back fast to the square where Nina was having a coffee and reading yesterday's *Times*.

"Where," she said predictably, "have you been? It can't have taken that long to ask for a phone." She looked at me and at her watch and then smiled at Nikos. "Will they be able to install it when we move in?"

I left it to him to explain.

There were matters to be decided: plumbing, electrics, and, above all, what Nikos called "the marbs". Pericles and Athina were coming down from Athens and would arrive around noon. As there was nothing to be done earlier in the morning, Nina elected to stay in the hotel and wash her hair. Nikos decided that I should continue my round of the public utilities.

And so to the water company. Water is naturally extremely important in the normally hot, dry climate of the Peloponnese. It is also, understandably, relatively expensive.

We had enquired before about the charges for turning on the water supply and for whatever standing, up-front disbursements were required. The rest was metered. Inflation was running at around twenty-five per cent so I suppose I should not have been particularly surprised at what seemed a rather larger increase on the water-rates. When I understood the new charges I must have shown some flicker of emotion.

It was a man this time taking the details and seeing to the business of assessing whether everything had been complied with – the relevant permission, the registering of the ownership of the property, the number of taps and outlets, the square meterage of the apartment, and my father's name. My flicker had rankled.

He said, "I don't know where you come from." This was patently untrue because at some point he had seen my passport, unless he meant what bog in the British wilds. "But here in Nauplion we supply water twenty-four hours a day. Every day. Without cease." This too was inaccurate, as we were to discover. "And we don't just give you the water, when and how you want it, we meter it and charge you precisely for what you use. And I don't know how you do it where *you* come from but here we look after the sewage too, *all the time*. We don't just collect it weekly or monthly but *all the time*. And not only do we take it away *all the time*." He drew breath and added triumphantly, "*We pump it out to sea.*"

Athina and Pericles arrived just as I was trying to tell Nina about what was clearly not so much a clash of cultures as a displacement of time and fashion. The Greeks had not yet caught up with contemporary anti-pollution right thinking, I was saying, that's all. Cleaning the sea is another chapter.

"Our sea was very clean," said Athina. "The Aegean was not like the Mediterranean. Very pure, very lovely. But," she added promptly, "must you not bath in the harbour. There are good *plages* and some not so good. I swim in a pool but I like better the sea."

Nina turned to tell Pericles how wonderful we thought the wooden roof was and how lovely it looked.

"Yes. Very lovely. *Very* lovely. And when," Athina looked round for Nikos as though to charge him with some heinous dereliction of duty, "when the floor is made and the windows and the bathrooms and," she cast around, "the doors were ready, very, very beautiful."

Pericles went round with Kosmas checking everything. Athina took us into what was going to be our bathroom and asked us what we felt about the floor and the walls and fittings. We did not feel anything very much, I suspect. We had agreed that it would be marble. What else were we to say?

"Yes, yes; marble. But how to put it? Big or small? And where is the bath, the toilet, the bidet? How you want it?"

"The marbs," said Nikos, joining us. "You want a design?"

"Design?" I said.

"Like flower or diamond."

"No," said Athina.

"No," said Nina.

Nikos looked at me. I was the one that mattered. I said no; I didn't think so, the room was too small for patterns.

"Perhaps the saloon, then," he said eagerly. "Plenty of room. I show you nice shapes and colours."

"No," said Athina.

"No," said Nina.

I said I thought Pericles had chosen some Ioannina marble.

"Why you not look at the marbs here?" said Nikos. "You come and see my aunt's son's house. Nice marbs, with colours and shapes."

"No," said Pericles, joining us. "Ioannina marble with no designs. The floor space in the living rooms is large. It must be plain with just traces of colour and variation. Which will be in the marble itself. In the bathrooms, a lighter colour; white I think. Good quality but not Ioannina. Perhaps local." He looked at Nikos.

"Big or little?" asked Athina.

Nikos said, "Little."

"He wants little," she explained to us, "because little marbles are easy to find and more cheap too. Big marbles are better."

"Big marbs are no good in little rooms," said Nikos.

The discussion swept into Greek. The tempo increased, voices were raised and it sounded as though a fierce argument was developing. Suddenly it died down. Pericles had intervened. A medium size was agreed.

We moved to the guest shower-room. There was another discussion about marbs. I decided I served no useful purpose and withdrew. Nina joined me at the end of the floor.

"You know," she said, "we don't really want a telephone here. People will just ring us up. It'll be as bad as being in London. We can walk to the OTE whenever *we* want to ring someone up."

"And what happens if someone wants to get hold of us urgently, like the children?"

"They can ring The Boatyard and leave a message."

Yes, I thought, but what about real emergencies and what if someone needed an answer quickly?

Nina and the others had moved on to electric plugs and lightfittings. Where? How many? Nikos asked the questions, Pericles decided, I nodded agreement and Nina said you could never have too many plugs.

Athina was impatient to get back to essentials.

"Must you choose bath and douche."

Nina said, "Now?"

I said, "Here? In Nauplion?"

"Must you come to Athens."

"We have a bathroom and cooking shop in Argos," said Nikos.

"Athens," she said firmly. "I take you to very good shop with Italian baths and showers. And another for kitchens."

"What about a broom cupboard?" Nina addressed the world at large. It ignored her.

"What about the dormer windows?" I said to Pericles. "Do we have to remove them right away?"

"Look," said Athina, "we appeal. I find something. Never mind."

Pericles, his usual judicious self, said, "It takes time. There are many decisions and appeals and more decisions, and perhaps more appeals. For now we stop work on the outside. A pity but there is work inside. We can hope."

"But all round us," I said, "I can see houses with structures on the roofs, coming out of the roofs, many of them are dormers. How can they say it's not a Naupliot style?"

"Because they're stupid," said Andreas.

"I have argued," said Athina.

"You *will* argue," said Pericles.

"I argue next time and I write letters."

"I speak and speak to them," said Nikos," but they didn't tell me anything. Only I find there are no permissions."

"Stupid," said Andreas.

"The process takes time," Pericles said. "*Telika*, at the finish?"

"Finally," I said.

"Yes, finally, perhaps it will be OK."

"Never mind," Athina said. "I have found something."

"Will find something," said Pericles. "Perhaps."

"*Then birazee*. Never mind. You like we go to Savouras?"

We liked. We went. Or rather most of us went. Andreas and Kosmas melted away, as I reminded myself they had done before. They were there as we started to walk down the *scala* but by the time we reached the harbour front, they had disappeared. It was never explained. There is an appealing casualness in Greek everyday social intercourse which is disarming but occasionally bewildering. You can never be quite sure that your invited guest is going to turn up. Or when. In the Orthodox Church services the congregation ebbs and flows; people come, people leave, others go and come back; everyone stands, walks about, chats; some pray. Not at all like the Church of England. Behaviour in church is mirrored in ordinary life, or perhaps it is that the Church is so much a part of life in Greece that there is no such distinction, even though most adult males never step inside a church from one Easter to the next, unless weddings, baptisms or funerals intervene.

We had ordered a dish of prawns cooked with garlic, tomato and cheese as *orektika*. The draught retsina, in its litre metal pot, the bread, the cutlery and the salad had been brought to the table. We were sitting outside having debated sun or shade or mixed and Nikos had gone inside to choose (but not for me) the fish. All Greeks are very keen and careful about their fish, Nikos particularly so. He believes that fish should only be eaten on the day they are caught or, if pushed, the day after the night they are caught. He says that you can tell from rubbing your hand over the skin. The flesh should be firm, of course, but the skin should still be rough; and then there's something about the eyes. As far as Nina was concerned Nikos' expertise was invaluable because he knew which fish were which. So, naturally, did Athina and Pericles, but they were not around all the time. This may sound simple, but Aegean fish are different. They also have different, and Greek, names. Dictionaries are not much help, nor for that matter are menus. Mullet on the whole is mullet and swordfish undeniably swordfish but others are variously labelled snapper or sea-bream. I have looked up three quite distinct fish under their Greek names only to find all three described as sea-bream. Even if Nikos could not be sure of their English equivalent, if any, he could tell Nina the ones to eat and their seasons.

There is a close season for small fry and shellfish and others are so seasonal they come but once a year. We were swimming in the sea one day and suddenly saw shoals and shoals of trumpet-nosed fish swimming in ordered line ahead, flashing in the sunlight, surprisingly close to the surface. The following day they had gone. Phaidon told us they were good to eat, if you woke up in time to catch them on the wing, as it were.

While we waited for the prawns to appear and for Nikos to return I asked whether people found bureaucrats easy to deal with. I thought this was a suitably neutral phrasing. Predictably it was Athina who replied.

"Easy? *Easy?* Easy for them not for us. You call them, I read, petty bureaucrats. Is that the same as French *petit?* Small. That's what they are. Small. And officers."

"Officers?" said Nina, breaking off her search for cucumbers in the salad.

"Officious?" I tried.

"Very, very. Many times they are not very clever and they have not helped." She paused to lend emphasis to the condemnation, but the pause was interrupted by the prawns arriving and Nikos returning. "Look," she said, "yesterday I go to the bank to pay the tax of a client. It was the due date. Must it be promptly paid. Then and there."

"Yes. The banks are like government. Talk, talk. Waste time. Lazy. Don't work." This was Nikos between bites of prawns eaten whole, tails, heads and whiskers. "They make you wait. Hours. But they make you pay on the day. Take your money quick, quick. You want something, slow, slow."

Athina had gone to the nearest branch of her bank, the Bank of Greece. It was not her own branch but she thought she would be able to pay the bill with a cheque. The teller thought otherwise. "And how could we be sure you had money in your account?"

Athina had replied by passing over her deposit account book which showed a healthy few million drachma in credit. This was dismissed as irrelevant. Athina had become stern. "I am a lawyer, an officer of the supreme court. Do you doubt my veracity?" Or somesuch.

The answer was an infinitesimal lifting of the head; no. "You may telephone the manager of my bank," said Athina. No, said the lady bank clerk, we do not accept telephone conversations for banking business. Not even from the bank manager of another branch of your bank? No. Athina had suggested that this was totally ridiculous and unacceptable. Why, asked the bank clerk disingenuously, couldn't the *kyria* take herself and her cheque to her own branch where no doubt a more credulous, or easily intimidated, official would yield to these importunate and patently unsound financial dickerings? Because, said Athina, with the slow, clear enunciation of barely contained fury, the bill had to be paid today, banking business would shortly close for the day and she was several crowded miles from her bank. Ah yes, said the teller, there was that.

Athina had stormed along to the manager. He rose and took her hand. Of course, what a pleasure it was to see *Kyria* Sideropoulou. And how was she? Yes, he knew her reputation well and, of course, he would be only too happy to accept her personal cheque. The word of a lawyer as distinguished as herself was as good as money in gold sovereigns. She relaxed a moment too soon with, I could imagine, a shy, refulgent smile. But he could not, of course, the manager went on, interfere with the teller on duty. It was up to her to take the decision and he was sure that as soon as Mrs Sideropoulou told her of his, the manager's, view all would correct itself.

Athina was by no means as confident. She was right. The petty tyrant refused to budge. The bill had to be paid a day late and the client had incurred a fine.

"It was jealousy," said Athina. "I knew it from the first. She is not pretty. Nor sexy. She has not had a man. She has not married. She has no children. And she is not very clever. Why else be still a bank clerk, eh? Of course she is jealous of me. Not only my marriage, my daughter – although this she did not know – but looks and fun and profession. I am sorry for her. It is a very dull life. But all this nonsense must stop. *You* are told the customer is always right. *We* are to believe that the clerk is never wrong. How silly. I complain to the big boss of the bank. We see. I think nothing happens."

"This problem is Greece," Pericles summed up. "Why Greece is not yet Europe."

XIII

Returning to the house for Pericles to have a last word with Nikos on site, Nina and I stood outside with Athina gazing up, imagining what it would be like when it was finished, not to say furnished. Would the dormers remain? Would permission be given? When? How?

"Look," said Athina. "Always there are problems. Difficulty with the permissions. Never mind. Your lawyer will find a way."

"Our *famous* lawyer," said Nina.

Athina smiled, but not for long. A first-floor shutter banged open, a head poked out and an imperious hand motioned us to ascend. This was Antigone, our future next-door neighbour, were we ever to move in. Athina did nothing. Nina smiled deprecatingly. I waved a friendly hand.

"She is your lawyer?"

"Yes," I said.

"Come," Antigone said. "Now." She beckoned. "Up."

We demurred.

"Come," Antigone repeated, command modulating just discernibly towards entreaty with more than a hint of the conspiratorial, heavy nods and winks directed at Number 19.

"This is not a good idea," Athina said, but Nina was already opening the door and going upstairs.

"It is not good," said Antigone as soon as introductions were made. "Look at my house. It is damaged. He digs under." She made a burrowing motion with her right hand. "The wall cracks." She made a splitting noise, like tearing canvass, and a separating gesture with both hands. "He hurts my house. It is damaged. He says nothing. He is not good. It is very bad."

Antigone's house was, as it were, in its unreconstructed state, both habitable and actually inhabited, floors and wooden ceilings intact. But then, despite Antigone's charge, it had not been undermined nor had its roof been taken off. Built on a more modest scale, it was nonetheless a comfortable eighteenth-century Naupliot family house on three floors with two balconies and three windows per floor. Antigone and her two sisters lived there; to be more precise, they lived there when they were not at their other houses in Athens and various summer resorts. This had been their childhood home and it was the family house; they returned to vote, and for Easter certainly, and at other times for quite long periods, but we were never quite sure when we got to Nauplion whether any of them would be there.

Antigone was always clearly in charge: it was her house, her affair. A retired dentist with an impressive career behind her, mostly in Athens, she must have been one of the first women in Greece to embark on such a profession. Their father, a cavalry colonel, had been killed in the Asia Minor offensive of 1921–22. His portrait in uniform hung prominently on the wall, together with his medals and a smaller photograph of King George II. The three sisters were unashamedly right-wing: Papandreou and his lot were a bunch of thieves and robbers. They probably remained royalist and I sometimes wondered how they had reacted to Papadopoulos and the dictatorship of the Colonels. No doubt about it, critical of many politicians though she was, Antigone was a Greek patriot. During the war she and her family had sheltered and hidden British officers while having German officers billeted on them. She was and is a formidable character.

She repeated, "It is very bad what he is doing to my house."

Athina looked at the portraits and predictably said nothing. Nina made an almost noiseless tut-tutting and looked sympathetic. I said I thought Nikos was doing his best not to cause any damage to her house; I couldn't see any cracks from the outside, other than those obviously of some age and, therefore, I should have thought of no great significance.

"You see up the stairs?" she said.

"No, I haven't. But I'm sure if there is any new crack Nikos will make it good and repair anything that needs doing."

Antigone harrumphed in Greek and made a dismissive, belittling gesture with her right hand. Neither I nor my message was approved.

"Something will be done. I cannot have my house tunnelled under, destructed. He has not *le droit. C'est insupportable. Je vais téléphoner à mon avocat. Immédiatement.* At once. *Grigora-grigora.*" Antigone changes languages a touch capriciously. She is of the generation that learnt French rather than German or English. Now she turned to Athina and asked her in Greek what she advised.

Athina advised nothing other than patience. She was not going to give anything away. We said goodbye and traipsed downstairs and into the street.

"This was wrong," Athina said. "I think you say conflicted interests. We are an interested party. She may take us to court."

"It's possible," I said. "But she's not getting at us. It's Nikos and I suspect he hasn't been particularly tactful with her. The fact that he's an ardent Pasok supporter won't have helped."

"Greeks like going to law," Athina said reflectively.

"Just as well for you lawyers," said Nina. "Every other office in Nauplion seems to be a lawyer's."

"Yes, many, many lawyers. Very crowded. But also many judges, many courts."

"I think Antigone has sued people in Nauplion before," I said. "That doesn't mean she's particularly litigious. She may have had right on her side. Or been provoked."

"I expect she has some right on her side right now," said Nina helpfully. "And I bet she's been provoked. Noise, dust, earth-shaking excavations and Nikos not being particularly careful of her sensibilities. Nor, I dare say, being very informative either." She paused. "Lovely man though he is."

"Look," said Athina, "we will see what happened."

Pericles and Nikos emerged into the sunlight smiling; all was well between them. Athina and Pericles made for their car to return to Athens where we were to see them later in the week. We waved them goodbye and *kalo taxidi*.

"Antigone thinks you've damaged her house," I said to Nikos.

"I try to talk to her. Never mind. No problem."

"I'm not so sure."

"No problem," he repeated emphatically. "She is worried perhaps because they are old."

"Not much older than we are," said Nina smartly.

Nikos smiled indulgently. "Never mind."

He was, as I reminded Nina as we walked back to the Amphitryon, the same sort of age as our older children.

Nauplion is not very large. The older part is so easily encompassable that sooner or later you get to know the externals of all the regular inhabitants, their shape, gait and sometimes voice, if not name or calling; and they of course likewise, only more so, know you. Strangers and visitors are instantly noticeable; only tourists seem somehow to merge facelessly into national groups. The Naupliotes will tell you that June brings the Germans, July the French and August the Italians. The English, like uncertainly migrant birds, drift in lesser numbers throughout spring, summer and autumn, some with noses deep in *Blue Guides*, Pausanias and Leigh Fermor, others with noses peeling from over-exposure at the beaches at Tolo and Assini. Whatever ruck, the Blishens were certain to stand out. We had not expected them nor they us, but even before Edward turned his head and those splendid eyebrows, a thick bunch of individualistic prawns' antennae, asserted his identity, I had said "Blishen", out loud, and Nina added with delight, "Edward and Nancy. How marvellous!"

We took them with what we thought was measured haste, after a cool drink in the *plateia*, to see the house. We were bursting with excitement and apprehension. They were the first of our friends to see it; what would they think of it? By the time I had run up the *scala* and waited for the others to catch me up I began to look at it with their eyes: a rather dreadful mess down below with a forest of concrete pillars rising bare for two floors to support a roofed platform that was to be our nest. What could they say, poor dears? That we were mad impetuous fools, romantic idiots, but all the more loveable because of it? Or the literary equivalent of "very nice I'm sure. If you like that sort of thing"?

"Ah," Edward said. "Aaaaah," one of those deliciously pro-longed open vowels. "What a delightful spot you've chosen. Right in the Old Town. And Nauplion itself. Such an elegant and –" he almost sounded as though he was surprising himself – "lovely little jewel of a city. I suppose it is a city. It has a cathe-dral, a bishop and his palace. But perhaps the Greeks use different rules."

I said I didn't know, and that I was delighted they liked Nauplion, and I wondered if they had seen all the local sites and sights. The archaeological museum with the only com-plete suit of Mycenean armour and the Lord of Assini? Yes, and they *had* noticed the so-called Lord of Assini, a small piece of pottery with a peerlessly arrogant face and high, thin, kingly nose, as well as the remarkable armour. Lerna and the House of Tiles? No. Tiryns? No. We decided to take them to Tiryns.

It lies just outside Nauplion, perhaps three miles from the sea, beyond the model prison farm. It rises above the main road to Argos and it has dominated this part of the alluvial plain for four millennia. It is not as well-known as Mycenae. No great riches were found in its tombs and it lacks the drama that attaches to the life and particularly the death of Agamemnon. Not to mention the longer catalogue of horror that belongs to the House of Atreus. This is not to say that wall-girt Tiryns is without its own atmosphere of doom, murder and mayhem, but we don't *know* of any king of Tiryns who served up his murdered nephews and nieces in a stew to his brother, as Atreus did at Mycenae. Tiryns does not figure as the background to any of the great tragic cycles. In the original 1972 *Companion Guide to Southern Greece* the late Brian de Jongh, contemplating the earlier inhabitants of Tiryns and perhaps sensing the lack of suitable gore, wrote, "At such a distance in time, it is not difficult to imagine the Argive women, driven mad by Dionysus, roaming the plain in search of their children whom they devoured raw." My rather less fervid imagination has more often been exercised by what sort of people choose to stay at the Hotel Tiryns in Nauplion. Do they know what they are undertaking?

The legends have it that Tiryns was founded by Proteus, twin brother of Acrisius, king of Argos. His successor, Perseus, who cut off Medusa's head, supposedly founded Mycenae, ten miles further north, towards Corinth, which came to dominate the Argolid and to which Tiryns later may have become a tributary. Tiryns meanwhile went about its legendary business, which included the king of the day setting Herakles – otherwise known as Hercules, and in modern Greek Iraklis – his twelve labours. In the tale Zeus, disguised as Amphitryon, Lord of Tiryns, fathered Herakles on Amphitryon's wife. The jealous Hera, Zeus's wife and sister, pursued the hero with an implacable hatred which was his eventual undoing. Herakles may well have been a minor king, perhaps of Tiryns, but we know very little about how the people actually lived then. By the later Bronze Age, the time of the Trojan War, brought to us by Homer writing probably 400 years later, another and perhaps more completely human hero, Diomedes, was ruling over Argos and Tiryns. We have much more information about this period from the archaeological finds and from the deciphering of linear B, and much of it, but by no means all, confirms tradition and Homer.

Tiryns may never have played a leading role, but it's an impressive enough monument to have in your backyard. The

Blishens were properly impressed, especially by the walls. Understandably, later countrymen thought they must have been built by giants, a band of visiting, contract Cyclops. They are massive, some twenty-odd feet thick, made of enormous, roughly shaped and cut limestone blocks, each of which must be around eight feet long and extremely heavy. There is, as at Mycenae, a ramp, a ceremonial and military approach wide enough to take chariots and horses, and evidence of a main gate leading to the upper ramparts. The site dates back well beyond the twentieth century BC but the walls belong to the fifteenth century BC. At the top, where there is a marvellous view of the plain, the mountains and the sea, there is the remains of an older circular building, presumably a palace, an early example of fired brick construction.

We showed Edward and Nancy the main palace, or rather the signs and traces in the *megaron*, of pillars and hearth, and the supposed bathroom and its drainage system. This great fortified Bronze Age palace, which had elaborate frescos of hunts, processions, battles and bull-baiting, was seemingly mysteriously overcome by fire, like the others at Mycenae and Pylos and at roughly the same time, around 1200 BC, and was replaced by a less evolved civilization. Contemporary Egyptian records blame the "Sea Peoples", their identity another enigma. The palaces were unrepaired. Trade, arts, organized government and literacy disappeared. Enter the Dark Ages. In the eighth century BC things started looking up again and by the seventh there were city-states, aristocrats and tyrants, and Drakon issued a harsh, or draconian, code of law in Athens. The arts were flourishing again and the Greeks were moving towards their great Classical Age.

Scrambling around the remains of Bronze Age Tiryns, we were saving the best for last: a marvellous vaulted gallery with doorways giving on to the orange groves below. It's in a splendid state of survival and is a wonder of construction. It may not have quite the scope and grandeur of the architecture of Atreus' Treasury, otherwise known as Agamemnon's Tomb, at Mycenae; it has rather more the air of "Let's have a bit more to the left there, Herakles lad. Now just you hold it steady while we fix the other side. Up. Up. Just one more block, boys. Up. Just a bit more. That looks about right. Let's give it a try, eh." Anyway it's a marvel and, like the Cyclopean outer defences, a monumental exercise in dry-stone walling.

The gigantic blocks have large patches of a wonderfully smooth and polished marble patina. The conventional wisdom is that although originally this casemate was used as a store-room, it had been a sheep pen for centuries, perhaps millennia, and the sheep with their oily woolliness had rubbed and polished the stone to the deep shine that television housewives aspire to. The sheep rubbing, if that be the explanation, has not produced a symmetrical or easily read pattern. Some of the more striking swathes of polished and veined marble are at eye height or above. "Some sheep!" said our visitors with Churchillian echoes and modified disbelief.

"They were climbing on each others' backs," said Nina, who knows about sheep from her wartime evacuee days in Wales and Shropshire. "You know, the way they do when they're all herded together and panicking."

"Maybe it was the rams," I said, "humping enthusiastically." Edward and Nancy looked, I thought, doubtful.

"Anyway," said Nina, warming to her role as sheep expert, "there are some extremely large Greek breeds. We once saw some sheep above Astros, the size," her hands shaped a giant shape, "the size of donkeys."

"Casemates," said Edward, rolling the word pleasurably round his mouth, "casemates and sheep the size of donkeys."

There was nothing credulous about the Blishens. Driving back to their hotel, Nancy told us about overhearing Edward having another conversation at a dinner party. He said that he and Nancy had had a very monotonous marriage. Even allowing for dinner party hyperbole, this seemed excessive. It rankled. Days later, she asked Edward what he had meant by calling their marriage monotonous. She knew they had been married a long time but . . . "Monotonous?" he said. "Our marriage *monotonous*?" He was dismayed, appalled, couldn't imagine what she had heard. Then it struck him. "My love, I said our marriage had been marvellously monogamous."

"At our time of life," Nina said later, "when we're all getting deaf, it's only too likely."

"What's only too likely?"

"The Blishen syndrome."

Nina elected to have an early night. I decided to ruminate while having a quiet drink. As it turned out there was no space for musing about senescence and decay. The bar at The Boatyard was filling up with the early shift of night owls, some of them familiar: the house painter drinking ouzo, the lawyer Vat 69. There was a German engineer, three local worthies of indeterminate middle age, two French girls, and a pair of *kamakia* chatting them up.

Kamaki means harpoon, and it is girls not whales who are pursued. The underlying assumption is that Greek girls are untouchable until spoken for – they have parents and brothers – while foreign girls are available. Seduction may still be an art but the current generation of harpoonists are not a particularly pretty sight, skins browned to a turn, muscles gross with steroids and weightlifting.

Conversations were being conducted in Greek and French. English was added by way of a greeting.

"You can help us," Phaidon said. "The origin of diplomat. But first what can I offer you?"

"A beer," I said. "Thank you. I don't know. I imagine ambassadors grew out of the heralds and messengers that kings used, very early on, in prehistoric times, to send messages to each other."

"And gods too," the lawyer said.

"No, no, no," said Phaidon.

"You mean they didn't?"

"No, no, no, no. Diplomat. The word."

"Oh," I said. "But isn't it Greek?"

"Of course," said one of the worthies, raising his head from contemplation of an empty glass. "We have the richest language in the world. More words than any other. We have seven words for stone."

"Nine," said someone else.

Phaidon took charge and wrenched the conversation back into English. "I think so." He paused, unsure whether to reflect on the richness of Greek or to pour another whisky in the lawyer's glass. "I think it must be like this. *Diplo. Matia. Diplo* – double. *Matia* – eyes." He mimed it energetically. "Double eye." He tapped his nose. "Two looks, just like a diplomat, eh? Not trusting."

"*Oxi*," said the lawyer. "*Non.* No."

"*Nai, nai,*" yes, yes, said the worthy who was still looking at his empty glass. Had it perhaps been refilled and re-drained?

"*Oraia,*" he said and handed his glass to Phaidon. "*Poly oraia. Diplo-matia.*" He laughed.

The lawyer said, "Nonsense. Two-eye nonsense."

"Well?" Phaidon turned to me. "What do you think?"

"Nice idea. Very engaging. But you're on the wrong track. The derivation can't be anything to do with eyes, not even double-eyes. Surely it comes from diploma, which originally must have meant something folded. A diplomat is someone who carries something folded, confidential, perhaps secret. A state paper." Phaidon looked dejected. He pulled a wry smile. "But," I went on, "I rather fancy the idea of the double-eyed, duplicitous envoy lying abroad for his country. Even though it's all eyewash."

Phaidon laughed. The lawyer half got up to go but then slumped back on his stool. "Of course, it's diploma," he said. "*Diplomat.* It's an omega not an omicron."

The French girls got up and went out with the *kamaki* pair on the way to a disco.

"*Then m'aresoun Angloi,*" said the other whisky-drinker, he of the rapidly emptying tumbler. And then, in case I had not understood him, "I don't like the English."

I was a touch taken aback. I had heard a certain amount of anti-American sentiments being voiced (not usually face-to-face), but remarkably few anti-British remarks.

"Why?" I said. "Because of Cyprus?"

"That too. Because you can't be trusted. Because you're full of pride. You look down at people. You pretend you protect people. Then you betray them."

"When?"

"Churchill." He spat the name out.

"You preferred Hitler?" I asked.

The German looked up. Phaidon poured him another beer.

"We fought hard in the War. Churchill encouraged us but we would have fought anyway. Then Churchill took away our arms. Churchill brought the king back. Churchill supported the rightists, the fascists, the generals. Churchill handed us over to the Americans." He got up, staggered a little but walked quite dignifiedly towards the outside world. "I do not like the English." And he was gone.

"*Ti krima*," said Phaidon. "What a pity. He was a good man. A brave man. A partisan in the War. He saw terrible things. Then and afterwards. In the *emphilio polemo*, the Civilian War."

"The Civil War," I said.

"Yes, civil. Brother against brother. Son against father. Father against son. For those who believed in a new world, a free Greece, you will hear many say Churchill betrayed them."

"And you, Phaidon? What do you think?"

"I am Pasok. Not communist, not rightist. I was born halfway through the second war. Churchill? I don't *know*, but I think so."

I started to tell him about many British friends and acquaintances, such as Colonel the Honourable C.M. Woodhouse DSO etc, known interchangeably as Chris or Monty, and their brave and difficult exploits in wartime Greece. I reminded him of the Battle of Crete. And Matapan. And I spoke of the younger unsung philhellenes like Freddie Matthews, Peter Storrs and all those correspondents who lost their hearts to Greece during the War and its aftermath, the Civil War, and were then confronted with Cyprus, Grivas, EOKA and a virulently anti-British Greece. And the older generations, more than a century and a half ago, during the War of Independence. The decisive role of Admiral Codrington. But it all got jumbled up, as points were scored and arguments exchanged, with the British rescue of President Makarios and the Greek military dictatorship's bringing about the tragedy of the Turkish invasion of northern Cyprus.

The lawyer asked why had Britain not acted *then*, as a Guarantor of the Treaty. And Phaidon said it was true, was it not, that Churchill had an anti-communist obsession. The German muttered something about Northern Ireland.

It is sensible as well as polite not to enter into arguments about other people's politics in other people's countries. It is also a mistake to go beyond the limit of one's linguistic ability, and mine in Greek is sadly lacking. Admittedly I had mostly spoken in English, admittedly I had understood the thrust of what had been said in Greek, admittedly too the Greeks love a political discussion, or argument, as it almost always turns out to be. I had been goaded on this occasion, flicked on the raw. Nonetheless, I thought, I should not have allowed myself to speak out quite the way I did. And then I thought, what the hell, I love these people, why should I patronize them? If they want to have a go at British foreign policy, fine. Why should I be politic and double-faced, if not double-eyed, and spoil their fun by not responding? I know that they know that I agree with them about a great many issues. Anyway I was on a hiding to nothing.

"And another thing," I said, putting my wallet on the bar ready to pay and leave. "You're wrong about the numbers of words. English is much richer than Greek. It has more words than any other language. By a long chalk." I thumped the bar. "Mind you, a good many of them are Greek."

That brought laughter and more drinks and the house-painter's insisting, "What did he say? What did he say?"

I got back to the hotel rather late. Nina stirred and asked sleepily what I had been doing. Practising my Greek, I said.

XIV

The road from Nauplion to Corinth runs due north, give or take a divagation or two to avoid mountains. It is not, however, a new road, nor is it a straight one. One of its more eccentric, if less endearing, characteristics is its tendency to cross and recross the railway line – the main line runs to Argos, Tripoli and all stations to Kalamata. Looking at the map (no easy matter since good maps are hard to find and the Greeks still consider ordnance surveys as military secrets, beneficial to an enemy and therefore to be denied to foreigners and not to be displayed or sold), the road crosses the railway line twelve times between Nauplion and the isthmus, a distance of about sixty-five kilometres. I have counted them lovingly, bump by bump, and made it an uncomfortable baker's dozen.

The line is single track, the trains are rare; the trouble is the height above the road that the rails, unevenly, are set. They are the least level level-crossings I know. They have, of course, to be taken slowly and carefully, many of them being carefully arranged to coincide with S-bends so that the car driver approaches them at a sharp angle. The Greek motorist, and often enough the Greek truck driver, being of a sporting and adventurous turn, sees them as a challenge to be taken with speed and verve. They also provide glorious chances for over-taking, and since the rest of the road is often narrow, as well as soaring up and down and twisting, the railway crossings are useful places to pass a vehicle or two by pushing safety, steering and suspension to their limits.

Blind corners are also much favoured on the mountainsides. One man slows down to take the corner and another joyously overtakes him – and it is almost always a male driver. I am not being sexist: Greek women drivers have their own little foibles, such as facing their passengers and talking spiritedly with hands, eyes and voices when joining main roads from side roads. Better still, I have seen Naupliot matrons making them-selves up in the driving mirror, lipstick in free hand, while bowling across the busy main street with a fine disregard for the traffic.

I was thinking as we drove to Athens this time how unwill-ing I was to leave Nauplion; how reluctant I was to say goodbye to this corner of the Aegean, the bare mountains with their bones showing, the rich Argive plain, green with orange trees and silvery with the shimmering leaves of the olive trees, the monumental solidity of Tiryns, the dominating bulk of Palamidi, the Bourtzi, the little fortified island in the bay. And, of course, our friends.

There had been no further news about the permissions. Activity at the house would soon reduce to nothing very much, since all outside work was, for the moment, banned. No elec-tricity, no water, not even for minor tasks. There was quite clearly nothing useful for us to do and Athina wanted us in Athens. So be it.

The towns and villages along the way are, on the whole, unremarkable, except for their lack of charm. Argos has an impressive castle on an adjacent peak, otherwise it is without grace, beauty or style, leaving aside the museum garden and the adjacent plantings in an otherwise undistinguished pedestrian area. It is not even spectacularly ugly, merely dusty and rather commonplace. Yet this is a city of great antiquity, surrounded by some of the most beautiful scenery in the world. In the fifth century BC it had a famous school of sculpture and was renowned for the profusion of statues that adorned the city. There is not much love lost between Nauplion and Argos – between the port, and sometime capital of modern Greece, and the seat of the nomarch and site of an ancient kingdom. There are continuous arguments and rivalries which range from the housing of the appeal court to good, old-fashioned football. But there is no contest when it comes to the aesthetic; even the law court in Nauplion is a notably handsome building set apart in trees and its own dignity.

Both towns have parking problems. In Nauplion, where we seem constantly to be trying to find a parking space which is both licit and cool, the courthouse has its attractions: it provides plenty of shade. Nina was trying to park the car one day in fierce sunshine and happened on a delicious unoccupied space outside the law courts. There were dozens of police on the other side of the road, so she shouted across to them to ask if she could park there. There was no reply. She tried again, slowly and loudly. Nina inclines towards the view that most people will understand her if she speaks loudly, clearly and slowly enough. "MAY I," she shouted, "PARK HERE? CAN I PUT MY CAR HERE?" No answer. "IS IT ALLOWED TO PARK HERE?"

This time there was an answer. "OK, English lady, you put your car there. Everywhere free here. You understand? Free country. Free parking for you, English lady, everywhere ."

It was a prisoner sticking his head out of the van in which he and several others were being kept until they were due to appear in court. The police had other things to do, like guarding the prisoners. Mind you, I doubt that this would have happened in Argos.

Apart of course from the occasional crusader castle, Byzantine monastery, classical temple or Mycenean palace, and

---

you do not see many of these on the road to Athens, there are no buildings of any size or distinction to set off the landscape. Driving back through Italy every hilltop seems to be graced with an impressive and usually fortified nobleman's residence. In Greece there are, in that sense, no noblemen and no grand residences. There are no manor houses, no extensive estates and consequently no landed gentry. The largest private estate in Greece is that owned by the sometime Labour member for Swindon, Francis Noel-Baker. Francis has given back to the Greek state a considerable amount of the family holding in Evia but I believe he is still accounted the largest private landowner in Greece. As our friend Plato says, modern-day Greeks don't go in for owning land: they make do with ships.

Not far from Nemea, where Herakles took on the lion and gained the lion's skin that he wore ever thereafter – to be seen on all carvings and statues of the hero, ancient and modern – the road turns abruptly right virtually at the railway crossing. Left takes you to Nemea and miles of vineyards, one of the most famous wine-producing areas, and another Mycenean site, right takes you to Corinth, through the mountains. A glorious drive, up, down, swooping round tight bends, with majestic vistas opening up round each corner; ancient Acrocorinth comes into view on a mountain-top and then the sea as you glimpse the Gulf of Corinth. From there it is downhill to the toll-road that links Patras, the Corinth Canal and Athens and where the traffic flows at about twice the speed. From Nauplion, the isthmus is only about a third of the way but it feels as though, leaving the Peloponnese for Attica, half the journey is over.

The first part of the road to Athens is picturesque, sea-girt; the rest takes you through sprawling industrialization, sulphurous smells, pollution and ugliness; it is best driven through at whatever speed the police and traffic allow, and then put out of mind. Until the return journey.

Athens was not badly polluted on this visit but a yellowish pall still hung over the city. It was a warm spring day, heating up appreciably in the afternoon but not yet becoming summer hot and, for once, there were no strikes; taxis and buses were functioning efficiently and so of course were the shopkeepers, who never go on strike. Athina had suggested we should go to various specialist stores, for example bathroom emporia.

Athina's suggestions are in the way of being commands, and just to make sure we understood she picked us up in her car and took us by the hand to each gleaming bidet and gilded battery of taps she thought suitable. The height, colour and aesthetic arrangement of low-flush suites; the pros and cons of various competing systems of mixer showers; the glorious symmetry of triangles, circles, step pyramids of taps; their finish and materials, stainless steel and chrome and what looked like ceramic hardened by being part of the nose-cone of a successfully returned spacecraft; their colours, gold, old gold, bronze, archaic bronze, silver, oxidized silver, and everywhere baths of unexpected shapes, girths and luxury.

"Of course," Athina said, beautiful with enthusiasm for making lovely our bathrooms and lavatories, "there are many, many other shops. Like this but not like this. I think I like another one better but this is just to see. See all, then decide."

"No," I said, "one will be enough."

I was shouted down.

"Italian," said Athina, an opera coach encouraging a dissident singer, "not Greek."

"What's wrong with Greek?"

"Not good design. Not good quality. Not chic."

"I bet they're cheaper." I had sneaked a look at what seemed to be the prices and was unnerved.

"I think they're all lovely," said Nina.

"Never mind the looks, just feel the prices." *Sotto voce.*

Athina heard me. "Never mind. We discuss prices later. They gave me special discount. Not so expensive." It was a phrase we were to hear often.

Nina repeated, "They're lovely."

"But not perhaps altogether suitable for our flat," I said tentatively.

"Apartment," said Nina quickly.

"A bit too much of the *luxe*? Even a touch decadent?" I went on.

"Look! We chose the best for your lovely house in Nauplion."

I gave up.

Three shops and several hundred baths, showers, bidets, lavatories and basins later, the taps had been decided: archaic bronze for our ablutions, modernistic chrome for our guests. I suggested we all needed a drink.

"No, no," said Athina. "We go back to the second shop. We get a coffee there. Or you like instead a cold orange juice perhaps?"

I liked instead a large whisky but there was no point in saying so.

Nina was entranced by the whole business. As she kept on saying, how often does one get the chance to plan a bathroom from scratch; to be let loose among all these amazing contraptions; to be able to buy a whole new way of life? Once was more than enough for me.

After a couple of hours of battering by Nina's and Athina's gushing delight at every spigot, faucet and plug I found myself becoming more and more austere. "No, not gold," I could hear my throttled and weakening voice saying. "Not black." "Surely not flamingo." "Thank God you didn't like the . . ." I was flattened, Nina uplifted and liberated.

We ended up with various handsome and expensive, even with Athina's special discounts, pieces of sanitary ware. There was a hand-basin, massively surrounded by marble, with marble-looking cupboards underneath, swinging open and shut with expensive clunks, and a looking-glass of dominant proportions surrounded by electric lights which would not have been out of place in a Hollywood dressing-room, or so it seemed to me. Nina professed herself over the moon.

The next day was to be kitchens. I felt weak at the knees. At dinner, at a taverna near the Plaka, an unexpected, small old restaurant with a collection of brightly painted hurdy-gurdies decorating the two rooms and a dazzling selection of hot *orektika*, I regaled our old friend Plato with the day's torments.

He said, laughing, that he must meet this lady lawyer of ours. "She really seems to have taken you under her wing. After a busy day at the courts to shepherd you on a shopping spree – I'd say that was well beyond the call of duty. None of *my* lawyer friends would do that."

"And," I said, "she's very good-looking too."

"And very determined," said Nina. "You really should meet her."

"What's her name?"

Nina said, "Athina."

Plato said, "No, her family name."

"Sideropoulos," said Nina.

"Soteriadis-Sideropoulou," I said pedantically.

Plato laughed and asked if I was sure of the stresses. He could, he said, help a bit with our search for kitchen equipment. A friend of his was general manager of Siemens in Greece. He would telephone him. Plato was sure he could be of considerable use to us.

So was I. A one-stop shopping expedition sounded admirable, and with a bit of luck there would be a limited choice; after all, I reasoned, how many varieties of grills, ovens, whatever, could any single manufacturer produce, let alone make available for export to Greece?

Nina, and Athina when I told her of Plato's suggestion, also thought it a good idea. We met at an early hour, before Athina's first appointment for the day, and swept into the main Siemens showroom. I thought I should take charge of this operation. I asked if we might see what they had in the way of ovens.

What kind of ovens, I was asked. Well, electric, I said. Yes, yes, they only had electric. But what kind of electric? What *kind* of electric, I repeated, like a bewildered schoolchild faced with relativity and asked what kind of time. Yes, yes; electronic, automatic, split-level, separate grill, ceramic, glass; or did we want double ovens or perhaps one with infra-red or microwave attached, convective, fan-assisted, remote-controlled and, of course, with automatic souvlaki fittings?

Athina intervened. She had every reason; I was dithering. Time would be saved if she took over and, she contrived to suggest, handled affairs properly, in Greek. She looked at her watch, she had an appointment. She whipped us through machines and catalogue variants. She persuaded Nina, at least, that we should be properly equipped. We ended up with a cooker with a console like Concorde, automatic functions galore but no plate-warming drawer or self-cleaning; a very fancy washing machine; a fine refrigerator with a large cool-drawer underneath, and a splendid dishwasher, all of them infinitely superior to our equipment in Islington.

"Why not?" This was Nina, an hour or so later, when Athina had gone off to her other law office in Piraeus.

"All right, if you think so. But do we really need a washing-up machine in Nauplion? What are all these dinner parties you're contemplating?"

This was below the belt. Nina had declared, vowed, that there would be no cooking of main meals, no food-time entertaining if Nauplion were to become our second home. No formal or informal dinner parties at Number 19. We would eat out. *Always*.

"Don't be silly. For once we can equip a place properly. And build it all in. And Athina was quite right; If we don't do it now, we never will."

I persevered. "But do we *need* a dishwasher?"

"It would be an advantage if we have to sell," Nina said perversely. "Athina says so. Having everything complete, built in. And anyway what about the grandchildren?"

This was a marginally more convincing riposte. Children do use an awful lot of plates, glasses and mugs, and we had eight grandchildren between us (nine now, at the last count) of admittedly assorted ages but still all using utensils. I gave up.

The next day Athina introduced us to our kitchen designer. He listened, in that order, to Athina, Nina, Athina, Nina, me. He would work out some designs and costs. When we returned in the autumn we could finalize plans, materials, all that. *Kalo kalokairi*. Have a good summer.

He was a tall, gingerish man with a receding forehead and plantations of freckles marching across his scalp, arms and hands. We had seen him in his office, a bright, austere room off his showroom, the latter gleaming with built-in kitchens of various sizes, qualities and styles. He was charmingly diffident until he had to take a telephone call when his voice dropped an octave, became forceful, at moments even strident; clearly he was conducting an intense, emotional argument.

"Sorry about that," he said in his light-voiced, amiably fluent English. "That was a difficult client. I just had to reassure her that she had chosen the right colours."

"What a nice man," said Nina as we drove to Patras to catch the ferry, Athina's *Kalo taxidhi* (have a good trip) and Come back soon ringing in our ears from the night before. "He even understood about my broom cupboard."

XV

We drove back through Italy in cold and rain, stayed with friends in the Auvergne where there was bitter frost and our nostrils iced up as we went for walks in the snow, and then as we moved north the weather got steadily better until we got back to England where it was warm and damply variable.

It was nonetheless, as Nina said, good to be home. She looked, I thought, a bit askance at the ageing dishwasher and the gas oven which had been known to go out during one cooking session and to burn up a meal in the next – a problem with the thermostat which we hoped we had solved but feared not. It was an imperfect instrument.

"Why," said Nina, "should we spend all our money on a house in Greece? I don't even know if I can write there." She was working herself up into a fine old taking. "And," she added, kicking the cooker and stubbing her toe, "we've never had anything new in our proper house. Let alone a *designer kitchen*. Most of this stuff we've had since the Flood." (At least I think it was the capital letter, Noah's or Deucalion's Flood.) "And what's more we need a new stair-carpet."

Much of this was true but a touch unfair since it was I had who had been trying to hold back the rush towards the all-electronic hi-tech gadgetry for Number 19's galley; but it was no time to say so.

"Couldn't we turn the stair-carpet?" I said helpfully.

"Turn it? We reversed it, moved it up, moved it down, darned it, cleaned it. Over and over again. Not that you'd notice."

Neither of us mentioned Nauplion for weeks.

I had written a letter thanking Athina for all her kindnesses and saying how splendidly we thought the apartment was coming along, how excited we were about it and how thrilled with the extra room or working space in the attic. I used the first person plural as a matter of politeness. I was not at all sure to what extent Nina was joining in the enthusiasm. It was wiser, I thought, not to ask. I had thrown in some comments about the bathrooms, the need for hand-grips and simple plugs, with chains, for baths and basins, and had congratulated her on choosing beautiful taps.

There was no reply. Nina kept up her Stakhanovite rate of work, without which as she tartly reminded me her books were neither written nor finished and without which the income we were so clearly going to need in spades to pay for my future excesses abroad would not materialize. Did I think books, or money for that matter, grew on trees?

I sent another instalment to Athina's bank in the Piraeas. I reckoned our account would be pretty low by then. I wrote another letter, this time to Pericles, saying how marvellous the wooden roof-ceiling was and how clever I thought his whole use of the space. Was anything happening? I was only asking because we were planning to fly out in September and he might think it better if we came later or, optimistically, earlier.

There was no reply. May gave way to June. Life went on normally enough. The 1988 Lord's test match gave me a chance to regale another group of friends and acquaintances with our Greek saga. I began to tot up the supporters. I played tennis with Michael Meyer and he confessed himself admiring; very courageous of me but not for him – too much travel and inconvenience.

At dinner parties, I kept the tally. John Sherwood preferred it to be called, as it always had been in his young days, Nauplia as in Nawplia. Phyllis James said they weren't taking all that long about it, were they really, considering the house had fallen down. Alasdair and Sheila Milne thought it capital and enthused about the Peloponnese and Nauplion and our determination. Chris Bell was thoroughly enthusiastic on our behalf and commended our energy while Carys said why didn't we join them at Port Madoc; Nauplion was lovely enough but Wales was much nearer. Richard and Duthy Tonkin thought it exciting and good for us but would it not mean we were away for months at a time? No, said Nina, firmly. My father flitted from Nice to Istanbul to South America, occasionally alighting in London. Travel was fine – he should know – but why buy a house, why tie ourselves to one place? Why, indeed, said Nina.

By mid-July I was restive. Doubts and anxieties were seeping into my dreams. Sleepless at three and four in the morning I was having nightmare arguments with myself about the amount of money we had already spent. How much more might I be letting us in for? I cracked and phoned Athina.

I knew that she was busy and would have let us know of any progress, I said. And I was sure she was doing everything she could. Which, of course, was absolutely true. But I would be glad of some sort of intelligence.

A week later a letter arrived. Athina and Pericles had gone to Nauplion together. "The work has been commenced," she wrote, "but not officially I am afraid. The reason is that there are some problems relating to the whole building and particularly the *traditional* aspects thereof.

"The Nondas brothers have referred the problems to a committee of the provincial authorities for a permanent solution of the problem. This committee had been constituted but it has not convened as yet. However Pericles is taking care of things.

"The only problem concerning you" (the *only* problem?) "is that you have two windows in your attic. I am trying hard to maintain them and I have found from an old photograph of Nauplion that there were in fact some sort of windows in the roof of the house.

"I hope that I shall be able to favourably argue your case and convince the said committee to allow us to keep the windows.

"I was going to write to you earlier but the developments with the above-mentioned problems and committee kept intervening and thus I postponed writing to you until I had a more clear picture to give you. I shall advise you further in due course."

Without being unkind to our famous lawyer, it was clear that the letter owed something to the excellent English of her daughter, Niki, a young lawyer just setting out on her career.

I replied at once, relief with hearing something warring with anxiety at the actual news. I said I realized it must all have been rather difficult and wished her and Pericles good luck. There were just one or two points. What were the problems, I wondered, relating to the "traditional" aspect of the building? I had thought there had been a new Planning Consent granted by the provincial authorities, allowing *modern technology*, i.e. bricks and suchlike, after the roof had been removed and the upper walls crumbled away. And if the committee, which, I assumed, was still waiting to convene, ruled against the dormers, would we be liable financially for removing the windows and restoring the roof? Would there perhaps be some sort of fine? And more generally were we to be held responsible for any modifications to or departures from the Planning Consent? What now was the timetable?

I hoped the heat was not too enervating. I knew they had been suffering but they could console themselves thinking of us and our appallingly cold and wet summer. For the moment I would make no plans to come out to Greece. I would wait to hear news and advice from her.

August came and went with another test match. My diary no longer notes people's reactions to what I had now decided was my own Aegean Sea Bubble. Good money down the drain. And more required. These after all, as Nina started to remind me, were no small matters. We would shortly, she announced, be down to her earnings and my pension. Words like extravagance and irresponsibility were bandied about. Nina almost shunned the sales except for a Jean Muir that was such a bargain that the savings it made were enough to kit her up in winter clothes as well.

At the beginning of September I went to launch the sixth-form year at Oakham. It stiffened my resolve. *Carpe diem.* I returned to London, put on a brave, smiling face and said let's book a flight to Greece at the beginning of October, come what may. We decided to make a proper holiday of it and take daughter Perdita who was, as they say in her world, resting, and granddaughter Ottilie. I booked rooms at the Xenia Palace in Nauplion and for one night in Athens. I telephoned Athina and said we were coming. She said nothing had changed that was why she hadn't contacted us, but not to worry, all would be/had been/was really all right. No problem, she said, signing off. No problem, indeed, I replied meaningfully, but she had gone.

Nina had a nightmare, a real one, not a half-waking one. She had gone into our new Greek, or rather Italian, bathroom and had seen this monstrosity, an enormous Hollywood mirror with flashing lights all round it. It was fixed, plumbed in together with an enormous marble basin with gold taps, and the lights wouldn't turn off. She woke, moist-faced with fear, and wanted reassurance: the looking glass wasn't really, was it, surrounded with flashing bulbs?

I calmed her. "They weren't flashing," I said.

"But there *were* hundreds of bulbs all round?"

"I don't think so. Only a handful or so. And only at the top."

I went off to play tennis for an MCC C-team against Petworth. I got back to find Nina temporarily unwell, whether because of light-fears or a bug. It seemed best to proceed with our plans. Seeing what was going on, and examining the looking-glass by light of day, might allay some doubts and anxieties. We left the following morning.

It was a good introduction to Greek culture for the two-and-a-half year old Ottilie; a not quite full Olympic Airways flight

4

44444

4

enlivened by a group of musicians with bazoukis. As soon as the
seat belt sign was switched off, a good half of the passengers
started to move around; the musicians strummed a bar or two
and then proceeded to play traditional songs. A few lively
young of both sexes and some older women danced up and
down the aisles. Ottilie grew bold with the music, joined them
and was made much of. The captain put his head into the cabin
with some amazement (I dare say the trim of the aircraft had
become a mite eccentric), grinned ruefully and withdrew.
Eventually the cabin staff imposed some kind of order with
their food trolleys, using them to bulldoze people back to their
seats. What with all this and the ecstatic applause on the captain's making a smooth landing at Athens, Ottilie found the
return flight on British Airways disappointing.

The next morning we picked up a car from Avis and drove
straight to Nauplion. I had booked the car from London and
was horrified to see the rates being charged in drachmas.
Admittedly car hire has always been expensive in Greece. The
country roads, some of them very much on the tourist map, are
not kind to vehicles and the price of new cars is horrific. There
was a one hundred per cent excise tax up to 1500 cc and then,
progressively, 150 and 200 per cent. In addition, inflation had
been running at a terrifyingly accelerating rate, nosing towards
twenty-five per cent. Any moment now, I thought, we should
have to use suitcases to carry our 5000-drachma notes – that is
if the banks were working long enough, between strikes, to pay
out the money we had sent on ahead of us.

Nina said, "Why is it the banks that always go on strike?
You'd have thought with the Greek economy the way it is,
everyone – even bank employees, no, *especially* bank staff –
would want as much hard currency to come into the country as
possible. Why don't you write to Mr Papandreou?"

This may have been a why-don't-you-do-something-about-
the-state-of the world, the house, the dripping tap, kind of
remark, or it may have been a sly dig at the occasions, during
the Colonels' dictatorship, when Andreas Papandreou came
to my office at Bush House and argued about the past, present
and future of Greece.

Mr Papandreou had other things on his mind. He had just returned from London and open-heart surgery. While he was in Harefield Hospital it had been announced that he was seeking a divorce from his second wife and intended to marry Dimitri Liani, the Olympic Airline stewardess who had accompanied him to London and elsewhere on the EC prime ministerial cir-cuit with much press attention and whom Greeks, the men somewhat admiringly, the women disgustedly, said was twice his size and half his age. Andreas Papandreou, Prime Minister, leader and founder of Pasok, was sixty-nine at the time. He had been married to his American wife, Margaret, for over thirty-five years and Mimi, as she was commonly called, his intended, was thirty-four.

There were other scandals which dimmed the glory of his return to Greece, snatched as he had been, according to the pro-Pasok press, from the jaws of death. Inflation was the high-est in the European Community. Although the massive austerity programme, which had come accompanied by a vast EC emergency loan, seemed a little less stringent, there were still strikes and a general feeling of unrest. The economy was in a grisly state. There were rumours of dissension within Pasok, even perhaps within the cabinet. And then the Bank of Crete collapsed with a deficit of over $130 million.

After two months in Britain with ministers whizzing to and fro between Athens and London and the opposition accusing Papandreou of absentee-premiership and government-by-fax, the Prime Minister had barely got back to Greece when the arch-swindler Koskotas, under a twenty-four-hour police sur-veillance and with charges of embezzlement, fraud, forgery and almost everything else hanging over his head, absconded in a private jet to the Americas. In those days, before the collapse of BCCI and the exposure of Maxwell, George Koskotas seemed quite a runner. With nothing behind him except income tax debts in the USA, this Greek-American had arrived in Greece, bought the Bank of Crete, persuaded government departments and state enterprises to invest their cash reserves with him at *lower* interest rates than his competitors were offering and, with the profits, bought the most famous Greek football team, a television station or two, a newspaper, *Kathemerini* (the nearest Greece gets to *The Times*), and achieved all kinds of influential support, not least among Pasok circles close to the prime minister. Then the bubble burst. It was all soap and water. How had it happened? How had Koskotas managed to abscond? How had Papandreou let it happen? How much was Pasok, and indeed the prime minister himself, involved?

The night we arrived in Nauplion the supporters at the bar of The Boatyard pooh-poohed all ideas of Mr Papandreou's personal involvement. There might have been some corruption elsewhere in Pasok. Who knows? Politics is a dirty business. And all bureaucrats are corrupt. The rest of the smears were just that, propaganda.

"I don't know," said Phaidon, having greeted us like loved but long-lost relations and enquired earnestly about our summer. "It's not good but I *think*," he paused to wipe the bar in front of us, "it's other people. Andreas says it's *foreign centres of destabilization*." This was clearly a quote. He poured our drinks and looked quizzical. Someone said it was the Americans. No, said someone else, it was the Turks. The Iranians, said another. The television news was on. There was a picture of Ms Liani coming out of some building; she dominated the screen. Someone whistled. Another said, "That Mimi."

Phaidon said whatever else, they had been impressed that not only had Papandreou survived the heart operation but that he still, at his age, intended to rule Greece and marry for a third time. It was a pity about the scandals. That Koskotas! How had he managed to get away with it? And how had he managed to escape? It must have been arranged. Probably the police had been bribed. But to let it happen with such an infamous prisoner with all the world's television on him. It must have been a very large operation, everyone bribed.

"Bribed with what?" said one of the beer-drinkers. "Mickey Mouse money?"

"It was the CIA." An ouzo with ice.

"Well, what happened to all that money?" said Phaidon. "Don't worry about the money," said the beer-drinker. "What's going to happen to Olympiakakos?"

Nina said, "What's Olympiakakos got to do with it? I thought it was a swimming team."

I took her arm and we walked back to the hotel. It was a fine, warm early October night, the sky full of stars. Our route did not take us past the house.

"It's good to be back in Nauplion," said Nina. "And nice to be walking back to the Xenia Palace."

Was this, I wondered, a return to the argument that we would do better to rent a suite annually at the hotel than to buy a house? A bit late for that. Or was it merely simple pleasure? The walk was certainly agreeable, away from the sea and diagonally across the marble-floored square, right, past the steps leading to the first parliament house, now a music conservatoire, past the knitting shop, along the wider road, always open to traffic, leading to the Hotel Amphitryon, left past Giorgos the jeweller, up the *scala*, and up, and up, past the Dioscouri Hotel, and up, and then almost level, turning right, along a narrow street with a dark, old-fashioned little grocer's shop at the corner, to the upper car park. And so to an astonishing tunnel hollowed out of the rock, wide enough to take a small car, which leads to the three lifts which go up to the summit of Acronaupliolan and debouch into the courtyard of the Xenia Palace. The whole arrangement smacks of James Bond and the lifts, somewhat dimly lit, take a long and juddering time to climb to the top. Somehow it's always a surprise to come out and find, after shops and the hotel itself, the sea and the town far below and the bay widened out, the arc of mountains circling round.

After breakfast we introduced the town to Perdita and Ottilie, and vice versa. Ottilie was much taken by the *plateia* but we dragged her away to see the house. We need not have hurried. Nothing much had changed. This time there was an even more marked sense of the unreal in that this was a house that was all top. I suppose it was because I had been dwelling on what might have happened since we last saw it that I had expected some sign of obvious improvement. But it was the same; the roof was on and most of the top floor, ours, was there, but, for the rest, there were the concrete supporting pillars, the curving concrete staircase, and in effect nothing else. Ottilie looked pretty bewildered, her mother taken aback. Could we go up? Was the staircase safe?

"Yes," said Nina in one of those maternal, and grandmotherly, phrases that bewilder nursery logicians, "if you take care."

In fact the steps were sound as anything, if rough-surfaced and sharp-edged, but they gave the impression of circling unsupported through the air for miles which must have been unnerving for a small girl. Undeterred, Ottilie clambered up as fast as her legs would take her, following me and occasionally holding my hand. Mother and grandmother leapt up behind fearfully and protectively.

Nikos greeted us at the top. He picked Ottilie up and whirled her around, way above his head. She seemed pleased. Still holding Ottilie, Nikos welcomed Nina and was introduced to Perdita who was looking around in some astonishment.

"You like it?" A question from Nikos requiring the answer yes.

"Oh yes," said Perdita, obviously surprised. "What a marvellous wooden ceiling."

Nikos went over to Kosmas, the young engineer. Nikos joined us, putting Ottilie down, whereupon she immediately began to run to the nearest non-existent balcony. I saw Perdita head her off and then look down into the street and turn pale.

"No permissions," Nikos said. Kosmas shook his head in agreement. "We go every week to Sparta. To the committee in Nauplion. Perhaps to Athens. Who knows? Many, many meetings. Much problems."

"Big problems." This was brother Andreas. "Big, big, big."

"For now," said Nikos, in case I hadn't got the drift, "much difficulty. What to do? We are stopp-*ed*. The plumber is starting but not today. He has hurt his leg."

"Broke his leg," said Andreas. "Here."

"Not here," said Nikos. "At his house."

"Here," said Andreas pointing to somewhere below the knee.

"Never mind. He comes with his son."

"How will that help?" I said. "Can't you get another plumber?"

"He tells his son what to do."

"His son is still no good plumber." Andreas, explaining.

"The son learns with the father. No problem." Nikos, removing doubt. "But we wait for your bath. Come. See."

He led me, reeling, into the irregular trapezoid that was to be our bathroom, where the much-lit mirror and the fancy taps in Mycenean bronze were to star. I saw the beginnings of what presumably would be the hole into which the waste-pipe would go. It was not particularly illuminating. Nina and Perdita looked round my shoulders. Ottilie darted between my legs, saying "Where? Where?" and then a disappointed "What?"

"That's where we put the bath. No?"

"Yes," I said.

"The feet there," said Nina pointing at the hole.

"Feet?" said Nikos.

"That way round," said Nina, determinedly. "Head, there," pointing at the other wall.

"Head?" said Nikos plaintively.

"Never mind," I said. "I'll get the bathroom stuff sent immediately."

"No, no, no. It's here." He pointed towards the rest of the house where indeed there were various packing cases haphazardly disposed.

"But I thought you said you were waiting for the bath?"

"Yes. We wait for your bath. Must it go in first." He spoke slowly, explaining to a bunch of dimwits. "Then the other pipes and basin and douche and bidet, isn't it?"

"Bath is most big," Andreas said.

"Biggest. Bath is biggest," said Nikos." We have to put it in, turn it." He mimed the manoeuvres. "No problem empty."

Heavens, I thought, were they really thinking of filling the bath with water first?

"Empty OK," he went on, "otherwise we maybe hurt the basin. So must it be bath first. Basin after."

I felt I had to retain some grasp on reality. Ottilie was chanting some refrain which sounded like, Bath first, telly after, Mummy says, Bath first, telly after, Mummy says . . .

"Fine," I said firmly. "*Entaxi*. So you put the bath in now."

"No," said Nikos looking pained, "the plumber who broke the leg is with the doctor."

"For how long?"

"Two-three weeks."

"Two to three *weeks?*"

"Then he comes with his son."

"Oh," I said. "Good."

It was deliciously warm in the midday sun outside. We went swimming at Arvanitia, the town beach. As we paused, balancing on some uncomfortably sharp stones at the edge of the water, I asked Perdita, who had been unwontedly quiet, what she thought of the flat.

"My God, they're beautiful."

I thought for a moment she meant the roof-beams. But no; it was the brothers Nondas. And so they were, quite astonishingly beautiful.

"It's their first job as builders," I said, having dismissed their looks and moved on to more important things.

"Oh stop mumbling and come on in," said Nina who was in the sparkling sea. "It's lovely."

"Hurry up, Grandad," shouted Ottilie, a favourite chorus that seemed likely to follow me down the years.

I counted to ten and plunged. It was almost as cold as Bexhill in midsummer.

Athina and Pericles were coming later in the week. There was clearly nothing much for us to do at the house, although I think Nina may have wanted to unpack the bathroom mirror. We spent the days lazing and idling and at the sea. We explored beaches. We went on small expeditions. In a friend's garden Ottilie was shown an old giant of a tortoise and its baby, about the size of her hand. She wanted to take them and the donkey home with her. Nina and I climbed up and down the various *scales* and found our way up through a fortified tunnel into the other end of Acronauplion where the older Xenia stands, ugly to the point of affront but marvellously sited on the saddle, one side facing the town and harbour, the other the great castle of Palamidi, looking down to the beach of Arvanitia. The prickly pears were ripening everywhere and the fruits were falling off and plopping juicily and messily on to the paths. Cyclamens, great clumps of them in places and tiny isolated single flowers elsewhere, were beginning to appear in crevices and cliffsides. From enclosed, secret courtyards autumn jasmine perfumed the air and blue trusses of plumbago fell over the walls. It was a marvellous season, the sun bright and hot but the air already cooling towards winter and the cobalt-blue sea perceptibly colder each day. The swallows had gone.

We advanced on banks. It was clearly sensible to have an account in Nauplion. As no one seemed to believe in cheques, or I suppose to trust them, like everyone else we opened a deposit account. We had had some difficulty in choosing a bank. Various friends advised us. All had different choices and appalling tales to tell of all the rest. The National Bank of Greece, the Ionian Bank, the Credit Bank, the Commercial Bank, the Agricultural Bank, and so on. We decided it would be sensible to have one within easy walking distance.

Nina chose the Ionian because it was in a handsome old building. I went to the National Bank in the belief that we could transfer money from London to Nauplion more quickly there. In fact we had between us picked the two banks most likely to go on strike.

We should, of course, have known better. A few years earlier we had unknowingly arrived in Athens in the middle of a comprehensive bank strike which had been unreported in the British press. It was illegal to bring more than a handful of drachmas into Greece. No one was changing money and everyone seemed to be running short of cash. We had arranged to go off to Hydra for a few days and we used our last few drachmas to pay the fare for the ferry.

Luckily our hotel on the island took Diners Club, but it had no restaurant and we had no money for food. Every day long queues, not only of foreign tourists, lined up outside the two banks. Neither of them opened. The shopkeepers must have been suffering but so were the visitors. We survived on two sandwiches and a shared beer for a couple of days. It seemed a ridiculous way to spend a holiday.

I remember standing on my toes, peering into one of the banks and seeing a middle-aged man with thin hair and a large yellow-tinged face sitting at his desk wearing a black alpaca jacket and apparently counting banknotes, like some Dickensian miser. We had been told there was no money in the bank so I jumped up to see better and realized he was just shuffling cheques which presumably he was unable to do anything with. My jump must have disturbed his musings and he made a dismissive flutter of both hands, as it might have been to say shoo to a cat. It was then that I saw he had very long, slightly curling down fingernails on both little fingers.

When I first visited Greece regularly in the early sixties you used frequently to see these long nails on men's little fingers. Here as elsewhere in the Levant it was a sign of not being a working man, of doing no manual labour. But the custom has now completely died out, in Greece at least. Even the *komboloi*, the so-called worry beads, are rarely seen and Greek men make do with their car keys, which they twirl, flip and catch.

Shortly after my encounter through the window, a side door opened and a much younger man came out, looked round rather furtively and said he could change a little money. I asked him how much. Five pounds sterling. We started eating at tavernas again.

Another year in Nauplion, we were coming out of the sea at Karathona, the bay on the other side of Palamidi, when we saw the manager of the Amphitryon in the middle of his daily run.

We exchanged pleasantries. I complained about the banks and just as he started to run off he said, "You think you've got problems. I've no money to pay my staff."

The problem was cash. He had masses of vouchers from the dozens of package-deal tours that arrived daily at the hotel and left after breakfast having spent nothing extra except the odd drink paid by credit card. Cash, as he said, there wasn't.

Most recently, in 1992, there was a protracted strike, I suppose political in motive. It was designed to make a fuss about the pension legislation that was being pushed through parliament by the right-wing and somewhat Thatcherite Nea

Demokratia government, which had a majority of two. Mr Mitsotakis, the Prime Minister, had taken on the minotaur by presenting a bill to bring Greek pensions more closely into line with those of the rest of the European Community. This, for example, would put paid to the expectation of many working women that they could, if they were mothers, retire after fifteen years' work. Understandably, many people were aggrieved, but the main thrust was straight agin' the privatizing and retrenching government.

The employees of the state-owned National Bank of Greece were foremost in the bank strike. Those of the Ionian Bank were barely half a pace behind. We had chosen well. Some smaller and more private enterprise banks were partly functioning, but none of them were taking drafts from abroad because all foreign dealings were suspended. All had to go through the Bank of Greece in Athens, and it was on strike. It had not been like that when we left London and arranged for our bank to send an adequate sum to settle our bills, taxes and what have you to the bank in Nauplion. It was sent in sterling.

The National Bank was not really closed. Some of the senior executives were working, including the branch manager, and one teller, a lady who lives further along our street, was dealing with the customers. Notices everywhere said *APERYIA*. STRIKE. Somewhere or other it had been decreed that there would be no cashing of traveller's cheques or Eurocheques and no currency exchange. Bewildered foreigners could either borrow on their Visa or Mastercard, or hope to find another more functioning bank or independent money-changer. Those with deposit accounts in drachmas, mostly local inhabitants, could pay in or draw out, that is if the computer was not down and as long as they did not mind standing in a very long queue. Sometimes it took two hours to get to the solitary teller.

My problem, to use a good Greek word, was that we had run out of traveller's and Eurocheques, that we needed quite a lot of cash, and that our money was lodged somewhere in Athens, and had been for weeks. I had to go in every other day to find out whether any money had come through and whether anything could be done. I was told there would be less delay if the money were sent in drachmas. I asked our English bank to send another transfer, this time in drachmas.

"Good money after bad," said Nina prophetically.

Could we perhaps, I asked the assistant manager on duty a few days' later, get the sterling sent back to London. "*Oxi. Aperyia.*" Was there any way at all we could get hold of some of our money? "*Oxi. Aperyia.*" Had the drachmas come through yet? He could not say. Why did I not give my bank book to the lady over there? I went back to the queue. No money had come through and by then there was no money left in the book. Marvellous.

Of course, we could borrow. All our Greek friends were enormously generous. But that was not the point. The bank had our money and was sitting on it. I worked myself up into a fair old fury and stormed into the bank the following morning at eight o'clock. A queue had already formed and there was a certain amount of jostling and jossing going on. The temper of the splendidly unruffled solitary lady behind the counter was, I thought, being slightly dented. I marched, undeterred, to the executive desk.

"What have you done with my money?" I said to the same assistant manager.

"Money?" he said. "No money. *Aperyia.* No change money."

"I don't want to change money. I want *my* money." I flourished my bank book. He took it, opened it, examined the balance and said, "You have 2400 drachmas."

"Thank you," I said. "I also have several hundred thousand drachmas not in the book" (which I thumped as noisily as I could on his desk) but *in your bank.*"

"*Then katalava.*" And to be fair I don't think he did understand, his English was uncertain. However, I was by then very angry. "I don't care about the strike," I said loudly. "You've taken my money. And it's downright dishonest not to give it to me. Plain, stark robbery." He looked uncomprehending but the crowd in the queue was reacting, supportively I thought.

"*Aperyia i oxi aperyia,*" I said, even louder, real fury overcoming me, "*pou einai ta xhrimata mou* – strike or no strike, where is my money? What have you done with it?" I drew breath for the kill. "Thieves," I shouted, "*kleftedes!*"

The only trouble was that in my fury I had got it wrong. The plural of *kleftis*, the word from which we get kleptomania, is *kleftes*, whereas *keftedes*, as habitués of Greek eating houses throughout the world know, are meatballs. If in my stuttering anger the phrase had meant anything, it would have been thieving meatballs. The rest of my audience was suitably amused.

The next day, perhaps not surprisingly, the presiding bank manager was waiting to introduce himself. He had heard, he said, that I was having some trouble. Could he help me? Yes, I said; I wanted my money. Ah, alas, he said, there was the matter of the strike. I had come armed with faxed copies of the transfers. I flourished them. How much money did I need? What bills were outstanding? Electricity, I said. Telephone. Dentist.

"Dentist?" he said. "He can wait."

He advanced me about a third of the money and I was very grateful. But still the transfers did not come through.

Some days after the banks suspended their strike – the bill had been passed by parliament – the drachmas came through. Then, a day or so later, the sterling. It had taken six weeks and the day it arrived was the day after Black Wednesday, in 1993, when we came out of the ERM and the pound had effectively been devalued by something over seven per cent against the drachma. We had, in effect, lost a couple of hundred pounds for no very good reason. I was not best pleased with Greek banks, nor for that matter with Messrs Major and Lamont.

XVI

Back in 1988, when we next visited Number 19 Kapodistriou, a new cast had been recruited and all was activity, or near-activity. The plasterer had finished the internal walls. They were drying out and he was admiring his work and, indeed, the layout of the apartment. It was the last free day he had, he said. Now he had to make the wine and then he was booked right up until he had to deal with his olives. And then there would be the oranges but with a bit of luck, if the permissions came through and if it weren't too wet, perhaps some days in December or January for the outside. He'd see. Like most Naupliot craftsmen and tradesmen, he was a man of parts, a shop here, an enterprise there, some property here and there, and always some land, some crops. It makes getting hold of a plumber, joiner or plasterer a major exercise.

The electrician was contemplating, perhaps with satisfaction or aesthetic delight, bunches of multi-coloured spaghetti sprouting from the wall next to what would be our front-door. He explained that the control box would be there. Would we go over with him the positioning of power and light points. And of light fittings. He had been told twenty points and nine lights under the roof. But surely we needed more in the bedrooms? And the bathrooms? Nobody had told him about extractor fans till now. And heaters. To be honest, he did not explain: Nikos did. I could not understand anything any of them said. A carpenter came to replace one of the balcony French window-frames which had warped out of true.

It was all very exciting. Even more exciting to Ottilie was one of the rickety ladders in which the Nondas brothers seemed to specialize, the long one, which was propped against the wall outside the guest shower room. It leaned rather precariously and led up to the attic and the disputed, and therefore left partially unfinished, dormer windows. She eyed it longingly and then, as fast as her legs and arms could take her, disregarding missing rungs and an unregulated wobble, she headed for the top. Nina and Perdita, both of whom profess no head for heights, had conniptions at the bottom but sensibly held on to the ladder as I climbed and caught up with Ottilie just before she stepped off on to the unprotected concrete platform which stood twelve feet above the ground. It was like the upper deck of a ship without stanchions or guard rails.

We walked over to the northern dormer, canopy and outline windowframe in place but with no side-boards. I held her up and we gazed down to the harbour and across the bay to the mountains. Then I took her across to the opposite dormer and showed her a stunning view of Palamidi. It was more difficult going down. I thought I had better go first and managed to miss the first convenient rung, trying to put my foot on one that was not there. Having overcome that fright I put her on to a safe rung and saw us both down.

Nina said, whether addressed to me or Ottilie I didn't know, "Don't you ever do that again." Perdita looked paper-pale.

The activity continued most of the morning. It was still going loud and strong when we returned from a coffee and

Coke break in the *plateia*. I began to think that it was designed to impress Pericles and Athina, who were driving down from Athens. I was wrong. By the time they arrived, Perdita and Ottilie had gone to the beach and all the workers had knocked off for the day except Nikos and Andreas.

There was, of course, no uplifting news. The committee had still not met.

"Never mind," said Athina, "Pericles spoke with the Minister. No problem."

We were all electrified, not least Pericles who said, "No, no. *Will* speak. If it becomes necessary. At the appropriate stage, and not before. Now, what about stairs to the working areas. We will believe the dormers stay and that you make best use of the upper floor. Then we need stairs. Where shall we put them?"

That took an hour or so, considering the placing and the construction. We decided, with Pericles' leading assistance, to put them against the wall of the bedroom area and to have them unboxed, uncased but with a bannister, newel posts and wooden vertical railings on the upper deck. The wood colour to match the roof-beams. Could Nikos find a good stairs joiner? Pericles would send the detailed design. But of course there was no point in doing anything quite yet until the permissions came through. Nonetheless it was sensible to make plans. To be ready when the permissions were granted.

Not *if*, but *when*. I realised this was said to reassure us but nonetheless I was partly reassured. Nina smiled. Athina said she had to talk to Nikos: money. I had noticed she was carrying her large handbag with her.

A few days later we said good bye to Nauplion for the year, to Phaidon, Nikos and our other friends, including some rather small ones with whom Ottilie had played, occasionally getting scratched and pushed over, in the square. She found it very difficult to understand why they spoke Greek and she didn't and why they didn't understand English.

We drove daughter and granddaughter to the airport and then settled down to really serious business: shopping. For years we had passed a shop on the way to the Plaka. Through

Austen Kark

windows made dark by quantities of furniture, we could just make out lace cloths, rich, red cushions, lamps of coloured glass and a dimly seen carved wooden bed which we had both hungered after. This time we determined to sit it out until the shop opened. There was, it is true, a card in the door which asserted in rather small Greek handwriting which days it was open and between what hours, but our experience had not coincided with its information. Luckily it was close to the Electra Palace Hotel where we were staying and so we hoped to surprise it at some point during the week.

It was closed the first morning, though long after its stated opening time. We had an appointment with Athina. When we returned, there was a different notice in the door, probably the card reversed. It said: *Epistrefo amesos*; the equivalent of Back in a Minute. I rightly reckoned it really meant Out for Lunch. So we returned to our hotel for a brief siesta. When we got back to the shop, shortly after four, the original card was back in place and it was clearly closed for the day. It took three days of close shadowing to catch it open.

Athina was much amused. She did not recognize the shop from our description, and indeed she had never seen it. Meanwhile we were on the trail of other game, Athina, a dedicated shopper, leading the chase. She was sparing us as much time as she could between what you might call paying customers, courts, arbitration, what have you. She could not be with us all the time. Sometimes we were, dangerously, on our own.

Nina said she had never had her own sofa. In her first marriage it had been her mother-in-law's and in her second it had been her predecessor's and post-war Heal's semi-utility to boot. This time, it was going to be *hers*. Make no mistake about it.

This entailed going into a great many shops, the quality and the price increasing each time. Perhaps this was better than looking at hundreds of baths and bidets; but not much. I was tiring and my feet were aching. After a more than decent while, I pointed out, reasonably I thought, that one over-stuffed and luxuriously sprung thingamabob was much like another. Whether sofa, settee, settle, recliner, corner conversation piece, Ottoman or Davenport, they were all basically for sitting on, or

— 156 —

putting things down on, or in. This enraged Nina.

"Typical," she said. "It's typical. The only time in my life I'm going to buy a sofa and you complain. And what's more you're not going to put things down on my sofa. So don't you think it, my lad. I'm going on till I find what I want. Even if it takes all day."

I looked at my watch. With a bit of luck the shops would shut soon and we could all put our feet up.

"And don't think you can slope off for a beer. I saw you eyeing your watch. I need you." I raised my eyebrows. "In case they don't speak English."

I nearly said that all those smart shops in Kolonaki had someone with good English, but kept my peace as we slogged onwards and ever upwards. At virtually the top of the street (we had climbed half of Lycabettus by then), Nina saw something she liked.

"I want something that will go with traditional Greek furniture," she said. "I think that might do."

The shop assistants, elegant young women, looked astonished. The notion that any of their chic, latest fashion, Italian things for sitting on and conversing would suit a traditional Greek anything was aggressively original. In addition, I don't think they knew which particular piece or pieces Nina had in mind. The combined confusion, I could see, was going to lead to their attempting some polite put-down. But then they didn't know my Nina.

Out of the corner of his eye, and at extreme earshot, while on the telephone, the owner, no fool he, understood. "Be with you in a second." After which, there was no going back. Nina chose three pieces, a two-seater, a corner seat and a one-seater which could be disposed into various arrangements. Just like a simple village house, I muttered to myself, but then we hadn't bought a simple village house.

"It's a matter of my being able to get them from the factory in Italy in time. We'll talk about covers in a moment. When do you want them? And where shall they be sent?"

He obviously thought we were mad and expected us to say Wiltshire or Suffolk.

"Easter," Nina said rapidly. "Nauplion."

"Oh, Nauplion," he said. "A very fine town. Quite beautiful. Used to be the first capital of Greece, did you know?"

Yes, we both said; we were buying a house there.

"I expect we can do it. Depends on the material you choose for the covers. Have a look over there. You'll find all the books and patterns. I'll just put the order in hand. How will you pay?"

"How much will it be?" I said. It clearly was the most expensive shop we had visited and I wasn't over-anxious to commit ourselves before we'd had a proper estimate.

"Again, it'll depend on what fabric you choose."

True, no doubt, but not helpful.

I hurried over to where Nina sat working her way through sample books and swathes of materials. Hours later, or so it seemed, we found some material we both liked and Nina with a fine novelist's eye reckoned would lend a traditional Greek colouring to the Italian masterpiece. Of course, it was English, from Osborne and Little, and our yards and yards of it would have to be sent from England.

I was surfeited with shopping, depleted of energy. I could have slid into a comfortable lethargy had not the matter of the price, including covers *and* piping, not aroused my least dormant emotion, anxiety.

I said to Nina, as quietly as I could, "We haven't got that much money in the country." I paused to gather breath. "I suppose," I added gloomily, "we've got just about enough at home. Or will have if we sell something."

"I'm having that sofa," Nina hissed at me.

The superior shopkeeper, receptive as ever, intervened in his classy English. "You may pay one half now and the other half before delivery to your address. You'll pay the carrier. I have no idea how much that will be. We'll advise you when it's ready. I'm sure you'll be very pleased with everything." He smiled. At that price we'd better be. "And how would you prefer to pay?"

"Credit card," I said optimistically.

"I'm afraid we don't take them."

"A cheque on my English bank, National Westminster?"

"Afraid not."

"I'll see our lawyer and try and arrange something."

"Remember," he said, "we really need to fax the orders off now."

"We'll be back tomorrow," said Nina, virtually pulling me out into the street. "Tomorrow morning."

We spoke to Athina. Was there, I suggested, any possibility of one of her special prices.

"Oh no," she said, shocked. "Not in that shop."

We decided she should pay the fifty per cent advance out of our joint house account in her bank. She would make all the arrangements. The following morning we were not in the sofa shop but back with the kitchen designer.

He had our plans brought in by his assistant. They were in a glossy folder, and looked very impressive.

"I went down to Nauplion," he said, "and saw your house. Very nice."

"Very beautiful!" said Athina.

"Yes, splendid," he said. "We can do a very good kitchen there. You were right; there's only one place for it. Now you see here on the plans how I've managed to build it in to blend with the wood of the inside roof and to be part of, yet not part of, the living and dining area."

Nina and I looked at a copy of the plan he passed over to us. Blankly. He passed over a drawing of the kitchen as seen from above. Another one as seen diagonally from the opposite corner of the room.

"Where . . ." said Nina.

"Here," he said firmly, "is the refrigerator. Here the dishwasher and here, since you want it in the kitchen" – he meant, instead of in the bathroom where God intended it to be – "is the clothes washing machine. This is the double sink. This is the oven and cooking top. These are cupboards and this is the concealed fan exhaust above the cooker. All in wood. We'll choose the type and colour in a moment. Here is a display cupboard, wood and glass doors. This is an open shelves decorative hanging unit. We must talk about the working surfaces."

"Marble," said Athina.

"What is this?" asked Nina,

"The divider. And serving area."

"Ah," I said to get in on the act. "What height?"

He smiled. I wasn't going to catch him out. "I remembered you didn't want any vertical structures. It's waist height, just right for serving."

Earlier we had seen great edifices of lattice work designed presumably to prevent any guest seeing the host or hostess at work in the kitchen. Nina had said that they looked like hideous temples to food.

"And," he went on, "it has useful cupboards on the kitchen side."

"Could we have bookshelves on the other side?"

"Bookshelves?" he said as though he had never heard of them. "I don't think so. We haven't got a unit quite like that. I suppose I could get one made."

Athina explained that all the units were manufactured in Germany. Nina backed off. The designer said that we had now got to the really important part. The finishes. The materials. The colours. Samples of different woods and varnishes were produced. He and Athina argued about their relative merits and aesthetic charms. Nina chose, was corrected by him and modified by Athina. Nina chose again. Everyone beamed. And now the main surfaces. Were we sure we wanted marble?

"Yes," said Athina.

Nina wondered what were the disadvantages of marble.

"It will be very beautiful," Athina said.

The designer said it was a wonderful surface. Always looked so good. But one must be careful with lemon. It destroys the surface.

"Must there be no citrus on marble," said Athina. "Other things fine. Marble is very easy, very lovely."

Which marble then? He summoned his assistant. Clearly we were going to go through the marble routine again. After all there were hundreds of different marbles. I looked at my watch surreptitiously and hoped that Athina had an imminent appointment. Instead I heard Athina saying she had met the best and most famous marble-cutter in Greece. He had a piece of Pendeli marble, just right for our house in Nauplion.

"Pendeli. *Po, po, po,*" said our designer.

Pendeli is the marble which was used to build the Parthenon. It still comes from the same quarry, near Athens. It is particularly white with some grey shadows. It is beautiful, rather rare and very expensive.

"Won't it cost an awful lot?" Nina said.

"I arrange a good price," said Athina. "Yes, expensive but not too expensive. You have a lovely house in Nauplion. Must you have lovely kitchen. Beautiful marb for beautiful home."

"Fine," I said. Might as well be hung for a bankrupt as for a minor debtor. "I think your kitchen will look smashing."

He smiled, acknowledging my coming to heel. "I'll arrange about the marble with Mrs Sideropoulou. I think perhaps it'll be quite difficult to get a piece of Pendeli big enough. But we'll see. I hope you'll be very pleased. Anything else?" He beamed encouragingly at Nina.

"A chopping block," I said quickly.

"It comes with the sinks. It's the top." Politely dismissive.

"A broom cupboard."

He turned and stared coldly at Nina. "And ruin my kitchen?"

Athina said hastily that we would see to that later. Meanwhile what about a special price for her friends? He said the price was the price. A discount, she suggested. Surely he could do something? This was quite a big operation. Yes, I nodded, it certainly was. For us. No, he said, his prices were honest, as cheap as he could make them. He was very fair. He would send us a detailed estimate but if we wanted everything ready by Easter we would have to return it – that is if we thought it reasonable – immediately.

We all shook hands. Athina said she would try him again but not till later. You never knew; he might do something. No but seriously, Nina said, what about the broom cupboard? Athina said never mind, we would find a solution. What mattered was our lovely house and it *would* be lovely. Certainly, I thought, if she had anything to do with it. She drove us back to our hotel before returning to her office.

We made a quick dash up to the enigmatic shop in the Plaka and caught the lady just turning the card and going out to lunch. I was able to ask her when she would be back and we made an appointment for three o'clock.

It was not, as we had thought, an antique shop, although it had some antiques and many embroideries, ornaments and lamps we had seen in the folk museums. Most of the stuff was contemporary but hand-made in the traditional styles. The furniture was made by the owner's husband at a workshop with, as far as I could understand, a co-operative of fellow craftsmen. The bed we had admired was beautifully carved but too small. It then turned out that we could have one made and could choose the design of the carving. We decided on a simple Peloponnesian flower design for our bedroom and a more complicated Naupliot design with birds and castle for the guest-room. And two bedside tables. No, four, said Nina. And then there were some finely carved and painted linen chests. We'd have one of those please. No, two. They were so useful, said Nina, and you could sit on them.

None of them was cheap. I was, frankly, stunned at the price, and said so to Nina.

"Well, when did you last buy a bed?" It was a fair point. Around 1950, I should think.

"Do you take credit cards?" I asked.

The lady smiled sweetly, her head moving delicately up.

"Tomorrow," I said. "When will you be open?"

She pointed to the card in the door. We had spoken throughout in a mixture of Greek, French and English.

"*Akrivos?*" I said disbelievingly.

"*Nai,*" she said. Punctually.

And at eleven o'clock the next morning she was there, as was her husband. We had decided to go the whole hog: a dining-room table and six chairs. And perhaps a looking-glass for the bedroom. We jibed at the price for that but we ordered all the rest – the beds and bedside tables, a simple mahogany dining table with carved legs and drawers and chairs which were a Greek pattern after Sheraton, sturdy and handsome. Emboldened by Athina's tactics, I asked if there would be a discount since we were buying all this stuff at one go. The husband had been measuring and calculating while the wife wrote down a list of the furniture and prices. They both looked up bewildered. Was this the wrong kind of shop? It seemed that whenever we slipped Athina's leash we ended up in shops that were twice as expensive and stood by their prices. He mumbled something about rounding down the total. It was still pretty formidable but then, as Nina said, we had bought virtually all we needed.

We sat for what seemed like hours signing traveller's cheques and Eurocheques till we ran out of them. And probably of money, as I said to Nina later.

"This was your idea," she said. "You wanted a house in Greece. If we're going to live here we need furniture."

I didn't disagree.

Athina came to dine with us that night. We showed her the shop. She was intrigued, peered through the window but could not see very much. It was, of course, closed. What had we bought? And how much had it cost? *Po, po, po.* Very deliberately. But then, judiciously, we had bought a great many things and if they were as good as we said they were, why that was a reasonable enough price. We had a very jolly meal. We were leaving the next morning. We told Athina how lovely we thought she was, how deeply grateful we were for everything she had done.

"I make sure your house was lovely; lovely-lovely," she said, hugging us. "I love you both. I feel naked before you."

I could think of no suitable response. Not even the useful Greek *episis*; likewise, me too.

"I see you soon," she said, "with permissions and windows."

XVII

Back in London, no one felt naked before us. Greece receded. It was November, wet, cold and wintry. The Nauplion saga was unending. No, I said several times a day to kind, enquiring friends, the Greek house was not ready to be moved into. No, I did not know how long it would take. Yes, it was splendid as far as it went. No, not even perhaps by next summer.

I was depressed. Seeing my GP about something quite else, she said I seemed depressed. Yes and no, I said. Not really depressed, just a bit down. Nina said briskly, "Of course you're depressed. You've been depressed for months, possibly years, long before you retired. You should see someone."

I knew what that meant. Expensive chaps in Harley Street, couches, Freud, Jung, Adler, Klein, Reich, primal screams. No, I said.

A day or two later I was sitting in an agreeable, light, warm consulting room with a charming doctor, young enough to be an older son. I wanted to say I wasn't much used to shrinks, except socially (some of my best friends were shrinks). I didn't really think I was quite ready for the funny farm, yet. But the language, even the sentiment seemed coarsely inept against his sensitive courtesy. No, I said, I didn't really think I was *in* a depression, just a bit depressed. Well yes, perhaps I was, I admitted after some sensible conversation, in a *bit* of a depression, but not a clinical depression. After all I had nothing really to be depressed about. The Greek house was taking a bit longer than expected but that was all. It would come right. I was busy. There were plenty of things I wanted to do. I was seeing more of my children and grandchildren and even of my father. It was a full, and should be satisfying, life. I was helping launch an exciting project, the first guidebook to London and the UK to be written in Japanese and printed and published here. And so on.

But that, he said, was precisely the point. There was no objective reason for my being cast down: I was, in a clinical sense, depressed. It was nothing to do with pulling myself together, with activity, with doing a job, with helping charities, with useful hobbies or any such popular remedy. It was not my fault and I was not responsible for how I felt. It was nothing to be ashamed of. Depression was depression and I was depressed. No doubt about it. I should accept the fact. (My name is Austen. I am a depressive . . .) But why, he said, should I suffer? It could be ameliorated. The gloom would lighten. I would be all right. Honest.

The happy doctor was quite right but it took some time. Meanwhile chinks of light appeared amongst the gloom, one of them a letter from Athens. "My dear Osten and Nina," wrote Athina.

> I wish my letters reach you in good health.
> I am starting my letter with good news since the Architect Committee of Tripoli has decided that the attic windows must remain as they are because such windows existed in previous years. We have succeeded in our efforts.

Therefore, there is no problem and the works are being carried on on all aspects. The bathrooms are being covered with marble and the walls are getting ready to be painted later on.

Mr Pericles has monitored this stage of the work and has prepared a plan for the staircase and the attic bars. I am expecting a price offer during the next few days. We must, therefore, make the payment of the fourth instalment to Nondas Bros during the next few days in the sum of drachmas . . .

And then it petered out into rows of noughts. It was always strangely disconcerting to see all those zeros. I knew we were spending millions of drachmas and I realized that we were not spending millions of pounds. But somehow all those clumps of figures clamoured for more attention than their sterling equivalent warranted. Divide by 225, I kept on telling myself, but the notion of the millions somehow survived the logic of the arithmetic.

Athina also enclosed the latest kitchen plans, awaiting our comments, if any. Nina expectedly said there was no broom cupboard but she was grateful that there was no temple erected to the culinary arts either, no vertical structure on the divider. But what did Athina mean by bars in the attic? Surely we didn't need a bar, let alone bars. And why in the attic anyway?

I sketched the fencing, as I supposed it to be, around the attic floor. Nina seemed unconvinced. Bars, I said, as in zoos or other prisons. Not bars as in pubs.

Christmas came and went. The normal January bills were swollen by requests from Athens and Nauplion for prompt payment. Plato telephoned from Athens to wish us a happy new year.

He thought, he said, as our oldest Greek friend, he ought to go down to Nauplion and see what was going on. "I gave your famous lawyer a lift. It was quite an eye-opener. Athina made Nikos remove every single knob and handle. They weren't up to scratch. I think it's going to be very nice. It certainly will be if Athina has anything to do with it. You know," he added, "when she's excited about something she occasionally gets a little muddled even with her Greek tenses."

I think he said this to reassure me about my Greek. I was going through one of my perennial fits of linguistic despair. Would I ever understand anyone? Would I ever be able to speak moderately fluently? Was there any point in going on? Nina had quoted Plato, our Plato, to the effect that there were dangers in becoming too good. Fluent foreigners sometimes made disastrous mistakes and just because they were so plausibly fluent they inadvertently ladled out insults which were then taken seriously. "Not, of course," Plato had said, "that either of you will find yourself in that plight."

Nina somehow fixed on this as a justification for not trying, or not trying particularly hard. After all one didn't want to get too fluent. Ha! I said in my bath. Ha! I said to my inert study on a cold morning. Ha! I said to unsuspecting, heavily wrapped up, would-be passengers waiting at the number 19 bus stop. I switc'.ed to a 171 and enrolled in a crash course at Morley College.

This seemed an admirable solution to the problem of how to get over the hump and make a breakthrough. A five-day slog, six hours a day, with relays of tutors to keep up the pace. Unfortunately it developed rather differently.

There were only five of us. One had quite good Greek; she was married to a Cypriot businessman who, she said, never spoke Greek to her at home and she needed practice in order to cope adequately with their annual visits to his family in Cyprus. She had taken time off work, as had a civil servant in his late twenties. A girl who had been island-hopping and was hoping to return to Greece to help run a hotel was not, I think, currently employed and the fifth was an athlete with her leg in plaster. She had, she said, done part of the course before and would drop in and out, between physiotherapy and surgical appointments. No harm in any of that, I thought, as we all sat, notebooks at the ready, and those of us that had them with us, the BBC *Greek Language and People* textbooks open in front of us. The first lecturer launched us quickly through a revision of the first five chapters. And then the exercise started to disintegrate.

"I don't see why," said the island-hopper, "when you speak to me the words change." Gender, dear, I said under my breath. "Gender, Louise," said the lecturer, turning round to the blackboard and writing out an assortment of pronouns, definite articles and nouns to demonstrate m. f. and n.

"Remember?" said the lecturer with a flourish and a painful squeak of chalk. The girl, who was perhaps twenty-three and whose name was actually Lois, still looked bemused.

"And I don't understand," said the civil servant, "why *diskos* goes to *diskous* in that bit you just rushed us through."

Rushed? I thought he had taken it rather gently. I had supposed it was just a warm-up until our mental muscles were toned up.

The lecturer swept round to the blackboard and wrote *Mipos exete diskous* in a fine clear Greek hand. "Have you any discs?" he said. "Accusative, Charles. Accusative plural, Charles."

"Giles, not Charles," said Giles.

"I find your writing difficult," said Lois. "Couldn't you do it in capitals?"

"I don't understand about accusatives," said Giles.

"Oh," said the lecturer, "Ah. These English schools. You were taught perhaps about subjects and objects in your grammar. I love you. You is the object, I the subject. Remember? I the nominative case, you the accusative."

"We didn't do English grammar at school," said Giles.

"Nor did we," said Lois.

"But perhaps you did French."

"No," they said in unison.

"German?" The lecturer was getting tentative.

"Babi –" It was the lady athlete – "I don't think they've learnt any language or any grammar. Lots of secondary schools don't teach them."

"They must teach a foreign language," Babis said. "For the GCSE." He was beginning to sound discouraged.

"I took other subjects," said Giles complacently, "and A-level English Constitution and Psychology."

"I only took one A," said Lois. "Art."

If Babis was disheartened, I was dejected. Apart from being

an indictment of the English school system, their education, or rather lack of it, threw a large spanner in the works. Clearly this could no longer be the crash course, as envisaged, for which we had signed up and paid.

"I thought," said Babis, "the prospectus spoke of some Greek being needed for this course."

"I've been to Greece for four summers running," said Lois, indignantly, "and my boyfriend says I've got quite a good accent."

"I'll confer with my colleagues during the lunchbreak," Babis said. "We'll try and split the course into a basic and an intermediate. For the moment, cases." He turned to the blackboard and wrote HE LOVES HER, SHE LOVES HIM. "You see. The word, the pronoun, he, she, nominative, the subject, changes when it becomes the object, changes into the accusative case, changes to him and her. Even in English. So far, so good, Charles? Louise?"

It might have been fair but it was not good. They were both bright and intelligent but grammar was an undiscovered universe. There was no breakthrough, not for them, then, nor for me later. Just a few more drops of water wearing a channel along the stone. An accretion of knowledge, I said to myself, nothing dramatic. It was, sadly, a bit of a fiasco: the course bombed rather than crashed. I expect in my depressed state I made rather heavy weather of what went wrong and of my disappointment. I expect it was not as wasted a week as my gloom made it seem. I had marginally improved my Greek.

The problems of the Japanese book were more to do with style than syntax. Various Japanese writers and journalists working in London were disagreeing with each other about language and layout. How formal? How literary? How journalistic? Should the book run from, in our terms, back to front in the traditional Japanese mode or should we espouse the new fashion of front to back? The typesetting had to be done in Tokyo and it was a nightmare getting the proofs corrected. Our expert advisers seemed to disagree about almost everything and after the book was printed, in London, the Japanese ambassador, who had been helpful and supportive at the beginning, was asking why we had published it in Britain. It would have been better if a Japanese publisher had done it. I said that we had published and printed in Britain because it was about Britain. My colleagues at CPC Guidebooks and I had determined to make it better, more accurate, more informative, more wide-ranging and better-looking than any of the Japanese competition. And so it was. It was the first new book to be printed in Japanese in this country but whether it was worth the considerable and devoted effort it took, I am not at all sure.

The news from Greece was good. The work was continuing apace. The dormer windows were finished. I spoke to Plato. He gathered the attic was going to crown our apartment. I spoke to Athina. Everything would be lovely but she and Pericles were watching the work very carefully. We agreed to the estimate for the stairs to the attic. The marbs were being laid on the floor. The balconies were being made ready. She signalled that more money would be needed soon to pay the next stage. More money was sent.

It all seemed strangely remote. Our excitement at knowing that the dormer windows were safe and that the attic would now be a useful working-space was muted. In my case it was probably just part of being glum. In Nina's, I think she was getting cold feet. Was she to be condemned forever to going to Nauplion, and only Nauplion? Would she be able to work there? And if not, what then? And all this money being spent when there were better things to do with it.

"Like what?" I asked when she finally gave tongue to some of these doubts .

"We could have travelled all over the world for our holidays. Now we'll never be able to go anywhere else."

She paused, waiting for a comment. I said nothing; there was nothing to say. "And anyway," she continued, "I don't suppose I'll be able to write there." She paused again. Nina has a nice line in studiedly abject despair. "Not that that matters. I don't suppose I'll ever write anything again."

It being a cold drab February, it seemed a good notion to book a flight to Greece for early April. It would be something to cherish in the gloom. We could look forward (with luck) to a change of climate as well as scene and we would be able to catch up on progress with the house and, according to Athina, make some important last-minute decisions. Like what? I thought we had decided more than enough already.

I reverted to my schoolboy self's habit of ticking off the days, and also to a new-found device for tackling insomnia: working out the shortest way for getting from Acronauplion to Kapodistriou without using the Xenia Palace's lift. Meanwhile there were friends, family, theatres and tennis. Travelling friends came and went. Nicholas Barrington came back as Ambassador to Pakistan and returned as High Commissioner. George Bailey, one of my oldest friends from Oxford, stopped over between visiting his New York publisher and going back to Munich, and envied us. He had thought of joining us in a Greek enterprise but Beate had been less than enthusiastic. Meanwhile there was the Lord's tennis weekend and the Queen's weekend. There were farewell parties for Chris Bell, who had been my, and my successor John Tusa's, immensely able, clever and loveable deputy. There was the boat-race, which we always – as long as they continue both to hold the party and to invite us – spend in Barnes with David, another 1946 Magdalen friend, and Sally Holloway.

And then suddenly it was 4 April and snowing as we joined the Olympic flight to Athens. For that or some other undisclosed reason we were very late arriving. But we woke up to a lovely morning, the Athenian light, the *nephos* not occluding the sky, being clear, sharp and precise in registration, just as one always hoped it would be, and as I always remembered, probably inaccurately, it being thirty-five years ago.

We went to the shops to check on the progress of our beds, sofas and other furniture. Athina, apparently delighted to see us, had found an early nineteenth-century marble-topped, four-drawer commode, a copy from the French made in Chios. She had thought of buying it for herself but had decided it was too large for her. It would look well in our drawing-room, she said, and it does, a handsome piece. She had also seen a large looking-glass in the window of an antique dealer in Skoufa, just round the corner from her office. Should we perhaps go and see it? We did.

"You like it?" asked Athina. "You really liked it?"

"Yes," we said. We thought it splendid. It was large, not over-ornate, and gold-framed.

"I ask the price," she said. Calculating the quietly spoken Greek in sterling, I reckoned it would have been cheaper in Camden Passage but Nina says I am out of date.

"Not too cheap," said Athina. Did she mean not too expensive? "I see if she makes a special price for me."

The lady, who wore tinted glasses and had girlish curls framing her face, peered into a drawer at the back of the dark basement shop and emerged with an exercise book. Her head went up a millimetre or two, a barely perceptible negative. Athina returned to the attack. It was clearly a very large and rather fine mirror. But was it worth this much? Surely not? The antique lady's chin lifted: no.

Athina was almost put out. "Never mind. I talked to her on the telephone tomorrow. Look. We arrange something."

I put in my ten drachmas' worth and explained that in any case we needed to think about it and we would have to arrange to draw some money. Did she take credit cards? Her eyes lifted and she smiled sadly and deprecatingly.

We agonized for a bit, Athina failed to bring off another coup and, of course, we ended up buying the mirror. At the last moment the antiques lady intimated in Greek (she had no English) that if we were paying in cash she would make a small accommodation. Athina said, rather complacently I thought when I reported back, "I tell you so."

We arranged, we hoped, for the sofa-cum-armchair arrange-ment to be ready to be sent to Nauplion at the end of May. "We can't be quite sure," a languid young woman told us. "We're in the hands of the Italian factory."

We also asked the shop in the Plaka for the beds, chairs, and tables to be available for despatch to Nauplion at the same time. And we bought another carved chest and two more wooden stools. Despite Nina's stated objective, which I heartily shared, to keep our Greek residence uncluttered, she seemed to find all sorts of irrefutable arguments for buying more furniture. I decided that she just liked buying furniture. More generally this was a sub-set of just liking buying. Whatever. Clothes, books, tables, pottery, glass, Christmas and birthday presents six months ahead of time. Anything.

Pericles drove us down to Nauplion. He wanted to see the wooden stairs leading to the attic which had just been completed and he wanted us to see the work that had been done. Once we were clear of Athens, it was a fine, sunny April day. In Attica wild flowers carpeted the fields and decorated the hillsides. The scent of herbs was heady. It felt as though these ancient mountains were annually reborn and were now decked with celebratory garlands of green and pink and yellow. In fact, spring was almost over and the grass was browning and beginning to die off. Summer was within reach.

Nauplion was sparkling, the sea glinting and the castle of Palamidi shining in the midday sun. We parked the car in the little squa re and walked past the church of St Spyridon, where a burst of candles lit up the shady interior, and along Kapodistriou. Number 19 was looking rather splendid. It had been rendered, plastered and painted a slightly yellowish cream, its approved colour. The front doors were there but they hung open on their hinges beneath a rounded wooden window arch with a wooden fan decoration. Four larger, rounded wooden-framed arches with narrow windows and space for double doors stood unexplained and empty, except for packing cases and the odd oil drum. Nikos had intended them to be shops, one small, the other quite large, on either side of the front door. It was not clear what kind of shop he thought would be attracted to the house. The idea of the bakery had gone away: the baker had decided to stay where he was. There were no other shops in the street. But Nikos had got planning permission for shops and the wide rounded arches, an original (in both senses) feature of the house, certainly continued to suggest shops or stores.

The neighbours from opposite greeted us. Antigone waved a welcome from her lower balcony. We waved back and then I suddenly noticed with excitement that we had a wooden floor to our front balcony. Inside, the entrance hall was now plastered and painted. A door-frame led to stairs which went down to the cellar. The ground floor now gave the feeling of a house rather than some rough-cast open-plan parking lot. The thirteen supporting pillars still stretched up, apparently unimpeded by any first floor accommodation, to the top floor, our floor. And there, in place but open, was our front door.

A carpenter was at work on the French window to the front balcony. Nikos and Andreas called out from the attic where they were apparently fitting the emergency water-tank. The wooden staircase was finished and in place, and very fine it was too: plain, good-looking and functional. There was no balustrade yet and the joiner, the stairs-maker, approached Pericles to discuss the design for the uprights. Nikos and Andreas leapt down the stairs four at a time and bounded up to us.

"You like it?" they said, one after another, "You like it?" We looked around, dazed. A vast expanse of marble floor. White walls. Windows everywhere. Sunshine and shade. Sharply defined shadows even in the early afternoon. The neat graceful stairs leading upwards. The upper deck illuminated by the dormer windows. The back balcony, bigger, finer than the south-facing front one, its ironwork the only remnant of the original house, also now floored and usable. Masses of wood to break up the white walls. All ten windows in the living room now had their wooden shutters fitted. The chestnut colour complemented and echoed the roof timbers.

"Gosh," said Nina.

"Wow," I said. "It's wonderful. *Poli, poli oraio.*" I searched my brain for Greek words of wonder and approbation. "*Thavma.*" A wonder. "*Katapliktiko.*" Breathtaking. "*Phantastiko.*" I knew the ancient Greeks had a word for it. "*Apithano.*" Phenomenal. But did *phainomeniko* mean it in that sense? I doubted and moved on to "*Yperthetiko*" which must mean superlative. I gave up. I thought they must have got the general drift.

The joiner beamed. The carpenter grinned. The somewhat alcoholic house-painter appeared from one of the bedrooms and smiled, vanishing again like the Cheshire cat. Andreas laughed with pleasure. Nikos' face lit up. He was pleased; pleased and proud.

Pericles said, "You have done very well," and then turned to the joiner and told him in Greek that his stairs were excellent.

Nikos said, "You come to the top." It was an invitation. He took Nina by the hand and led her up the stairs. She whooped with delight. It was the first time she had been up to the attic and she ran to the south dormer to look up to Acronauplion and across to the great fortress of Palamidi.

I meanwhile was peering out of the other dormer and looking over the roofs towards the harbour and the mountains. I was wondering who had objected to our dormers because it was surely not just the architectural purists. Was there someone out there that did not want to be looked down upon? I was trying to work out if there was anywhere obvious which we could see from the attic and not from the balconies or ordinary windows, some additional intrusion into privacy. But we did not seem to be any more invasive than from the lower floor.

"Go on," said Nina, plucking at my shirt, "let me have a go. I've never looked out of this window." I gave way with my usual gracious good humour. "I can see a bit of sea," she cried, "and lovely mountains. And the roofs of other people's houses. And some windows and balconies. I must remember to bring my binoculars. Oh, I think I can see the parrot."

We had assumed there was a parrot because whenever we had visited the apartment we had heard what seemed to be a child calling out "Mama. Mama." Iambus. Short-long. Unaccented, accented. Mama. Mama. Exactly like a fractious child, a fractious Greek child. You could hear them all round the town, querulously demanding their usually beleaguered mothers. But this particular cry, although at first remarkably convincing, was a bit mechanical in its repetition, mechanical and unvarying; indeed parrot-like. In addition we could never see the child who was crying out for its mother. Hence we deduced a parrot.

Nina was unwilling to go too near to the edge of the unprotected platform. She held my hand tightly. "It looks good from up here, doesn't it. Spacious. Elegant. Pleasing." I nodded happily and we went down the stairs to explore the balconies.

The front balcony overlooking the street and facing south

was wide enough to take two or three people standing. It was not really deep enough for anything except those very narrow *kafeneion* chairs, the kind that Greek villagers perch on, balancing on two of the legs. "Or stools," said Nina. "Lucky we decided to buy three in that shop in the Plaka."

Opposite us, and almost close enough to shake hands, were neighbours. We could see into their rooms, so presumably they could see into ours. Directly opposite were a couple of around our age. I thought I had seen them on occasions with married sons in the forces who were living elsewhere, probably Athens. Almost everybody lives in Athens or has relatives who do, except for those who have never been more than five kilometres from their birthplace. Various other people lodged with them: the chief waiter at one of the tavernas and a man who had a tourist shop selling romantic views of Nauplion and the surrounding countryside. In summer they had a room which was let to tourists who wanted a bed for the night. Behind their house rose the streets and houses that marked the different contour lines up the slope, culminating in the walls of Acronauplion. Here and there were small gardens and terraces and most of the balconies were bright with pots of green shrubs and flowering geraniums and pelargoniums.

In our excitement we had hardly noticed that the kitchen area was almost finished. The divider was there, but not quite in the right place, so we moved it. The fridge, oven, washing machine and dishwasher were wired and plumbed in. The final touches, the wooden cladding and the marble tops, were still to come. The marble expert was bringing the slab of Pendeli with him. He would cut and finish it on site.

"But alas," I said, getting in first, "no broom cupboard. Still, there's always the bathroom."

"And just where in the bathroom do you think you're going to fit in a broom cupboard?"

I marched Nina firmly to the other balcony. It was wide and deep enough to take two large chairs and a table. "We can breakfast out here," I said. It faced north, towards the harbour. There was no one, and no house particularly close, looking straight ahead and because of the slope down to the sea we were higher than all the other buildings. At the next street down, on the corner and above the bakery, was a room with one shutter open and a flapping curtain, grey and flimsy with age. Inside there was furniture – a table, chairs, a *chaise longue* – but all of them with the dusty air of long disuse. Yet these were not rickety rejects, the discards of an affluent family. They looked well cared for, loved and looked after. True, the room had been abandoned, furniture, trinkets, ornaments and all; but it had been an unexpected, unplanned leaving. Perhaps like Miss Haversham someone was keeping the room as it was, as it had been. The curtain fluttered, the half-shutter swung in the breeze. Slightly further down, on the next street down, the parrot, if parrot it were, sung out Mama, Mama. This was a house with keen gardeners. There were plants everywhere, pouring over balconies, climbing up walls. Coming back closer to home, down the *scala* was a house apparently divided into lodging rooms or small flats. On the balcony outside the top one lay a well-behaved young Alsatian sheep-hound, basking in the sun. To add to the rich variety of sounds, and Nauplion is not a quiet little town, was the unmistakable clucking of a hen. Or was this too a parrot?

We met the hen before we saw the mina bird. The hen was being taken for a walk. Or rather it was being brought back from a walk. It seemed that it was living in our cellar, which was open to the *scala*. The hen had a piece of string round its neck and was connected to its keeper by another length of twine looped through the collar. The woman at the other end of the leash was an artist, so she told us, who had a room off the *scala*, opposite our cellar.

I asked her why she took the hen for a walk.

"Well you wouldn't want to stay in a cellar all day, would you, if you were a hen?" She spoke with some indignation and with an Australian accent. "And I suppose you want to know why I keep her in a cellar. *Na sas po.* I'll tell you. My room's too small. That's why. We only come for a few days at a time."

"Where do you live?"

"Athens," she said. With an unspoken "Of course. Where else?"

"And Australia?" I ventured.

"My father had a job in Sydney. We spent five years there."

"What was he doing?" I was rapidly catching the Greek habit of asking personal questions without any show of hesitation.

"Baking bread."

"What do you do with the hen in Athens?"

She looked at me pityingly. "I've got more room there."

The mina bird was marginally more conventionally housed in the window of a printer's shop. It occasionally moved around the job cases of type and could be seen to speak but no sound was audible from the street, and certainly not from our house which was three blocks away. In any case, whatever the bird was saying it was not Mama, Mama.

We had agreed to meet Pericles and Nikos for lunch at three o'clock at Noufara, the Greek-Italian restaurant in the *plateia*. Meanwhile we had time to stroll round and check up on what had happened since we were last in town. The mayor's assiduous tree-planting (he was apparently particularly fond of palms) was going well, the trees growing fast and healthily. In fact Nauplion looked eminently well cared for. The seamstress who lived in the little square near Agios Spyridon greeted us as she hurried into her shop. The cobbler who worked in a little cubby-hole next to Vassili's taverna responded to our "*Herite*" with an enthusiastic "*Yeia sas, yeia sas*" as though he recognized our voices, although Nina had only once asked him to repair a heel and he was very nearly blind. (I don't think Greek cultural sensitivity extends to what we used to call, in an earlier euphemism, the handicapped: it is rather more taken up with marbles from the Parthenon and the composition of Philip's, and today's, Macedonia). Vassili and his father, who works as head waiter, shook our hands enthusiastically and asked how the house was going. When were we going to move in? "In the summer," I said and then added, "We hope."

Could this really be true, I wondered. Were we tempting the Furies? Summer was only a few weeks away, even in English terms. Perhaps I should have suggested autumn. Nina said she couldn't believe that it would be so soon. It suddenly seemed imminent, she said, and she wasn't sure she was ready, not quite yet.

"Don't worry," I said, "there are bound to be more delays."

But in truth there was no reason for any further hold-up. And Nikos and Andreas would want to finish as soon as they could, and get paid. Anyway, even if we hadn't given any coherent thought to it, we had already arranged for furniture and suchlike to be delivered at the beginning of June.

Pericles confirmed this as a realistic date. Nikos said, "*tin proti Iouniou?* Sure." He paused. That had been an instant response. Now came the considered verdict. He smiled. "OK. *Entaxi*. June one. No problem."

Before waving Pericles off as he drove back to Athens we told him what a marvellous job he had done and how grateful we were. He told us in return that he had been very impressed with what Nikos and his craftsmen and workers had achieved. He hoped we would be very happy in Nauplion. He thought it would turn out to be a lovely and comfortable home. "A place," he went on, "where you, Mrs Nina, will find it good to write books. I shall feel proud to have played my part in your beautiful literature."

Nina looked as though she didn't know where to put herself. In embarrassment, she very nearly simpered. We made our farewells and waved energetically till the car was out of view.

"It's not quite goodbye," I said, largely to reassure myself. "We're not on our own yet."

Down at The Boatyard they had other things to think about. They were putting the world, and Greece, to rights. The Koskotas affair was still gusting away. Was Mr Papandreou involved or was he not? Koskotas, in gaol in America and trying to avoid extradition, had said in an interview in *Time* magazine that Andreas Papandreou was directly and personally tied up in the scandal.

"But why should we believe that crook Koskotas when he talks about Andreas when we don't believe anything else he says?" This was Phaidon. "It's logical, isn't it?"

"All Cretans are liars," I began, but it was an unfortunate intervention. No one picked up the allusion and the house-painter's friend, hitherto unknown to me, came from Crete.

"What's he saying? What's he saying?"

Phaidon dismissed him with a wave of his hand.

"Ah," said a dark-suited visitor from Athens, "but what about the box stuffed with 5000-drachma notes?"

"They were in a box of diapers. Nappies," Phaidon said to us before rounding on the Athenian. "And how does that make Andreas a criminal? He had nothing to do with it."

"It was allegedly given to a senior Pasok official," said the resident lawyer. "Truth is no one *knows* anything."

"Well what about the other scandals, then? The Sale of the Century? The frauds on the Community?"

Phaidon ignored the Athenian and explained to us that the Sale of the Century was the purchase of forty F16 and sixty Mirages at what was said to be huge and uncompetitive prices plus hefty supposed kickbacks for those who negotiated the deal. The Athenian gave up, knocked back his ouzo and said he was going to eat. Phaidon said we mustn't believe everything Nea Demokratia said. He asked after the house and our family. He had been to see the marble floor and the staircase to the attic. When were we planning to move in? We must have a new house party, and meanwhile he would introduce us to some of the people who happened to be eating or drinking in The Boatyard tonight.

A few were English or American, some married to or living with Greeks, others were Greek couples and singles, and there were a few singular Germans, Dutch and Swiss. It was difficult to take them all in at first introduction but some stood out. There was the corpulent Greek restaurateur, a familiar feature of Constitution Square; an English couple who had sailed out ten years before and had built a house near a village some four or five miles from Nauplion; the willowy Norwegian blond and her more compact Naupliot businessman husband; the manager of the Amphitryon Hotel and his dark, pretty fiancée from the far north of Greece; an American archaeologist; a German archaeologist; a tall Athenian designer and maker of jewellery and his petite German silversmith helpmeet; and an assorted Naupliot cast of lawyers, workers and drinkers. We floated up to our hotel on a sea of good wishes and Metaxas seven-star brandy.

Athina was involved in some protracted court case in the Piraeas. She could not get away to join us in Nauplion. Plato came down for the weekend and brought us the message. They seemed to be getting on well together. As usual when Plato was around we had marvellous meals. Plato always seemed to get the best out of restaurants, tavernas, bars and indeed people: he has an air and an elegance of speech and mind. We returned with him to Athens, bidding Nauplion an encouragingly happy-sad farewell. We would be back in two months' time, with the semi-permanency of our own place in the community, a stake, a property.

"You know," said Nina, as we shot round some steep mountain bends in Plato's Lancia, "I'll miss the hotel, the Xenia Palace."

"Which bit of delight?" said Plato. "The plumbing or the absurdly portentous Colonels' architecture?"

"I'm very fond of the place," Nina said spiritedly. "And I'll miss staying there. Seeing that glorious view." She paused for dramatic effect and then slid into bathos with a "whatever you say."

The next evening Athina came to our hotel for a drink. We discussed finances and the progress of the house. Then we all dined with Plato in the Plaka. The restaurant (or was it a taverna? Certainly it was only open at night) was unexpected. The door was almost invisible and there was no sign or mark to show what lay inside. It was small, with no more than a dozen tables. It was apparently not only difficult to find it, but also difficult to reserve a table there. They specialized in game and were closed during the summer months.

"Hardly a tourist trap then," I said.

"I never," said Athina, "shall be here before." Plato shuddered. Athina tried again. "Never I was here before."

"No," I put in hastily, "we've not been here before either. Very good it looks too."

"Austen, why you say *weave*? Weave not been. I thought weave was with cloths."

"Clothes," said Nina, a reflex correction, precisely as Athina corrects her Greek pronunciation.

"*Cloth*," said Plato. "You weave *cloth*."

"They say," said Athina with something of a giggle, "only the old Athenian families can book tables here."

Plato pooh-poohed this simple snobbery. He thought you just had to be someone known to the proprietor. He busied himself and us in the mysteries of the menu and tried to tease out the English names of the game birds and mammals. The food when it came was remarkably good.

It seemed a suitable moment to tell Athina how splendid the apartment looked. Plato congratulated her on her masterly attention to every tiny detail, including the door furniture which he was sure was no part of her legal duties. I wondered how after all the planning difficulties the log-jam had come unstuck.

"Your lawyer," said Athina, "cleverly found the right picture, the earlier photography. This shows attic windows on the house. I speak and show the planning court. The court over-rules the refusal of the local authority. But there is still further appeal to the ministry." Plato interrupted and corrected her. "Yes, sorry. The person, the minister. He still will decide. And the planners are still opposing. Look. Pericles knows the minister. So I say to him, not to interfere but just perhaps to speak a few words. And you shall see it came out OK."

I said, "Our lawyer is famous and clever and Pericles is a prince."

We flew back to London the next day on the lunchtime Olympic flight.

XVIII

The following day I was at the London Information Forum. This was a rare bird: a CSCE (Conference on Security and Co-operation in Europe) meeting, within the Helsinki process, dealing only and specifically with such matters as freedom of information. For this reason, amongst the delegations there were many journalists, editors and media folk. Some of the big battalions, like the Soviets and the Americans, flew in stars of press and broadcasting. Others had a few not so tame journos sitting on the reserve benches waiting for their managers, and the referee, to let them on to the field.

Great Britain, as host country, had gone further than most in this momentary liberalization or aberration, depending on how you feel about us hacks, and had neither politician nor diplomat as its leader but Lord Rees-Mogg, who not improbably would regard himself as being both political and diplomatic.

Nonetheless William was clearly head of the UK delegation, given always, of course, that he was high on the Thatcher approved list, as an ex-editor of *The Times* and a former vice-chairman of the BBC, as well perhaps as being chief nanny of television morals at the newly established Broadcasting Standards Council. There was a pleasing diplomat as deputy, Sir Anthony Williams (as ambassador to Argentina he had not altogether read the portents aright over Argentinian intentions towards the Falklands), who was something of a CSCE buff, having led the delegation at the meeting in Madrid in 1983. There were some very agreeable minders from the Foreign Office, captained by Patrick Roberts, professionals who knew what they were doing and who got and kept the show on the road. Otherwise the UK delegation was made up of journalists such as Neal Ascherson and Malcolm Rutherford, academics like Geoffrey Hosking, John Vincent and Jonathan Eyall, broadcasting and film heavyweights like David Nicholas of ITN and David Puttnam, and telecommunications experts like Adam Scott and John Harper.

All of which was why, the day after we got back from Greece, I found myself sitting next to the Greek delegation in the Queen Elizabeth II Conference Centre, Westminster, listening to a rather relentlessly boring speech by the leader of one of the then Soviet bloc countries. The UK was placed between France and Greece, because under CSCE rules we appear under G for Great Britain or, more likely, G for Grande Bretagne rather than R for Royaume-Uni or U for United Kingdom as we do in other international organizations. There must be a learned paper somewhere called "The influence on international relations of variable positioning at conferences, dependent on the linguistic predilection of differing organizations."

This was the late spring of *glasnost* and *perestroika*. High summer was yet to come but there was a strong sense of ice-floes breaking up, of pent-up waters poised, waiting to break for the open sea. There was an excited anticipation of change; how far, how much, how fast, no one knew and no pundit in his or her wildest dreams compassed the reality. Back then, of course, nothing truly dramatic had yet happened – if you except

Academician, Nobel Laureate and noble dissident Sakharov's giving a press conference at the foreign ministry attacking the Soviet record on Human Rights – but Mr Gorbachev had been talking about openness and introducing tentative reforms and new approaches since 1987. And now, after meetings with President Reagan and the first steps taken towards disarmament, Mr Gorbachev was saint of the month, and indeed of the year.

In the Queen Elizabeth II hall there were recurrent buzzes of excitement. A senior Soviet delegate had publicly condemned critics of *glasnost* and had argued for freedom of information – admittedly more strongly for Soviet correspondents abroad than for Soviet journalists at home or for foreign correspondents in Moscow – and others took up and ran with the idea, intoxicated with the whiff of freedom until it seemed to embrace everyone, everywhere. But not the German Democratic Republic (otherwise known as East Germany), not Bulgaria, not Romania, not Yugoslavia and not, altogether, Czechoslovakia. Meanwhile Hungary and Poland showed distinct libertarian tendencies but were periodically reined in by the surviving old guard, the thought police.

It was a funny, odd moment in history serendipitously to hold an international conference on information. At times the American anti-communist stalwarts sounded antiquated; the world had changed between their opening remarks and their perorations. At times Honneker's men sounded more Stalinist than the horrific old Georgian himself. The Soviet Union had not altogether lost its theoreticians and party hacks, in both senses, but the Russians, and they were of course mostly Russians, were flying kites, the more adventurous flying them very high indeed, and even the time-servers were speaking more in the language of Arbatov than the *Pravda* we knew and despised.

It was funny too to be holding such a conference at such a time under such cranky rules of procedure as the CSCE had devised during the years of the Helsinki process. They were needed of course to get this most encouraging movement going. Nothing could be done except by consensus, by unanimity. All delegations naturally had a right to address the conference at length, a right which was fully utilized, and, indeed, a right of reply to something that another delegation had said. This too was thoroughly, acrimoniously and tediously exercised. Limits there had to be but these could only be imposed if they were in the original Helsinki rules or could now be established by total agreement. All this took considerable time.

Plenary meetings, which brought out the worst in tendentious and declamatory rhetoric, were held every Friday. For the rest of the week we met in committee, usefully and, mostly, sanely. I was taking the chair in the broadcasting group when we decided to debate a primary question of Conference information policy. We all professed to believe in open communication and, to a greater or lesser extent, in freedom of information although we in the UK delegation were in a very fragile glasshouse here, the Government having just got a new Official Secrets Act through Parliament which to many of us seemed even more restrictive in some crucial particulars than the old one. The Americans on the whole kept quiet about what they believed to be the absurd British addiction to secrecy; not so our European partners, nor of course the Russians who enjoyed teasing us and jabbing our ribs with less playful remarks about Northern Ireland. Many of us in the UK delegation had made clear to our minders our own disagreement with the new act and our unwillingness to defend it.

Nevertheless here we were at the London Information Forum intending to discuss how we could best improve present, and often restrictive, practices and facilitate the free flow of information. Meanwhile, under CSCE rules, we were going into closed sessions, banned to public, press, microphone and television camera, to discuss the freedom of press and broadcasting. It was a ludicrous inconsistency.

The recognition of this was, we thought, general; we had discussed the matter off the floor. Now I raised it in an official session. I thought we could take a simple step: establish a unanimous motion that this and all subsequent sessions of the broadcasting committee could be thrown open to public, press and broadcasters. Well, yes, in principle, said the USSR delegate, but it posed certain difficulties. No, said the East

German: it was unacceptable. All CSCE working sessions were held in private. Even ones taken up with freedom of information? Yes, I was told, whatever the topic. And there was the question of setting an undesirable precedent. After what seemed a day of argument (it was probably only an hour) I adjourned the session for a five-minute private discussion. We returned with a compromise. Every session would begin as a closed session. The chairman would then seek the agreement of all the delegations to close the meeting and start an open session. Thus the precedents would be preserved but debates and discussions would be held in the open. And we went through this routine for every single session.

In between this unsought education in CSCE conference diplomacy and the exercising of an unaccustomed largeness of patience, there was the pleasure of new acquaintances, of a variety of nationalities, of catching up with news from old friends and colleagues, and of talking Greek politics with the Greek delegation.

Mr Papandreou had survived yet another vote of confidence in March and was set clear to weather the onslaughts of the opposition and the growing weight of scandals to the end of his term. In Greece the period is fixed at four years and the next election had to be held in June, at the end of Papandreou's, and his creation Pasok's, second consecutive term in office. It could be, and was, argued that Papandreou himself was the victim of the scams. Certainly, his supporters could not accept that the great social and economic revolution which Pasok had seemed to usher in, the first left-wing government that post-war Greece had seen, was going to be frustrated by a fraudster like Koskotas. They could not understand that their glorious party had, as one Greek diplomat put it, blown it. To the less partisan there was Papandreou's health, too, to be considered, as well as his matrimonial difficulties – the divorce was being discussed, angrily rather than amicably; the suspicion was also still prevalent that he had been directly implicated in the Bank of Crete fraud, and, not least, there was the disastrous state of the economy or, as many would say, his disastrous handling of the economy, despite vast EC aid.

Following a well-worn tradition, Andreas Papandreou was in the process of establishing a whole wide raft of temporary, i.e. politically appointed, civil servants, effectively turning these jobs for the boys into permanencies and pensions and, of course, votes. He was also ardently engaged, another traditional Greek pre-electoral gambit, in moving the goalposts. In this case, he was altering the method of proportional representation, the intricacies of which escaped me but, as my mother would have said, as sure as God made little apples the effect was not going to help Mr Mitsotakis's New Democracy party win the election. Naturally enough all this was argued over, presented, repudiated and re-presented by the various Greek delegates in between anxieties over inflation, Cyprus, the Middle East, the Balkans, and, on the floor, answers to Turkish statements or rights of reply.

One of my old friends and allies in many a short-wave broadcasting battle, Leonard Marks, was leading the US delegation. Ambassador Marks has always been a great and valuable supporter of the BBC World Service. He could whisper to presidents who would phone prime ministers, a word from the American wise being infinitely more effective in Mrs Thatcher's ear than brave evidence from Europe, the USSR or the Commonwealth. Leonard was another CSCE buff but in the interstices of the conference we spent odd meals discussing not just the state of the world and our respective countries but the possible outcome of the deregulating of broadcasting in the UK. Leonard saw this as an exciting time of adventure and opportunity, with rich seams of profit and power there for the mining.

Casting aside predilections and predispositions, I could see he was right but I failed to summon up energy or enthusiasm. I disappointed him, I saw myself disappointing him. Here he thought was something that I could be, should be, beavering away at, thinking up ideas for, exploring the future. Here, he foresaw, was a new and suitable career for me, one in which I could properly deploy my talents and experience. He foresaw wrong.

It was, I supposed, underneath all the fascination with the

conference and with what the underlying theme really meant to all of us, that I was still not able to emerge from the sludge of depression. I decided this as Nina and I were being shown round Battersea House, which the Forbes family had bought and had done up, by Malcolm Forbes Jr. The young Forbes was giving a party for some of the delegates in his role as chairman of the Board for International Broadcasting. The BIB was the Washington-based, government-backed organization through which Radio Liberty and Radio Free Europe, both of them established in Munich and thought by much of the world to be arms of the CIA, were funded and, in a sense, overseen. Despite, or perhaps because of, the occasion, Forbes sent each of his guests home with a party bag of goodies, not balloons, toys and sweets but scarves, umbrellas and ties all labelled with an enigmatic message: CAPITALIST TOOL. Saying goodbye to Forbes, I suggested that the ordinary British working man more often used "tool" in quite another sense. He didn't laugh.

At a farewell party at the US embassy I found myself saying to Leonard Marks that I thought I'd just go steadily on with my plans for Greece.

"Good. Good," he said. "But then what? You can't stay in Greece for month after month. For ever. Fine for a holiday. But what are you going to do then? You're only, what ? Sixty-two, three? You're not thinking of *retiring?*"

It reverberated within my head. It became a heavy word, an aural assault; a word like disease, infection, cancer, AIDS. But the truth was that if I could lever myself out of the slough of despond, I was going to do just that. Retire, or rather retire from the kind of compulsive activity to which I would otherwise be prone. I wanted to change course and speed. I wanted, if I could ever achieve it, to relax and think. About what? Well, the usual: string and sealing-wax, cabbages and kings, Bishop Berkeley's tree in the quad, Marvell's wingèd chariot, Milton's *Areopagitica*, Pericles' address to the Athenians, $E = mc^2$. I wanted to say that I rather hankered after contemplating my navel for a while, learning Greek, enjoying sun and sea, and people and food and drink, and children and grandchildren, friends and relations, paintings and books and music, and old films. But it sounded feeble and trite and I felt guilty at even allowing myself to have such thoughts.

"Oh well," I said out loud. "I think we'll just try out Greece and see how it goes. It'll be an alternative workplace rather than a holiday home." I could hear all the unspoken responses. You ought to get yourself a proper job. It's much too early to retire. Just because the BBC thinks you're ready for the scrapheap at sixty doesn't mean it's true. Doesn't relieve you of the responsibility of doing something, getting off your butt.

I told some of our American friends the story of the Greek fishermen standing on the pier at Miloi looking across the bay of Nauplion, rod in hand, thinking not very seriously about going fishing. A second generation Greek American who has made his pile in the construction industry and is visiting his father's village, partly as an act of filial piety, partly searching for his roots and partly wondering what he can do in the way of some grand act of charitable benevolence (while not closing his eyes to any profitable investment), contemplates the fisherman contemplating fishing.

The American Greek speaks. "You a fisherman?"

"Yes," says the fisherman. If the American were not a stranger, a guest, he would have added, "what else?"

"You got a boat?"

"Yes," says the fisherman, gesturing towards a small boat, one of only two or three that have not gone out.

"Make a decent living?"

"Not too bad."

"Why've you not taken your boat out today?"

"Caught enough fish yesterday."

"What d'you mean, enough?"

The fisherman mimes a decent size basket.

"If you caught more, you'd get more money."

"And what would I do with the money, eh?"

"You could buy a bigger boat."

"What for?"

"To catch more fish. To make more money. To buy maybe two, three boats."

"What would I want two-three boats for?"

"You could catch many more fish. Make much more money. Then you could sell the business. Retire and do whatever you've always wanted to do."

The fisherman makes a gesture of fatalistic incomprehension. It annoys the American.

"Well, wouldn't you like to do whatever you've always wanted to?"

"Of course I want to do what I want to do. So?"

"Well," (infuriated now) "what do you want to do?"

"Sit here and think about going fishing."

The conference, which had lasted four weeks, ended the next day, a Friday. We arranged to leave for Greece a fortnight later. It was a time of great activity and equal anxiety. How much should we take? What should we take?

Books figured largely in our thoughts. We played safe. A set of Dickens and of Jane Austen; an assortment of Trollope; Gibbon's *Decline and Fall*; a variety of books about Greece; a range of thrillers, crime and detective fiction to suit most tastes; an eclectic and haphazard basket of recent novels, the only condition being that we wanted to read them or at least would be prepared to read them if afflicted with book famine.

This was the easy part, giving rise to no more than a minor spat or two about the selection of this book or that. But what about dictionaries and reference books? We argued angrily. I wanted to take, at least, the *Shorter Oxford*. Nina held out for no more than the *Concise*. Nina won. I wanted to take a clutch of Greek dictionaries including a *Modern Greek Etymological Lexicon* which Plato had given me. I also thought of taking an out-of-date *Who's Who* which Nina wanted to throw in the rubbish bin. I won the lexicon but lost what had become the Who-Was-Who-in-1986.

Nina laid down that we were not to have television in Nauplion. I argued, but without overmuch conviction. I insisted however that we should have a decent audio system and promptly went out and bought one.

I had been to the Greek consulate, established our status as the owners of a property in Greece, made out a list of the household goods we wanted to import, duty-free, and received a document detailing what had been agreed.

"Oh, go on," said the consular official, "put down a video-recorder and a television set. You might change your mind. You know how expensive they are in Greece."

I added them to the list but Nina did not change her mind and by the time I had re-thought their usefulness we were out of the six-month period covered by the entitlement. And that was that.

We were not at all sure how long we should be away, so we tried to do as much as possible before we left. My diary was peppered with meetings: the Japanese guidebook was in a critical state, final corrections to proofs having to be made, one way or another, at the typesetters in Tokyo before the printing began in London; Sir Michael Caine was reporting on the state of play with the One World Broadcasting Trust; the BBC Alexander Onassis Bursary Trust was deciding how much money should be apportioned to bursars coming from which parts of the world and whether to use capital or stick only to revenue. There were meetings of a group trying to raise money for the continuance of the Research Council for Complementary Medicine at a proper level. The RCCM needed to be able to conduct more clinical trials seeking to establish to what extent less conventional (and often less expensive) forms of treatment could, or could not, help in the treatment of a variety of conditions. Then there were friends, children and grandchildren, doctors and dentists, chiropodists, hairdressers. I played as much tennis, mostly at Lord's, as I decently could ("indecently could," said Nina).

We dined with Robert and Linda Milne-Tyte at Hurlingham. Would we, they asked, go to see the Sumners who had retired four years before to a village in the Pelion? We said we would.

Michael and Annie Sumner, both members of the Bush House mafia, had bought a village house, high up, overlooking the sea, and had started to restore it, make it comfortable and, in Annie's case, to try to make a garden out of the terraced and steeply descending land, rich in rocks. It was remote and beautiful and they had barely moved further than Volos, the nearest city, a two-hour drive away, in the years they had been there. We had visited them twice and spent several happy days with them; we hoped we might entice them to visit us in Nauplion. In general Greek village life had turned out well but they had encountered the odd difficulty with bureaucracy. For example, the importing of cars.

They had gone to Greece for good; they had emigrated and become permanent Greek residents. Different rules obtained for residents and they were allowed to import, without duty, everything they wanted. They naturally assumed this privilege extended to their car, a not exactly new Citroën. After eighteen months or so officialdom intervened. They were summoned peremptorily and told the privilege only allowed them to keep their car a year and it was well over that now. They would have to pay the duty and, of course, be registered with Greek numberplates. They were taken aback. How much would the duty be? A hundred per cent of the list price, unless it was over 1600 cc. or had special luxury features in which case it would be at a higher rate. No, it wasn't and it hadn't. But one hundred per cent of the list price when the car was several years old? Yes, the price when new. But nobody had told them. The regulations, authority said, were quite clear. They could have taken the car out of Greece and re-imported it later. But since they had not done this, and since it was well overdue, the duty must be paid now, and in full.

Reminded of this incident, I phoned the Greek consulate the next morning. Visitors, and this included those with a second home in Greece, could bring in a car for six months but then it would have to be taken out of the country for six months before it could be brought in again. That sounded clear enough, even if not terribly convenient for us. But then why, I said to myself, should the rules be drawn up to suit us? And anyway the single market should be operating by 1993 and meanwhile there would surely be some convergence before then.

I was confidently credulous. It was a paradox I found difficult to resolve. I was optimistic in the longer term about important issues like the European Community and nuclear armageddon but my personal black Fury kept on kicking me in the kidneys, reminding me that the immediate was what counted and there was no hope or health in anything. Rubbish! Pull yourself together! Get on with something!

I got on with packing and repacking the car, and gradually excitement and the pleasure of looking forward reasserted themselves. Our adventure was going to be achieved. Our place in Greece was virtually ready and so were we, apart from a nagging doubt about whether Nina was actually going to be able to write there. What was the equivalent of buttering the cat's paws? Or taking the child's sucking blanket? We were travelling with the lap-top and all obvious comforters, although it was clear that nothing was down to computers, everything lay in the lap of the gods.

It rather looked as though Poseidon was trying to warn us off. We had decided to put the car on the train from Boulogne and travel with the SNCF to Milan, comfortably sleeping the hundreds of miles away. At Dover, where we were booked to travel with Hoverspeed, the clouds were scudding across a stormy sky, the wind was gusty and the sea well-covered with white horses. The service was, we were told, suspended. But if we hurried, there was a ferry just leaving. We shot out of one part of the docks and screeched into another and joined the ship just as she was raising the ramp. We drew breath and smiled with relief.

As the ship emerged into the Channel we felt the swell and the stiffening wind and understood the reluctance of the hovercraft to sail. In fact, it was quite a struggle to climb to the upper deck. We discovered an officer, poised between activities and thus vulnerable, and asked him when we were due to dock in Boulogne because, as I explained, we had a train to catch and were booked on the now abandoned hovercraft which presumably had a much quicker crossing.

He looked warily at me. "We don't go to Boulogne," he said and looked at his watch. He was French. "We anticipate arriving at Calais at four-thirty But with the wind and the sea . . ." He shrugged.

We sought out the purser. Could someone get a message

through to the train ferry? Perhaps. One would have to see. It would be tried. No one, of course, told us whether they had suc-ceeded or not. It was a very uncomfortable ship. Nina became anxious; I grew fretful.

We arrived an hour late and were sitting in what seemed to be a gridlock in Calais at the time we should have been driving on to the train. Another forty minutes at least, I reckoned, if and when we were able to clear the traffic jam. Calm replaced the angry anxiety. I secretly thought the train would wait for us, assuming that there were other cars and passengers in a similar plight. Train ferries must be used to the vagaries of wind and weather. Nina, whilst putting on a face of grim resolution, clearly nurtured no such belief.

"It's not the end of everything if we miss the train," I said cheerily.

"No," said Nina, "but we'll miss the Ancona–Patras ferry as well and lose our booking and our cabin."

"We could phone the shipping office in Ancona, if we had the number."

"Well we haven't."

Round about then the traffic started to move, slowly but steadily. Soon it began to thin out. Steadfastly I drove, over not very fast roads, to try and make up dead time.

"If we're killed," said Nina, "we won't catch the train either."

I said, with restraint I thought, "I'm going very slowly. If I touch forty it'll be a miracle." It would have been difficult to drive at any great speed.

"You're racing," said Nina.

When we arrived at Boulogne and fought our way over bridges and down to the train ferry a very civil lady welcomed us and said the train was waiting and would be leaving in ten min-utes. I handed over the car and it was driven on to the upper deck of the carrier. There was one other late arrival whose car followed ours. We were whisked along to the train and settled in our compartment. Minutes later we were *en route*.

"There," said Nina not altogether accurately. "I told you we needn't have worried. Of course the Railways of France would wait for us." She had a moment of what I hoped was decent doubt but then she added, "or is it the *Wagons-Lits*? Anyway it's much more comfortable than driving."

And so it was, and is each time we travel that way. We had not gone as far as Milan before; the service only starts in June and this was the first of the year. They had advertized a buffet-restaurant car, a departure as far as we were concerned. Previously we had brought a hamper. A whole new adventure, we thought, in additional comfort if not luxury. Dinner was called. We waited, doing the decent thing and letting families with children eat first. It was a touch early and we summoned the marshal of the coach and ordered a drink, in anticipation of our food. I suppose they are really called controllers or conductors, but I find myself shying away from both terms, suffering from the inhibition of having at one time been a BBC controller, which meant something rather different, and with being brought up on red London buses. "Sleeping car attendant," Nina said firmly after he had, from earlier trips to Nice or Narbonne, recognized me but not her.

After a reasonable interval and when the dining car steward came through the train for the second time, crying his wares, we sauntered along towards food, feeling agreeably hungry, breakfast a long way behind.

We had an awful meal. They had underestimated the demand. They were not expecting so many, said the steward. Why, we asked? It was an experiment. Apologies. In concrete terms it meant no bread and only one dish left, *faux-filet*, a steak of teeth-breaking toughness.

This was a strange lapse, because the train-ferries are otherwise very comfortable and very well run. We returned to our compartment, to our bunks neatly turned down and welcoming, and to the familiar attendant suggesting cognac as a nightcap. The brandy and the biscuits, which Nina thought particularly delectable and finished before I looked round, sent us happily to bed.

There is something peculiarly comforting about speeding through the night, waking occasionally to watch the lights of stations flashing past and allowing the repetitive rhythm of the train on the rails to sing you back to sleep. We both awoke to a bawling baby and to find the train stationary at Lausanne not once but twice. The third time I struggled to lift my head, after drifting off again, and got up to find out why we were still stuck in the same station after an hour and a half. As I opened the door and stumbled into the corridor, failing to allow for movement, the train pulled out and accelerated. I returned to bed and woke up to daylight and the Alps.

After breakfast we discovered what had happened. A passenger had died in the lavatory. He was going on holiday with his son and daughter-in-law and grandchildren. When his family discovered him, the train was in Switzerland, so in addition to the tragedy itself, and to their having to return home with the body, there was an extended debate with the authorities as to whether he had died in France or Switzerland. Eventually an English doctor who was travelling in our sleeping car intervened and decided in favour of Switzerland. The shocked family left the train at Lausanne and we moved on towards Italy.

Nobody wanted to be thought insensitive but we were running very late. We had been the best part of two hours late setting out and then there had been the unavoidable stop. People looked at their watches anxiously. The older ones relentlessly asked each other how their fellow-passenger had died and what was his age. A massive coronary, said the doctor, and much his own age, sixty-seven. Those younger looked suitably mournful and said, "Poor fellow, what rotten luck, just at the beginning of the holiday." Would they have thought it any better, I wondered, half-way through? Those older than sixty-seven were clearly relieved, and felt guilty at the relief, that the Grim Reaper had missed them out and that they had outlived that dangerous age. His contemporaries were ambivalent and muttered about how there but for the grace of God went they.

We arrived subdued in Milan a bit before eleven o'clock and disembarked. Carrying our overnight cases and books we made our way underground, below platform and tracks and then up and along the station, to the docking bay where the car-carrier was to come in. There was a general air of release. Voices became louder and more enthusiastic. Passengers exchanged visions of the next stage of their holidays. Drivers talked of the quickest route to the mountains, the sea, the antiquities, the glories of paint and sculpture, the south. No one else was going to Greece. No one else had a boat to catch. But there was time enough.

The shunting engine took some considerable time to bring the cars round. It was Sunday, an Italian railwayman explained, and the schedule had been put out by the late arrival of the train. There had been talk of a strike, nothing to do with us, but, more important, the morning shift had gone off and everyone wanted their meal break and, we gathered, a siesta. No matter; the carrier was placed in position, the engine went off, railwaymen removed shackling bolts and laid down plates and ramps. Eventually the cars started to roll off, bottom row first.

We were on the top row, second from last. The bottom row emptied itself, the railwaymen lowered and adjusted the upper flaps and arranged new ramps and unbolted the restraining chains. All the rest of the drivers clambered along to their cars and made themselves ready to move off. Slowly the head of the queue juddered along, but it was only after some minutes that I noticed that the car ahead of me was not starting its engine. Not surprisingly, since it was empty. I shouted to attract attention. No railwaymen came but a few other drivers got out to see what was wrong. It was a new Mercedes. Word went down the line to summon the driver. Where was he or she? I tried the door: it was locked.

No embarrassed driver came hurrying along. Slowly consternation turned to alarm as we collectively began to realize that the Mercedes must have been the dead man's vehicle. The others got back into their cars, the Italian railway staff shouting for them to hurry up. This left the owner of the final car and myself stymied, wired, balked, immobile. There had been a recent *Which?* survey in which Mercedes had come out on top for the security of their locks. The tame *Which?* burglar had cracked every other car in under twenty seconds. I don't remember precisely but I think it took him over a minute to get into this model Mercedes. It did not augur well. We tried coathangers, bent wire and small screwdrivers. We could see a set of keys on the driver's seat. It was easy enough to reconstruct what had happened. At Lausanne the poor bereaved family had opened the car to collect their things, had left the one set of keys on the seat and had locked the car and taken the other set with them.

The only hope was that they had given the keys to one of the train staff. I walked back towards the disembarkation point, following the last car on the move.

"What's wrong with you?" Nina shouted. "We haven't got all day." When I got close enough to talk, I explained.

I went off to find the railway staff. No one had the key. No one knew anything about it. Stuck behind a dead man's car? They made it sound somewhat obscene. I said I did not know for sure but I assumed it was the dead man's Mercedes. Otherwise where was the driver? It was a mistake to let in doubt. He could have gone off to have a drink, they said, looking meaningfully at their watches. Or to make a telephone call. He could have got lost. It was notoriously difficult to find the car-loading platform. They had pointed this out to management on numerous occasions.

"Let us assume he is dead," I proposed. "Let us assume we cannot get into the car without breaking in. What are you going to do to get the last two cars off?"

Who? Us, sir? No, sir. We can't do anything without Authority. I contrived what I hoped was a winning smile and added, "Well how about getting hold of Authority?"

Again they looked at their watches. Clearly they expected everybody to be having their Sunday dinner and not wanting to be interrupted. I became more forceful. Eventually, and very reluctantly, the foreman, who luckily for me spoke reasonable French, walked off towards the station proper.

Sunday midday staffing did not include a shunter-driver. One had to be summoned. While we waited, some obviously disputatious union business was transacted. They decided not to stop the engine that was going to rescue us but there was only a half-hearted attempt to quicken things up. Finally the engine arrived and towed the almost empty car-wagon away. Ten minutes later it reappeared, having turned the wagon round and shunted the carrier in to the unloading bay with the remaining three cars in the front, stern first. I climbed up, got into the car again and waited with something less than equability while the other driver had trouble getting his car to start.

We were the last to leave the yard. As we pulled out, one of the railway officials shouted out that he did not know what he was meant to do with the locked car. Or had he called it the dead car? It looked peculiarly abandoned, alone on the upper deck of the car-train.

Being a Sunday, there were almost no trucks on the road – an excellent law this – and we made very good time, driving rather fast and relentlessly. We only stopped for petrol and grabbed a coffee and a salami sandwich standing at the bar at an *autostrada* stop. We arrived at Ancona at a little after seven o'clock, drove straight on board the *King Minos*, sank into the beds in our cabin and slept away the better part of the two nights and intervening day at sea. We were, as we said to each other, determined to land in good heart.

XIX

It was Tuesday 30 May 1989 and a lovely, clear, cool morning as we drove through Patras and out along the main road with the blue Gulf of Corinth to our left and the purple mountains to our right. By the time we turned off the highway to head south it was warming up and a heat-haze was reducing the horizon. We arrived in Nauplion at eleven-thirty and, feeling deliciously warm and summery, rushed to the house to find everyone working at unexpected speed, rather as though one of them had been keeping an eye out for us and had blown a whistle, jerking them all into hyperactivity, as we drove into the little square. But this was a superficial and unfair impression: they had been working flat out all morning.

There were white ceramic tiles laid out on the floor. They were to go on the wall above the cooker. We both looked doubtfully at them. Wouldn't they look a bit funny next to the marble? Nikos, who had welcomed us with a winning smile and warm embraces, tried to reassure us.

"Mrs Sideropoulou chooses them," he said. "They are Italian *plaka*. Very good." He looked at us, considering the matter dispassionately. "Very expensive."

The plumber was there in person. He appeared, all these months later, still to be having trouble with his leg. He was sitting on a box, instructing his son who was tightening, with a wrench, the fitting which transferred water from the bath mixer-tap to the hand-held shower. He seemed to be tightening it rather too strenuously. His father, who radiated frustration and criticism, yelled at him. I moved away.

Nina meanwhile had been peering down the loo. "It's filthy," she cried. "*Filthy*." Nikos was reassuring. Lots of stuff had been poured away, down the drain. All would be tidied up, cleaned and polished. Nina smiled, unconvincingly.

"It was *unbelievably* filthy," she said to me in a whisper.

"Never mind," said Nikos, who had keen ears. "The girl, I make sure she clean everything up."

The girl was Albanian and had a marked, if thin, moustache. She also had an unattractive child standing disconsolately by her, a girl of about seven who picked her nose with the perseverance of a miner scraping for diamonds. After surveying us bleakly she made for Nina's skirt and there was a fine *pas de deux* as Nina tried to avoid her without appearing to reject an unfortunate.

As a timely distraction I swept Nina and Nikos off for lunch. We then drove up to the Xenia Palace where we were, not surprisingly since we had been bouncing back like yo-yos every few months for the last three years, greeted as old and missed friends. After a glorious swim at Arvanitia, the pebbly town beach, I said to Nina that I reckoned the apartment was looking rather good. She made some Ha!-like interjection but smiled tolerantly. She was, she made clear, indulging my little games.

We had a cheerful dinner at Savouras with Laura, Phaidon's wife. Nina said that if we were going to live in Nauplion I really should have another try at eating fish. I said I was quite happy with the prawns but was goaded into nibbling a small piece of a not very large red mullet. Nothing dramatic happened. I merely felt that I did not want any more.

Laura asked if we had seen the new Olympic swimming-pool. From a distance, I said. It looked pretty impressive.

"It is," she said. "It's great. Every comfort. Heated. Shiny new. Full Olympic size. Just what the town needs. Except you can't use it."

"What do you mean, can't use it?" both of us said, in unison.

"Adults can't use it. Only the swimming team. If you call them adults. The children have to join a club and go for organized lessons. That's it."

" Why?"

"Well, all this is a bit embarrassing but since you're going to live here, you might as well know what kind of a society you're joining. I got mad when I thought of all the money that had been spent and how little the pool was being used. Most of the time it's empty. So I went to see the president of the swimming-pool committee. He's one of the local butchers. I went to his shop. It's not one I normally use. Standing among the hunks of meat, I congratulated him on the pool. It's fine, I said, marvellous, except we can't use it. Why? So he said, not particularly flustered, you mean people can't use it? Yes, I said, people like me can't use it. Of course not, he said, just think what would happen if people used the pool. Like what? I said. It would get dirty, he said. You wouldn't want an old man, an eighty-year-old, dirtying our new pool? Now would you? End of conversation."

The furniture from Athens was due to arrive the next day. It didn't. I walked to the *periptero* off the main square. In Greece these newspaper, tobacco and sweets kiosks almost invariably have a telephone. I managed to get through to the shop in Athens. Sorry; it was not their fault. The carrier had said Thursday but now it might be Friday or even Saturday. They hoped we would not be too inconvenienced. No, no, I said; of course not. Was there not perhaps somewhere they could phone and leave a message? Well, there was The Boatyard but it did not really get going till after they shut the shop.

Nonetheless they took the number. This was going to be the main inconvenience in not having a telephone in Nauplion, I thought; it was difficult for anybody to get in touch with us. Not so much the calling as the being called.

I walked back through the *plateia* and exchanged greetings with Vassili and his father, with the cobbler and, taking the longer way round, with the seamstress who seemed to be working away at a shirt. Nauplion was still a town where you could get your shoes properly mended and your cuffs replaced and, indeed, where you could buy a nail or two and a single needle. Purchases were carefully and skilfully wrapped in paper without tape or string. Plastic bags were still a rarity, except at the seaside and any picnic spot, where they compounded the litter. They were not really strong enough for the groceries they were meant to carry. Hence perhaps, I thought generously, the busted bags at the beach. Later, when plastic became more common and the bags marginally stronger, I saw there were even more of them despoiling beaches and mountainsides. It is an oddity about the Greeks that they do not seem to notice the mess they leave behind and, indeed, return to, and yet they take pride in their streets and their houses shine with polish.

Civic pride in Nauplion, much encouraged by the mayor who puts up signs exhorting the populace to urban cleanliness, is evident in the daily collection of rubbish and the number of Naupliotes that put their garbage in a bag and lower it, in the early morning or late at night, on a hook from their balconies. It has to be nicely judged so as to be too high for prowling dogs and climbing cats but just right for the dustman. There is great feeling, jealousy even, about the rare wheely-bins. It is not thought proper to use one in a neighbourhood not your own; indeed any such attempt will be fiercely repulsed. But none of this admirable communal pride extends to the bathing beaches, although owned and regularly if infrequently cleaned by the municipality.

Back in Number 19 the electrician had arrived. He was connecting the night-storage heaters to their circuits and thermostats. Nina looked happier. The kitchen tiles were up and looked rather good in place, agreeably setting off the marble.

"Come," she said, drawing me to the larger, north balcony. "I think I caught a glimpse of the parrot. It's green."

I looked and saw nothing but a balcony full of plants, greenery and flowers and a door leading into a dark room which might have been a kitchen or a living room. No sign of a green, or any other colour, parrot. I could however quite clearly hear the cries of Mama, Mama. It might, of course, have been a real child and not the invisible parrot. We went out and climbed the next *scala* along, towards Palamidi, struggled up past the Catholic church, up and up until we passed through the arch which led into Acronauplion, and then we climbed down the road leading from the Xenia to the Xenia Palace and found our way to the pebble beach at Arvanitia. It had taken ten minutes from the house.

Later, much later, after a lively dinner with Greek friends at The Boatyard, I startled myself awake, anxious at three o'clock. Had Nina felt anything of the same elation at the thought of moving in? How much had I harouched her into doing something which she didn't really want? Was the outburst about the lavatory really about something else? Perhaps she would have preferred the business of choosing and planning and buying and preparing to have gone on forever. She had doubts about whether she was going to be able to write in our Nauplion attic. Had I just propelled and prodded her into my change of life scheme? Was she the actual victim of my depression?

By the time the sun was up my pulse had slowed and the acute circular anxiety – *Ti na kano?* What to do? – had given way to a tentative linear stoicism: it was too late to do anything, so why worry? Easy to say, not so easy to still the nagging doubts. The weather, as always, helped, daylight despatching the worst of the ghouls. It is a harking back, I suppose, to atavistic memories. The nights must have been full of terror, the adults staying awake to tend the fire and guard the young in the cave while outside in the fearful dark wild beasts roared. Daybreak was a time to relax as the sun drove away the night. And here in the Peloponnese the miraculous Aegean light heals like Apollo himself.

We went for a swim in the sparkling sea and got to the apartment at noon. Just about everything had been done. We spent the Thursday making lists, planning what food and household necessaries we had to buy. Friends and acquaintances sent flowers, masses of them. We had no vases and nowhere except the marble top of the kitchen and the sink to put them. Friday we waited for the furniture. Saturday it came, around five p.m.

Nina said the table and chairs were much too dark. I said I thought it was only the wood stain. The sunlight would soon perk them up. We both agreed that our bed was too narrow. But everything was there: the mirror for the small bathroom, the sofa and its companion pieces, the grand mirror, the commode. Nina swept and swept and swept. I tried to adjust the furniture that had been roughly put in position. Nina kept on sweeping. Finally I dragged her away and we retreated to the hotel where she tried to telephone the shop. It was, of course, shut. There was an answer-phone but the Greek rapid fire instructions were daunting.

It was a day or two before she made contact.

Nina: "I don't know how it happened but the bed in our bedroom is too small."

The shop, from what I could overhear, said they had sent the right bed.

"No. There's been a mistake. I know what we ordered."

The problem was compounded by Nina's having little Greek and, as we knew, the lady at the shop almost no English. I took over and enthused about the rest of the furniture. Clearly the lady, still perplexed, reckoned we had forgotten which bed we had chosen. On reflection I thought she might be right. I'm not sure that Nina came round to this view for some months.

The Sunday morning, we paid our bill – the last one, Nina murmured sadly – and said farewell to the Xenia Palace. We drove to Tolo for a swim. Tolo, which we remembered as a pretty fishing village with one hotel, has a beautiful sandy beach, a glorious position and view and has been messed around by developers. It is now a package holiday resort, stuffed full of everything that a kind of holidaymaker, frequently British and, these last few years, often lager-loutish, wants. On this first Sunday of June before the worst of the recession it was already crowded and, threading our way through sunbathers and discarded plastic bags, we flung ourselves into the unspoilable sea.

With relief we returned to Nauplion and, with dozens of suitcases and parcels, took up residence. First things first: I set up the audio system on the floor in the attic, the speakers overlooking the space below. The CD I put on, the Takacs Quartet playing the Haydn Op.76, B flat major, sounded remarkably good in the living room, the music rich and clear. I was less successful with my much-travelled and reliable Sony ICF-7600D short-wave set. There was nowhere convenient to run an external aerial without, as Nina put it, ruining the decor. As the walls were painted white, I thought this something of an overstatement. The extendable aerial gave an excellent signal on the balcony but only an adequate one inside the house. However, we heard "lillibullero" and the news from London and felt that we had established our base. We played house for a while, a long while, and then went out to dinner in the *plateia*.

It was odd to be walking back to Kapadistriou, a mere stone's throw away instead of climbing up to Acronauplion. It was even stranger to be going home rather than to a hotel, here in the heart of Greece.

We were the only people in the house and when we shut the front door it was dark and silent. It took a second or two to turn on the light. Nikos had fitted a time-switch and we discovered that we had to hurry to get to the switch on the next floor and could hardly make it to our door before the light went out. Two flats were being laid out on the middle floor, a medium-size one that the brothers hoped to sell and a smaller one, a *garçonnière*, for Nikos. Andreas had a wife and child, and flat, in Athens but his older brother was still cast in the role of a bachelor playing the field while living with his mother in Neo Kios. In fact, life was already on the change. Nikos had met and taken up with Célestine, a French lyceé-teacher.

Looking back, he had always rather fancied French girls. There was one occasion I treasured. We had happened to go to The Boatyard one autumn evening and had found Nikos pinned uncomfortably, but nonetheless rather enjoying it, between two French girls. They clearly were not friends but equally clearly they had both had affairs with Nikos during various earlier visits to Greece. Now they had coincided and anyway I suspect he had an extant girlfriend.

Célestine was a rather different, more formidable character. As it turned out, Nikos was to marry her and Phaidon was to be best man and in time godfather to their first child, a singularly beautiful daughter, just as Nikos had been Phaidon's best man at his wedding to the American Laura and godfather to their first child, also a daughter. I often wondered to what extent the two fathers had suppressed the traditional desire for a son, which in many cases was an overriding obsession. For most Greeks, a daughter is a dowry, even now when dowries have been legislated away, and a son is a gun.

XX

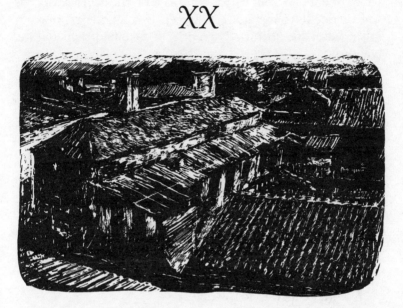

On that first night Nina slept well in the narrow bed and awoke all sunny to a bright summer's morning and a new life. I fell out of bed (I felt as though I had been falling out all night) with a crick in my neck and several grouches.

"You'd have thought," said Nina brightly, making tea, since we had brought an electric kettle with us and had not yet bought a coffee machine, "you'd be over the moon. Here we are in our own Greek palace on a lovely bright sunny day and all you can do is moan about your aches and pains."

"And another thing," I said. "There's that dog."

"What dog?"

"The one on the balcony. Down the *scala*."

"And?"

"You were sleeping so deeply you'd have missed the Last Trump. But it barked and barked non-stop. For hours. I exaggerate. For about half an hour."

I don't think she believed me. After two more nights she was joining me in clamorous complaints to Nikos and asking what we could do. Nikos was dismissive. What dog? It was midday. He went out on to our balcony and saw, on the other side of the *scala*, a docile young alsatian, agreeably somnolent – not surprising after his nocturnal activities. Looked all right to him. Nice dog.

A day or two later Nikos spent *his* first night in the house. The alsatian, who once again had been left alone virtually all day and confined to the balcony all night, barked and barked and, when he wasn't barking, whimpered. By the morning Nikos was in a fine taking. He hadn't slept a wink. It was disgraceful. Terrible. How could anyone sleep through a noise like that? It was antisocial.

"And cruel," Nina added.

"Yes, cruel," Nikos was glad of a new word, "cruel that I cannot sleep." He paused and decided to be generous. "And you too."

"No," said Nina.

"No?"

"No, I meant cruel to the dog."

"Cruel to the dog?" Nikos was winding up to a real fury. "I shoot that dog. But first I find the man. Perhaps I shoot him first."

"What about the police?" I thought this a calming line to take.

"The police?" Disbelief.

"Our other neighbours?"

"Look. No one sleeps on this side where is the *scala*. And the dog. Who hears him? Who cares?" He cut the histrionics short. "Never mind. I do something."

We never found out what Nikos did but two days later, the owner took the dog away.

The neighbours on Kapodistriou were friendly and welcoming, wanting to know how long we were staying, how old we were, how many children we had, how many grandchildren, where we were from, what we did and how much we earned. They waved from their balconies and from their windows as they closed the shutters in the morning to keep out the sun and keep the house cool, and again as they opened them in the early evening. At times like these we seemed, so narrow is the street, to be entering each other's bedrooms and living rooms. You coexist, I learnt, by observing the conventions. Once people have settled down for the evening you don't acknowledge them or show yourself aware of their presence or proximity until plant-watering or shutter-closing time the following morning.

Now that the dog had gone we became more aware of the other night noises, normal human activity such as jolly singing from tavernas by German and Italian groups overnighting, and the frenzied shrieks of cats. Nauplion is full of cats. To castrate or spay is too expensive. The cat population grows, domestic kittens are put out to die, the semi-feral struggle to survive. The toms fight, the females get pregnant. During the day there were other sounds. The swallows and swifts, with their vertiginous aerobatics, were fewer now but still noisy. The green parrot, if it were a parrot and green, called Mama dozens of times a day. Fish, shellfish, vegetables were cried aloud every morning as the itinerant sellers on bicycles or vans went past. Church bells rang at surprising times. And the high-volume loudspeakers carrying electioneering addresses and encouragements became more frequent, and frenzied, as the first General Election of 1989 approached.

There were plenty of political discussions, noisy enough to be arguments, at The Boatyard. The nightly television, above the bar, showed politician after politician mouthing silently. Much of the time Phaidon had the sound off and preferred to play tapes, perhaps for the benefit of his non-Greek customers, but when Mr Papandreou appeared, which was frequently, and Mr Mitsotakis, rather less frequently, they were allowed to harangue us in full voice. The debate was highly polarized and important for Greece. But other events were stirring the world. One night we watched the Ayatollah's interrupted funeral with crowds snatching at the body. It was curiously chilling and in Greece you could feel the almost palpable hatred, and fear, of militant Islam, rooted in centuries of hostility and subjugation and renewed by the exchanges of population with Turkey in the twenties and the Turkish invasion of Cyprus in the seventies. It was not quite Christian-good, Muslim-bad, but almost. The Greeks would instinctively side with the Serbs partly because they were a fiercely warrior people who had gallantly taken on the Turks and with whom they could iden-tify but mostly because the Serbs were Orthodox and the Bosnians Muslim; and for that matter the Croats were Catholic.

More shatteringly horrifying at the time, with a sadness shared by all, were the events in Peking. That brief flowering of hope for a new, young China, the seven-week occupation by the pro-democracy students of Tiananmen Square, the impos-ing of martial law by the gerontocratic old guard and the mowing down of the students, probably in their thousands, by the army's tanks. And all on the world's television screens. Pain, anguish, the tragedy of hopes betrayed. The poignant pictures of all those frail, sweet, young students.

The children of Nauplion were thinking of ways of taking themselves out of the seriously depressing world of the adults. One group of them had discovered our cellar and the empty, putative flat on the ground floor. It was a paradise of cardboard boxes, oil drums, water pipes, bags of cements and bales of wire. They were able to play there, creating a splendidly deafening cacophony by banging on everything within reach. Now and again a neighbour, or a mother, would call the children away. It wasn't the sort of thing a father would interest himself in. The children would slip back, one by one. The din would start up again. Once Nikos appeared and shouted at them to get off his property. It was also rather dangerous. There were holes every-where, loose bits of chicken-wire to catch on you and trip you up, unfinished electric wiring, partly connected, and, of course, it was comparatively dark.

One late afternoon, as much worried about their safety as infuriated by the banging, we went down to get them out of the building. I shouted at them to get their attention. Nina went to help them out. Somehow one young girl tripped and fell on her arm. Her brother took her home. We asked if we could do anything. They said no. The next day we saw the child with her mother, her arm was in a splint and bandaged. I asked how she was. Bad, said the mother. I said we were sorry. The mother spoke angrily. I assume she thought it was our fault. I tried to explain that the cellar was dangerous but my Greek was not up to it. I wished the child well. She was playing with a skipping-rope within a few days.

Friends brought offerings and house-presents. Phaidon arrived with two small daughters and a jar of olive oil. I suppose this is what would be called extra virgin although I have never understood how a virgin can be more virgin. Virginity is absolute. Extra virgin can only be the beginning of some linguistic game of relativity which is matched, at the other end, by the Edwardian housemaid's "a little bit pregnant". This was virginal, the first pressing from Phaidon's own trees. It was delicious and not at all like the French or Italian oil: lighter, cleaner and more delicate of taste, somehow less clinging. Others brought flowers, plants, honey, wine, a silver nut dish and, when we threw a small house-warming party, no less than five ice-cream cakes which could not be fitted into the small freezer compartment of the refrigerator.

We bought and bought and bought. Essentials like irons, stepladders, Hoovers, brooms, mops, washing-lines, pegs, buckets, crockery, glasses. We paid in cash, there was no doubt that paper money was the thing, and we ran out. So there were endless visits to banks. The Eurocheque came into its own when we ran out of traveller's cheques. We came to know all manner of shop and shopkeeper. Every now and again Nina would lose her way. One day we both lost the little supermarket we had taken to using for everything from milk and eggs to washing powders. It had disappeared. Strangely disorientated (was Nauplion a city of magic, mystery and mirage?) half an hour later we realised it was on a parallel street, one down towards the harbour. We discovered a series of postcards, coloured photographs improbably captioned "Nauplion – Fun City". We ate and drank rather too much, often at other people's expense. We hung the grand mirror with grave doubts about its safety as it was rather large and given to sway in any current of air above the noble antique commode. We washed and swept and garnished the apartment and worried about the marble.

Everybody had said that marble floors were marvellous and easy to look after. Ours were beautiful but they showed streaks and marks. You just wash them, we were told, and then mop or swab them dry. Do you put anything else on them, we asked. Oh yes, of course, you can put on Awverlye. This turned out to be Overlay, an Italian polish, but we found it left even more streaks. Meanwhile the very beautiful white Pendeli marble in the kitchen seemed to be marking badly with everything we rested on it. We were, as instructed, being terribly careful about citrus fruits, but everything seemed to mark the marble except water and milk. We got ourselves into a great state, preparing for Athina who was coming to spend the weekend and carry out a tour of inspection as well as tying up some legal loose ends.

She was due to arrive at eleven o'clock. Nina woke up feeling none too well. I told her to stay in bed. At about eight forty-five I was preparing breakfast and watering the plants on the balconies when the entryphone buzzed.

"We want to come up and see your apartment." A male, English voice.

I paused, taken aback. Nina by now was pottering about and she took the receiver out of my incompetent hands.

"Yes," she said, a bit brusquely, I thought.

"Are you," said the voice, loudly and slowly, "the lady who does a little bit of writing?"

Nina could barely answer. But they came up anyway and gave the place a once-over. Nina was still mouthing, "And without as much as a by-your-leave. Lady who does a little bit of writing, indeed!" long after they had left.

Athina arrived at something after twelve. She admired everything, thought that all the furniture looked superb where we had put it, marvelled at the completed attic and said, "I will tell you before how brave you are. And look. It is very lovely. You are right. It is not just air. It was your Greek house. I wish you were very happy here." And then in splendid, pure Athina style, she added, "And I too happy here."

After the reciprocal congratulations and many hugs and embraces we summoned Nikos and went through his accounts. All then being settled and in order, we arranged to meet at the notary public's office at six. We lunched, bathed in a delightfully bouncy sea, and got to the office on time. Nikos and Andreas were already there. Documents were produced. I flipped through one of the English translations and came across a paragraph which said, "It is further stated that: no real estate broker interfered in the present agreement."

The brothers Nondas signed, in front of the notary public, that the account was settled. Then the notary declared that the property was ours and shook our hands. We gave a celebratory dinner for as many as wished to come.

Plato arrived for the weekend, admired the finished flat but preferred to stay the night at the Xenia Palace, despite its architecture and plumbing. "Full marks," he said. "I never thought you'd pull it off." He said that Athina had obviously kept Nikos up to the mark but the two brothers had done an extremely good job. We were, he pointed out, very lucky in having Pericles to mastermind the whole thing. "But," he summed up, "you owe an awful lot to Athina, you know."

I said we knew. Plato advised us to change the door-lock – "You never know who may still have a key" – and to double-lock every time we left the flat. I thought then, and I still think now, that it's not necessary in Nauplion where some people leave their front doors open and their cars unlocked.

There was more to buy. Athina had no easy prescription for the marble floors. In fact the more we questioned her, the more reticent (not a mode much associated with our famous lawyer) she became. Finally she owned up. She had a firm in, every month, on a contract. She wasn't sure that we'd find anything like that in Nauplion. Never mind; there was a special red polishing mop. We must go and buy one. (We did and it made no difference.) We also had to buy, according to Nina, underblankets, more sheets and carpeting for the attic.

Luckily they were all to be found in the same *emporiko*. Unluckily all the sheets and pillowcases either had red hearts on them or messages along the lines of His and Hers or Not

Tonite Joe/Josephine. Nina said she wanted plain white and a better quality cotton too. Great rolls of the stuff were presented for our approval. The material was fine but, said Nina, she wasn't going to measure it, sew it up and hem it; no, not she. Of course not, said the one of the amiable brothers who owned the business. There was the seamstress just round the corner and she'd run them up in a trice. Should they arrange it for us? Yes, please. We had them a day later. As for the carpeting, they would come and measure up the attic whenever it suited us. Perhaps we would care to choose from one of the rolls. We chose. How should we pay? Later but in cash, please.

The brother dealing with us had remarkably good English. It turned out his wife was English. But there were other requirements, other *emporika*, and not every shopkeeper spoke English. It could only be assumed in the so-called tourist shops and we were mostly not buying keepsakes from Nauplion-Fun-City for Aunt Aggie. There was, for example, the furniture shop, one of several in the new town, along or off the main roads that radiated from the crossroads. The crossroads were notable for no one agreeing on who had priority. The traffic lights had been switched on once, for what one can only imagine must have been a truly disastrous day for accidents, and never again. On Saturday mornings, market day, a policeman imposes some kind of idiosyncratic order; for the rest of the year it's like stags exercising their antlers at the beginning of the rutting season, playing violent games of territorial aggression.

The furniture shop was a minute or so away from the trial ground of the crossroads. It was as much a manufacturer as a retailer. The showroom was the size of a small village post office and was jammed with tables of most sizes and a few descriptions. They were all varnished with a high gloss, the colours varying from yellow-brown to dark mahogany. The air was heavy with varnish and turps. The work was not highly skilled cabinet-making but it was serviceable enough and all I wanted was a long, low table to put in the corner of the attic to take the radio, CD player and speakers. There was nothing quite the right size.

A man wearing a T-shirt which said Harvard on it came forward, smoking a rather brown-coloured cigarette, perhaps, I thought, from the varnish, but there was another smell hanging in there to complement the sweat. He was short, quite slim and very, very hairy. Hair crept up from his T-shirt to meet the hair climbing down his neck. His arms and hands rivalled his legs in the luxuriance of their pelts. The palm of one hand was wiping paint or varnish off on to the glistening hair on the back of the other hand.

"*Ti thelete?*" he said.

Well, I said to myself, what did I want in his terms, and could I put it in Greek?

"*Ena trapezi.*" At least I'd got that right. It's a novice's nightmare. *To trapezi*, neuter, is the table, *i trapeza*, feminine, is the bank. But *trapeza* feminine, also means table but of the more grave kind, such as conference, operating or mortuary, and the two words of course come from the same root. Banks originally were tables. He pointed to two or three dining-room tables and I knew I had got it wrong.

"*Ena trapezaki,*" I rushed in. He pointed indiscriminately to all shapes and sizes of little tables.

"*Oxi,*" I said. "*Yia to . . .*" How was I going to say tuner and amplifier in Greek? I tried "*radio*". He looked perplexed. Perhaps he was seeing a transistor. I wanted to suggest that it was more of a ghettoblaster. I had another thought. "*Radiogrammophono.*"

"*Radiogrammophono,*" he said incredulously, automatically correcting my stress. That was clearly no good. He was visualizing a self-supporting edifice, a Fred Astaire and Ginger Rogers model. The Greeks have a good run of old movies on television.

I went over to the only table close to what I was hoping to find. Like that, I said, only wider and lower. He repeated wider and lower as though either he or I had gone rather more than mildly mad. When? Tomorrow, he said, and then looked at his watch and corrected himself. Day after tomorrow. Early evening. "*Methavrio to apoyevma.*"

It was just after six when I went back to the shop. It should have been open but the door was locked and the lights out. The shopping hours in Nauplion have to be learnt. On Mondays, Wednesdays and Saturdays shops are open till three p.m., and that's it. On Tuesdays, Thursdays and Fridays they close at two-thirty p.m., open again at five-thirty and stay open until half-past eight. I knocked a few times and eventually a light came on in the front of the shop. I waited but no one appeared. So I decided to go to the end of the block, turn left and left again to see if I could find the back of the shop. There were several workshops. One smelt of wood-shaving and varnish. I walked in. There were bright naked lightbulbs swinging, one large, muscles-going-to-fat man in his vest sawing a flat piece of timber, smoke drifting up towards the nearest light from the cigarette at the corner of his mouth, and in the opposite corner, sitting on a stool and reading one of the evening newspapers, his younger slimmer brother with whom I had had the conversation two days before.

We exchanged good evenings. "*Oriste*," he said. And there it was, perfectly good and solidly made, the right size but the wrong height. "*Pio hamilo.*" Lower, I said.

"It is lower," he said.

"I want it still lower."

"It is for a television, no?"

"No. A radio."

"Is low enough, then."

"No," I said.

After some minutes, he believed me. He still thought I was mad but he was prepared to humour me. He turned the table on its side, grabbed a saw and asked me to show him how much he should cut off. I showed him. He took no notice and cut off less, muttering. The radio was going full blast, a sad Pontic song of death, disaster and passion. I wandered around the workshop while he sawed off, or rather down, the other legs. They went in for tables and sideboards exclusively. The only decorations were a series of coloured photographs of unclothed young women pinned round the walls. Actually they did not show much of the girls, just their thighs and vaginas and pubic hair, pornographic rather than erotic.

The legs of the table were reduced but, unfortunately, were not level. He tried to persuade me that it was the floor not the table that wobbled. After a few minutes filing and sandpapering, the legs were almost level, the wobble reduced to a slight rocking movement reminiscent of most taverna chairs and tables.

"*Koitaxe*," he said, "look. The television is heavy."

"Radio," I said feebly.

"The TV is heavy." He sat on the table and demonstrated its stability. "Look. No move."

"*Entaxi*. OK." It wasn't but it would have to do. "How much?"

He went off to get paper and pencil. I paid out all the cash I had on me. It was just enough. He licked the pencil and, holding the small piece of paper against the wall, wrote out a receipt, mandatory in Greek law for every purchase, even a loaf of bread. I raised my head to the picture above where he was writing, anticipating another anatomical pose. But no: it was a yellowing newspaper portrait of Colonel Papadopoulos.

I felt as though I had been punched hard in the solar plexus and was going to vomit. I had been feeling queasy, I realized, for some time; the scent of sweat, cigarette stubs, varnish, the intensity of the naked bulbs and the sound of the electric saws were all a bit befuddling. And then to find, amongst the masturbatory icons of vulvas and pudenda, the complacent face of Papadopoulos was too much. I picked up my table and fled.

Colonel George Papadopoulos was not a Hitler, not even a Mussolini, but he was a nasty enough little dictator. He seemed the embodiment of the partially educated lower middle class on the make. "Who else these days," said Plato then, "goes into the army and becomes a full-time colonel?" Papadopoulos was quite clever in executing plans. In his way he was decisive and sure of his rightness, until things went wrong which, for several years, they did not. He was ruthless in repressing opposition. Under him torture, cruelty and petty tyrannies flourished; under him politicians, intellectuals, journalists, musicians, civil servants and army and navy officers who did not support him were imprisoned or exiled under extremely rigorous and unpleasant conditions; under him the student occupation of the Law Faculty of Athens University was brutally broken up, and under him the sit-in at Athens Polytechnic was crushed with many students killed. His was the first, and only, example of a *coup d'état* overthrowing a parliamentary democracy, however imperfect, in the West since the Second World War, a war fought to safeguard freedom, tolerance and democracy and finish off the fascist dictatorships.

Papadopoulos was in power from, 21 April 1967 until he was arrested and replaced by Brigadier Ioannides, the sinister, brutal and sadistic chief of the secret police in November 1973. The dictatorship collapsed on 24 July 1974. It is true that Ioannides was a horse of quite another colour: he would have done well in the Gestapo. It was Ioannides too that tried to oust Archbishop Makarios from the Presidency of Cyprus and impose an ex-EOKA terrorist thug, a chain of events that led to the Turks invading Cyprus and occupying the north which, in turn, was the beginning of the partition of the island which has endured till today. But it was Papadopoulos and his anti-communist obsession that established the regime and allowed people like Ioannides and the prime police torturer, Inspector Lambrou, to flourish. Papadopoulos, and his chief supporters, and of course Ioannides, were eventually tried and sentenced to death, although the sentences were later commuted to life imprisonment.

Papadopoulos' aim was to make Greece a nation of Christian patriots with short hair and long skirts. He also made the trains run on time, abolished the monarchy, outlawed strikes, banned the smashing of plates in nightclubs and tavernas, rewrote the history books and made long, incomprehensible speeches. Some of these measures were undeniably popular with some, but not always the same, parts of Greek society. Right-wing royalists found themselves over a barrel. They approved of much that the Colonel had done but, the young King Constantine having packed his bags and fled the field, Papadopoulos usurped and eventually deposed him. The King, to many observers, had been ill-advised in helping create the political crisis which brought about the coup, wrong-headed in signing the decree legitimizing the Colonels' takeover and inept in the manner and timing of his abortive and unsupported counter-coup.

After a due breathing space, Papadopoulos abolished the crown, substituted a phoenix and, jettisoning the Regent he had appointed, made himself President, as well as Prime Minister and Minister of Defence and at one time, I seem to remember, Foreign Minister and Minister of Education too. By then he had relinquished his military rank and style and had become common Mr Papadopoulos, very common in a country where Papadopoulos is as popular a surname as Smith in England, but there was no doubt that when you said Papadopoulos everyone understood whom you meant.

Papadopoulos had an astonishingly good conceit of himself. He saw himself as guardian of the Christian Greeks, a worthy heir to two great, and in his mind strangely and confusedly interwoven traditions: classical Greece and Byzantium. He was ambitious to the point of megalomania. His behaviour bordered on the psychotic, the language excessive, the gestures inappropriate, the emotions transparent, violent and raucous. He was a dangerous pygmy who did uncounted harm to the Greek social and political psyche.

I met him early on in the evolution of the military junta. He was a still shadowy figure, keeping away from the cameras and the crowds, lying low in Parliament House on Constitution Square. There was a civilian prime minister, as a front, a brace of generals for military respectability, and martial law to keep everyone happy. Shrewd observers, so it was said, had expected some move by the right wing via the generals. Papadopoulous and his fellow Colonels – only one of the conspirators, Brigadier Pattakos, who commanded the tanks in the Athens district, was above the rank of colonel – pre-empted them.

A general election had been planned for 28 May 1967. It seemed highly likely that George Papandreou, Andreas' father, and his Centre Union would win a majority. Rumours abounded: a left-wing plot to take over the army – there had been a trial of members of *Aspida,* said to be a left-wing conspiracy within the army; a selection of right-wing plots to take over the country. There was plenty of suspicion of the right wing, who had been in power virtually uninterrupted since the Civil War, and there was the bitter aftertaste of the murder of the left-wing EDA deputy, Grigorios Lambrakis, four years earlier.

Lambrakis had been killed in a street in Salonika by a motorcyclist after a peace rally. His assassins were underworld members of an extreme right-wing terrorist group with direct and sinister links to senior officers in the *gendarmerie.* The brave and unrelenting investigation by Christos Sartzetakis, later, in Andreas Papandreou's premiership, President of Greece, led to some of them being charged and found guilty of culpable homicide, although not of murder. This disturbing political tale was the basis for a novel by Vassilikos and a good, passionate film, Z, with Yves Montand playing the Lambrakis part.

There were plenty of rumours, too, after the Colonels' *putsch.* It had been a NATO plan; a CIA plot, with American connivance; a devious ruse of the King, the shipowners, big business and the army; a desperate throw by right-wing politicians frightened of a Centre Union victory shared by the Papandreous, father and son.

My friends and contacts were not completely immune to some of these wilder flights of fantasy but most of them were more down to earth in their analyses. A state of hysteria, they pointed out, had been manufactured around the notion that there was a vile and despicable communist plot to take over the country, aided by the USSR and all the Soviet bloc. George Papandreou was cast in the role of Kerensky. Therefore a Papandreou victory must be avoided at all costs; there must be no general election. The Colonels acted, or rather Colonel Papadopoulos acted, with a little help from his friends.

Colonel Papadopoulos, I asked; who he? Oh, they all said, when he was a major he organized a ballot-rigging fraud in the army during the 1961 election won by Karamanlis. More recently he had unmasked a non-existent communist plot in a tank unit which created great publicity, enhanced fears of the communist menace and, on investigation, turned out to be totally false. He was the ruling intelligence in KYP, the Greek CIA, and a willing pupil of his American counterparts. He was not exactly an intellectual nor particularly personable and he certainly was no politician but he was the Man.

It turned out that nobody actually knew him. So I decided to try and interview him.

I applied officially and got nonsensical answers such as there was no such person in government; I put out unofficial feelers in various directions; I sounded out a few politicians still in circulation; and I spoke loudly in public places, saying I should like to meet this Colonel Papadopoulos. Nothing. I spoke to diplomats. Nobody knew him. Oh yes, they had heard of him, of course, but . . . No one knew how to make contact with him.

I had packed my suitcase and was getting ready to leave the Athenee Palace Hotel to make a couple of last calls before going to the airport when I got a telephone call from the office of the Minister to the Prime Minister. This was the ministry that traditionally looked after press and information, and probably general intelligence, and particularly the foreign press and broadcasters. They gathered I wanted a special briefing. Would I please come this morning. When? Right now. To Zalacosta Street, I assumed, where the ministry always had been. No: to Parliament House.

I was there in ten minutes, not knowing what to expect. There were soldiers all round and sentries at the side door. I was admitted somewhat reluctantly. A young officer (everybody was in uniform) met me and took me through to a large office where to my dismay I was thoroughly searched. Not that normally I would mind being searched (although it seemed a touch excessive). Perhaps they wanted to make sure I was not carrying a concealed recorder. I had a small tape-recorder with me but it was in my briefcase and I displayed it. The trouble was that thinking I was going almost directly to the airport I had disposed about my person packets of letters which friends, who quite rightly, as it turned out, thought they were going to be arrested and sent off to one or other of the prison islands, had asked me to post outside Greece. I also had my own not altogether discreet notes and some apparent evidence of torture. I was decidedly nervous. It was not sensible to be going into the lion's den, as it were, hampered in this fashion.

However, the military did not find anything they were looking for. Together with my escort we moved on, through grand corridors and up and down stairs and into smaller corridors. I breathed deeply, and my anxiety state reverted to a yellow alert. Not for long. Another checkpoint; another search. This time they peered into my pockets, looked at my pipe – I still smoked then – emptied the briefcase and again patted me all over. No sweat, I said to myself; they're not looking for documents. At that moment, a major came over and started to examine the papers from my briefcase. But he lost interest, perhaps because they were all written in English. There was a third search in the antechamber to Papadopoulos' office. By this time I was thoroughly twitchy although I was now reasonably sure that they were looking for guns or bombs. Colonel Papadopoulos was nothing if not paranoid.

He was not unfriendly to begin with. He admired Britain. He respected Winston Churchill. Did he now, I thought? He had thought highly of the BBC – the pluperfect was significant. But now, he spread his hands and paused. I interspersed a question. Could I record him?

This set him off. His interpreter had trouble keeping up with him. This was not an interview. *He* wanted to see *me*. Not the other way round. Whatever he said was between him and me, not for newspapers or radio broadcasts. Off the record. Not for writing. Otherwise, no conversation. Perforce I agreed neither to broadcast what he said nor write it up for publication.

Having got that out of the way, he proceeded to attack the West in general but mostly the Western press and, above all, the BBC. We failed to understand what the new government was about and we were misleading the people. He got to the nub of the matter: the Greek people listen to the BBC World Service. I nodded agreement but said disingenuously that surely only a small proportion of Greeks listened in English, knowing full well that those who did were both educated and, under normal circumstances, influential. But, he said accusingly, you also broadcast in Greek. You broadcast misinformation in Greek. And in English too. Could it perhaps be that the BBC misled others because it itself was misinformed?

After a tirade that lasted over an hour, I was thoroughly informed. Yes, Athens was the seat of democracy but when danger hovered at the gates firm government was needed. What danger? The communist menace. And then there was the decadence from which the people, and particularly the young, must be protected. What decadence? It was typified by long hair and miniskirts. (And this, I have to remind myself, was the Swinging Sixties). The evil in society must be extirpated. The nation must be purified. Was this why all sorts of people were being arrested, interrogated and imprisoned? Yes, the people must be protected from dangerous elements. Anarchy must be prevented. But why did this need imprisonment without trial? Decent men do not need to hide behind the minute intricacies of the law. I reluctantly let that one pass. Why had there been so many reports of violent interrogation amounting to torture? I waited for the explosion. He paused and thought. The police can be enthusiastic in pursuing their enquiries. Even your Scotland Yard are sometimes criticized for their treatment of suspects. Evil, the criminals that support it, must be fought on its own ground with its own weapons.

From time to time he thumped the marble table at which we were sitting and the coffee cups jumped and so, I hope less obviously, did I. The interpreter looked strained and tired, as well he might. I thought at first that perhaps he was not a very good linguist but I soon came to the conclusion that any confusion was not his but his principal's. Papadopoulos started by referring all the time to "we" but shifted to the first person singular as soon as his temper was aroused. Which was often.

His mission was the nation's: to build a Greece fit for Christian Greeks. All steps, *all*, would be taken to that glorious end. When would he contemplate a return to an elected government? Elections were irrelevant. Unsuitable. What was important was building a righteous society. Why did he need to censor the press? The press is free to print the truth, but they write lies. That's why. It is necessary to guide the newspapers. And the broadcasters. To show them their duty. But is not a free press an attribute of a civilized society? Greece, he said angrily, is the heart of civilization and had been so for thousands of years. The world had learnt philosophy from the Greeks. Look at Aristotle.

I looked. This was not to be a meeting of true minds; it was a chilling experience.

As I got up to go I took out my pipe and a pocketful of letters fell out. One of them, I think it was addressed to Amnesty International, contained photographs of a political prisoner the soles of whose feet had been beaten to a pulp. They were no longer recognizable as feet. Lady (Amalia) Fleming, a Greek doctor and the widow of Alexander Fleming, with whom she had worked at St Mary's, Paddington, told me on some later occasion that after prolonged *bastinado* walking would always be a torment, standing a continuous pain. But at that moment of absurdity I was not thinking of tortured prisoners: I was wondering when Papadopoulos, his ADC or the interpreter would reach for the letters. I was thinking of the dreadful repercussions for my friends, the authors of the letters. How could I have been so careless? But it was not so much rashness as that I had not expected this interview and had made myself ready to leave for the airport. As slowly and normally as I could manage, I stuffed the letters back into my pocket, not trusting my luck, and got up to go. When Nina later in the day met me in Rome, where I posted the letters, she said I looked as though I had seen a ghost.

Before leaving Greece I spoke to Leslie Finer, the courageous and perspicacious Athens stringer for the BBC and the *Observer* who was expelled shortly thereafter, and to the British Embassy, briefly rehearsing my interview. Interestingly enough at this point neither the British nor the American Ambassador had seen Colonel Papadopoulos. I returned to London expecting the worst to happen in Greece; most of it did.

Running into my then overall boss, Sir Hugh Carleton Greene, Director General of the BBC, I told him about the Colonels and my interview. "The trouble with you, Austen," he said, "is you're too young to have met a real dictator." Hugh had been the *Daily Telegraph*'s Berlin correspondent in 1939. It was not till after he had retired from the BBC and undertaken a series of interviews for the *Sunday Telegraph*, which included Papadopoulos, that he changed his mind and became an influential critic of the junta.

But all that, I said to myself as I waited in some sort of queue at the OTE, the Nauplion telephone exchange, the new low table up-ended beside me, was over twenty years ago.

"No," said Plato firmly when I finally got through to Athens, "there is no resurgence of support for the junta. That was all over years ago. Your furniture-maker is an aberration and probably a pervert. Or mad."

"No," said Phaidon that evening, "not that I've heard of. You did say Papadopoulos? No, no. Of course not. Naturally, there are extremes, right and left. But no."

"No," said a Greek friend who had had some of his fingernails pulled out by the Colonels' henchmen. "Absolutely not. Of course we have right wing fanatics but I don't think anyone would seriously now support Papadopoulos."

Certainly democracy was in full cry, as heard from our apartment. Cars and vans with loudspeakers mounted on them rushed up and down blaring incomprehensible messages at full and therefore hideously distorted volume. Sometimes the names of the parties could be decoded. In the *plateia* large platforms had been erected and every evening they were political meetings with noisy sound systems and blaring music. All the main parties and groups and some of the smaller ones set out their wares in this way. The General Election was to be held on Sunday.

The electioneering seemed no more passionate than usual; politics in Greece is always very passionate. There were comparatively few new issues, programmes or platforms. Andreas Papandreou's new electoral law under which the election was being fought was an immensely complex variety of proportional representation which, his critics said, made it virtually impossible for the main opposition party, *Nea Demokratia*, to get a majority. The extra 100,000 public service posts created by Papandreou in May was thought to be a nice little earner in terms of votes for Pasok. The opposition ND were locking on to their promise to investigate more thoroughly the financial scandals, particularly Koskotas' Bank of Crete's alleged connections with Pasok and Papandreou personally. In this objective, ND were joined by the Coalition of the Left, *Synaspismos tis Aristeras*, which combined two wings of the old KKE, the Communist Party of Greece. Greek politics being what they are, fissiparous, this still left another three or four Greek communist parties fighting for votes.

In The Boatyard, Phaidon's view that Andreas had done well to survive his heart surgery, his affair with Mimi Lianis – Papandreou's divorce came through just in time for them to get married before the election – and the allegations of corruption, which he and all good men and true, he assured us, believed to be false, were applauded by the regulars round the bar. It was no mean feat to be able to go out on the punishing canvassing campaign that we saw every night on The Boatyard's TV after all that: Andreas was seventy.

Although it was all around us and the town was decorated with the flags and colours of the parties and littered with the thrown-away handbills, we only intermittently gave our attention to the election. It was like the economy. We knew it to be in a parlous state but having acknowledged the fact, we put it aside and went on with the business of setting up house. This is to say we had more humdrum preoccupations, like the marble and how to find someone to come in once a week and do us over.

"Once a week while we're there, once a fortnight when we're away." This was Nina to all and sundry who she felt might have access to some miraculous pool of responsible labour.

We heard from a variety of sources about Janet who everyone said was marvellous. Janet was Scots. She had been working in Glasgow as a secretary but her company had contracted and she was made redundant. She had come to Tolo on holiday and had decided to stay. She put her redundancy money down on a flat and had got work mostly with one of Nauplion's leading families but also with some non-Greek residents. Three or four intermediaries approached her on our behalf but no; she was sorry but she had quite enough on her plate.

"Oh well," said Nina, "the economy the way it is there must be lots of suitable people."

We asked Nikos. His face lit up.

"That Albanian woman I got to clean . . ."

"No," said Nina before he finished. "What about a Greek lady?"

Nikos looked taken aback. Had we shocked him? Perhaps it was not done, perhaps it was patronizing to offer housework as employment.

"I don't think," said Nikos, ruminating. "What Greek lady? You know her?"

"No. I don't know anyone. I thought maybe you could suggest someone. You or your mother."

"My mother," said Nikos, genuinely affronted.

"No, no, not your mother," I said quickly.

"Not your mother to clean," said Nina, making matters worse.

"To clean my mother?"

"Someone your mother knows."

"My mother knows no one."

This was not strictly true. Two days later the doorbell rang. I picked up the entryphone and a shrill voice said that she was a friend of Nikos' mother. I buzzed but she did not open the door. I looked down from the balcony. She was a lady in black, elderly and unaccountably carrying what seemed to be a large suitcase. I shouted to her to come up and buzzed again but to no effect. I went downstairs and let her in. Had she come about the work, *douleia*? No reply. Perhaps she hadn't understood my basic Greek. I tried again. Still no answer but she gestured that she wanted to go upstairs and contrived to suggest that the suitcase was heavy. It was.

Unencumbered, she flew up the stairs. By the time I reached our floor, she was surveying our property. "*Oraio, poly oraio, poly, poly oraio.*"

"Yes it is, isn't it?" said Nina, and then to me, "Has she come about the housework?"

"She says she's been sent by Nikos' mother." I turned to our visitor. "*Oxi poly douleia.*" Not much work.

She smiled and agreed. "*Oxi poly douleia.*"

Nina said, "How do I ask her if she wants to do some work for us?"

"Try it in Greek."

"Don't be funny. You know I can't speak Greek. Not *speak* Greek."

"*Thelete na doulepsete edo?*" I said. Would you like to work here?

"*I* work here?" she said. "Why I work here? What work?"

"Housework," I said. She looked nonplussed. "Why did you come?" I said.

"*Kyria* Katerina, the mother of Nikos, said to come and to ring the top bell. I did. You, *kyrie*, came down and said to me to come up."

By now I was as taken aback as she had been.

"Ask her why she's here," hissed Nina.

"I have," I hissed back.

"What did she say?"

While we were thus engaged she had lugged the case up on to the dining-table and opened it. Seconds later she was taking out of tissue paper a large and finely worked lace tablecloth. This was followed by a set of matching napkins and place-mats. Then there was a long narrow runner, to go down the centre of the table, she explained. And a round lace cloth to go on a round table.

Seven tablecloths later, fatigue had set in. Nina had started, in a ladylike way, to bargain for one of the tablecloths. She directed asides at me. "They're very expensive", "But they're beautiful, of course", "Too expensive", "But hand-made. Just look at all that work." In the end, Nina failed to move the price by more than a couple of thousand drachmas and the expensive but beautiful cloth was ours. The lady in black blessed us several times, asked how many children and grandchildren we had, and blessed them while she carefully folded all her lace into tissue paper and packed it away, then picked the case up and tripped lightly down the stairs, refusing my offer to carry it for her.

"Well, it's jolly nice," Nina said, a bit defensively, I thought, as she tried it out on the table.

But we were no closer to finding a cleaner. Laura said she knew of a Bulgarian lady who was looking for work. No doubt she was. Like most of the other East Europeans she was probably an illegal immigrant. We heard no more.

The same could not be said of the election, which got noisier by the day. The town filled up with natives rather than visitors, Greeks returning to their family home to vote, as they do to celebrate Easter. It is compulsory to vote, so people fly back from abroad and swarm down from Athens. Sanctions can involve confiscation of passport or driving licence, neither of them light matters.

Antigone and her sisters were back next door from their various houses. We greeted each other and then, almost immediately, she drew us aside and said Nikos was behaving badly. Her house had been damaged. What was he going to do about it? The way she looked at us made me feel she wasn't altogether best pleased with us either. Nor was she pleased with Mr Papandreou, whom she regarded as a scoundrel running a corrupt government. She, of course, supported *Nea Demokratia*.

Passions were running high even among the non-Greek residents. James and Barbara, the couple who had sold up, sailed their boat from Plymouth to Nauplion and lived on board whilst they built a house in a stunning position above the Argive plain, when we ran into them in the *plateia* told us they would have voted for ND too had they been Greek. Their views of Andreas and Pasok were at least as extreme as the three sisters'.

Nina and I were still preoccupied with putting our house in order, getting to know the shops and trying to learn how to work the various machines. The washing machine and dishwasher were relatively easy to crack. The cooker defeated us. Its technology was so high that nothing as simple as popping a chicken in the oven could be contemplated. It had a control panel of flashing lights. It wanted to know by when the food was to be ready, how much it weighed, and whether it was fowl, flesh or good red herring. Nina, who finds video recorders too difficult to programme, gave up first. I persevered, discovered a manual override and proceeded dangerously to undercook the only meal I embarked on. After that we stuck to grilling toast and boiling eggs, and dined out.

XXI

Every morning was an adventure. What time would the sun strike the large balcony? It was better to take breakfast before it got too hot. How many lines of mountains would be visible, three, four, none? Sometimes even Argos castle had disappeared into the heat haze and it took an act of faith to believe that we lived in anything other than a flat world of sea and plain. It was only, we were to discover later, in winter that the full range of mountains in their ordered ranks could be seen, the peaks marvellously powdered with snow. There was one which looked as though it rose, sparkling white, at the end of our street; in summer it was almost invisible.

Going to get the bread was a sort of extended tumble from bed to front door, down the stairs, out into the street, right, down the *scala*, and then right again and into the baker's. Then there was the actual choice of loaf. We discovered an extremely good and rather unusual bread apparently called *lagana*, which my dictionary defines as flatbread or bannock. Unexpectedly, after several days, perhaps weeks, there was no more *lagana* being baked. Why? What had happened? Nina tried to find out. I asked the pretty wife of the baker, only to be told that they were not baking them now. Why? They had only made them around Easter. Or was it after Easter? Or for Easter? But we were in June, long past Easter. The mystery remained unsolved. We took to buying another very satisfactory bread, a round firm loaf called *karveli*. Nina still forlornly asks every once in a while for *lagana* and is met with a kind, sweet, regretful smile.

In the button shop Nina asked for a packet of needles and was told they hadn't any. They sold needles singly. How many would the lady want? Surprised, Nina said ten. Ten, said the lady who kept the shop; *ten*, what would you want ten for? Nina shifted to six and still felt she was being sinfully prodigal. In the ironmonger's shop I saw the problem coming and asked for eight nails and six screws.

We swam every day and varied the beaches but mostly, since we still had plenty to do, we stuck to the two nearest bathing places, Arvanitia, the pebbly town beach, and Karathona of the non-golden sand. Coming back, happily exhausted and rather hot, from Arvanitia the Thursday before the election we found water pouring through the ceiling light-fitting in the bedroom. I turned off all the electricity. It seemed to be a crack in the union of the pipe with the hot-water tank. Luckily Nikos was coming, bringing a carpenter who, we hoped, would make us desks and bookcases for the gallery.

Nikos felt the water, agreed it was a cracked hot-water tank union, turned off the water and said he'd get it fixed. The carpenter, a cheery man with shiny brown eyes like polished pebbles, measured and sketched and said he'd send us estimates for the work.

"I like him," said Nina. "I expect he's competent and quick. He looks reliable. The sort of person who'll always do a craftsmanlike job. Not a botcher-upper."

This fulsome spiel was provoked, as much as anything, by the less than happy plumbing. I found myself saying that the poor old plumber had after all been working at a disadvantage, like a broken leg or two. Nina's response was a snort and a toss of her head as she went off to wash her hair in the rapidly cooling water.

On the Friday the furniture and books sent from London arrived. Or rather, to be precise, they arrived in Nauplion at the customs. The load had arrived in Athens some days before but the agent for some unaccountable reason was reluctant to send it down and wanted me to come up to Athens to see it through customs there. I demurred. They found excuses for not transshipping it. Hence some excitement when I phoned them and was told that the load would be at the customs house before noon. They would have phoned the day before but we had no telephone, wasn't that so? It was becoming repetitious.

Local lore had it that to deal with the customs you needed a customs agent. To confirm the tale there. were three or four agencies in the street behind the customs house with, it seemed, numerous staff, presumably gainfully employed. As our stuff, which did not amount to very much anyway, was coming in under a no-duty rubric I could see no possible use for an agent. Nikos was less sure. Phaidon was suspicious of the customs. Others, perhaps they had relations who were customs agents or perhaps they were just being solicitous on our behalf, thought it was essential to have an agent. Finally I went to see one of them.

She was a bright, brisk, competent lady and she heard me out. Since, she said, I had what amounted to a duty-free import licence, there was nothing for her to do except take my money as a commission. And that would be stupid. Thank you and good day.

Nikos saw the sense in this but felt I needed to be shepherded over the bureaucratic hurdles. He would come with me. We went down just before twelve o'clock and took ourselves into the long and narrow main office. It gave the impression of being crowded, mostly with people on the other side of the counter. There were two what might be called customers: a lorry driver and ourselves. We waited perhaps a quarter of an hour before anyone took any notice of us. And not for want of trying either. Nikos had started with greetings and cheery chat – he had been at school with many of them – but there was no response. He moved on to jovial shouts along the lines of "Who's meant to be running this place, anyway?" and "A good thing you've all got something to talk about." Thwarted, he progressed to the downright critical, not to say opprobrious. "There's a woman boss. Women? Look at them. Playing with paper, painting their fingernails, gossiping. Bah. Nothing works. They don't work. Is why."

Finally one of the men took notice of Nikos. Greetings were exchanged, and *badinage*. Yes, the load had arrived. Yes, everything was ready for customs inspection but, alas, looking pointedly at wristwatch, it was too late to think of starting today. First thing tomorrow. Ah, no. Tomorrow was Saturday. How silly. How could he have forgotten? And Monday morning there were lots of trucks. So how about twelve o'clock on Monday, eh?

"But," I heard myself bleating, "we came today at twelve o'clock." I was ignored.

"Damned old women," said Nikos outside.

"Who?" I said.

"The men."

There was nothing we could do, except come back on Monday as they suggested.

"We come here at eleven forty-five," said Nikos. "And make a noise."

We returned, at my insistence, at eleven-thirty with a small pick-up lorry borrowed from a neighbour. The town was awash with discarded posters, handbills, party ribbons and plastic mini-flags. The election had come and gone. On the day itself no alcohol was served in bars or restaurants, except in a couple of tavernas left open to satisfy the tourists' known thirst for beer and retsina.

When the results were announced, no one was happy. Mr Mitsotakis' *Nea Demokratia* had won the largest share of the vote, forty-four per cent, but translated into seats in this latest amended form of proportional representation it only gave him

144 out of 300 and he was unable to form a government. Mr Papandreou gained thirty-nine per cent, thus giving Pasok 125 seats, a remarkable result given his heart operation, his divorce and the Koskotas and other scandals. He too, in turn, was unable to form a government, as was the third group the *Synaspismos*, the Alliance of the Left. And so we were into coalitions. The obvious one, Pasok and the *Synaspismos*, was not a runner. Mr Florakis, the leader of the Alliance, a septuagenarian communist survivor of the wartime resistance, was insisting on catharsis, a cleansing of the body politic and thus vigorous prosecution of the corruption charges against Pasok and its leader.

Just in time to save the follow-on, a rerun of the election, Florakis and Mitsotakis agreed on the unlikely Conservative-Communist government that took office and set up a parliamentary investigation of the charges. Perhaps the most significant achievement in this shortlived but useful coalition of political extremes was its partial burying of the deep division between Right and Left which had endured since the Civil War and had bedevilled Greek life and politics.

Waiting at the customs, the conversation, in so far as I could make it out, was about Papandreou's and Pasok's feared defeat and about the future of public-service employees.

This particular group of public servants was demonstrating its devotion to work and to productivity in fine style. There was a queue of lorries on the dockside and a fury of inspection of cargoes. Inside the building there was an equally furious continuity of conversation and argument. Nikos, who was not best pleased by the elections, was visibly, and increasingly audibly, restive. Eventually one of his schoolfellows chose to recognize him. Was there something?

"Yes," exploded Nikos. "We've been here since eleven-thirty. No – since twelve o' clock on Friday."

His interlocutor blinked. He didn't know what Nikos was on about. Anyway it wasn't his department. He would try and see what he could do. Like finding the appropriate person. He disappeared. Another quarter of an hour passed. Everyone was smoking, except me. Nikos was about to light his third cigarette since our brief contact with officialdom and I was trying to calculate how many weeks of direct smoking was equivalent to an hour of this kind of involuntary inhaling with twenty dedicated chainsmokers simultaneously on the go, when a lady approached us from the other side of the counter, stubbed out her cigarette and took us through to an adjoining room. Name? What is being imported? I gave her the inventory and the signed, stamped and countersigned permission from the consulate in London. She disappeared.

"What now?" I asked Nikos.

"*Oti xereis, xero.*" His guess was as good as mine.

A while later we were summoned into the warehouse. A customs officer went through the list, asked me questions and kept up a running commentary. Another man opened each crate in turn. I started to unpack everything, sometimes helped by Nikos. Everything? I asked whether it was really necessary to examine every single item. Yes, it was. And unpack every box? Yes. But I had this duty free import licence from the Consul. Yes, even so.

I could only suppose they thought this was an original way for drug-smugglers to bring the hard stuff into Greece. First you buy a falling down house. Then you get planning permission. Then, a year or two later, you go to the Greek consulate and start stuffing your furniture with controlled substances.

Luckily there weren't that many boxes. A couple of crates of books; a Piper; our buhl desk; an Afghan runner; a pair of slender bedroom chairs that Nina's mother had been fond of and a few kitchen implements (pots, teapot, cups and saucers). None of it very exciting. Or so I thought as I unpacked and described virtually every item on the list.

They wanted to start with the roll.

"It's a rug," I said. "A small carpet."

"Unpack it." Or the equivalent: Let's be having it, squire.

It was more of a tussle getting it out of the tube than I had imagined.

"*Oopah,*" said the customs officer, watching the penultimate tug, "a fine carpet. What rich colours." And then in an aside to Nikos. "That must have cost a pretty penny."

I was still struggling to get it out. "Won't that do?"

"No," said Nikos, "all the way." And laughed until he coughed, remembering, I resentfully imagined, stripclubs in seaports around the world.

When I finally unrolled the carpet, the officer measured it roughly and said it was a funny shape. I said it was a runner, meant for a long narrow hall, for example.

"*Khali, nai.*" (Yes, a carpet). He mused over that for a bit. "Where from?"

I explained it was not from a shop but from the hall in our house in London. Nikos translated.

"No. From where?"

"It's an Afghan," I said. That was a mistake. Nikos translated: it comes from Afghanistan.

"Afghanistan," said the customs officer. "Problems." He took the rug up and shook it. There was a flurry of dust. I sneezed. Nikos coughed. The rug was cast aside and the other helper spent the rest of the time, when he wasn't at work with his mini-crowbar, trying to roll it back into its container.

"How much?"

I guessed an appropriate sum. "Four hundred pounds."

"*Bamphtino.* Very cheap in England."

Was he making a joke? Or warning me that he knew what things cost.

"But there's no duty to pay," I said.

"Never mind. Let's see that." He pointed to the very clever packing-case built round the buhl desk to protect the delicate legs and the inlaid brasswork which had just been expensively restored.

It was relatively easy to unpack and in a minute or two it stood on the concrete floor of the warehouse, half of it in shade and half catching some diffuse sunlight. It looked splendid, black, red and golden. It glowed.

We went through the *po-po-po*-that-must-have-cost-a-drachma-or-two routine again.

"What is it?"

"It's the buhl desk," I said, referring to the list he held in his hand.

"Yes. But what is it?"

"A desk," I said, "*ena grapheio, ena thranio*, a bureau. *Escritoire.*"

"That," he said, pointing to the inlay, "gold?"

"No, no. Brass."

Nikos said, "I think the same as bronze, like bronze statue. Isn't it?"

The customs officer asked him what he'd said and he repeated in Greek that it was like a statue cast in bronze. Or so I thought. At any rate there was some confusion and Yiorgos the customs man started demanding to see the statue.

"What statue?" said Nikos.

"The statue cast in bronze. There is no mention here," he slapped the inventory, "of any statue."

"There is no statue," said Nikos, spacing the words as though he were addressing an educationally disadvantaged child.

I was trying to persuade the manual worker to help me parcel up the desk. He was demurring, waiting for an OK from the boss. It didn't come.

"How much?"

I said I didn't really know. It was old. It had been in the family some time.

He walked over to it, opened the flap, tried a drawer or two.

"Old, eh? *Oraio.*" He closed the flap, ran his hand over the inlay, flicked his nail on a piece of brass. "Not gold, eh?"

"No," I said in what I hoped was a firm, no nonsense voice. "Brass." Like all customs officers, he was making me feel guilty.

"How much is it worth?"

"I've no idea. It's old but it's a copy," I said. "Real buhl is valuable."

I heard Nikos translate valuable as *akrivos*; dear, expensive, pricey.

The customs officer shook his head in agreement. "*Poly akrivo.*"

"Tell him something," whispered Nikos. "Anything. *Oti theleis.*" Whatever you like.

"But," I said, "there's no duty to pay. So why?"

"*Then birazee.*" Never mind. This was the customs officer. It sounded more like, "Never you mind, my lad. You just get on with answering the question."

I plucked a figure out of the air. "A thousand pounds."

He sucked his teeth, tried it out in drachmas, decided it was expensive but probably right for England, and said, "Not gold, eh? OK."

The rest was coasting downhill. What is this Piper? An English artist, John Piper. What is the painting? A ruined church. Greek? No, English. Why paint a ruined church in England? Not archaic?

Books. I heard him ask Nikos why anyone would want so many books. To open a shop? Nikos shrugged. I said we had many more books at home in London.

"*Po, po, po.* Many, many books. Are you a professor?"

"No. My wife's a novelist and I write a little."

I heard Nikos say something about my being the Director of the BBC.

"Much money. You earn much money?"

"No. I'm retired. On a pension."

"How much?"

I busied myself putting things back into crates.

Nikos hissed, "Tell something."

"Five hundred pounds."

"A year?"

"No. A month."

"Too much," said Nikos. I smiled apologetically. What would have been right?

By half-past three we were unpacking and taking everything up to the flat. The final proceedings had only taken another half-hour or so. I had to sign various documents in triplicate. Stamps had to be found and paid for, and then the whole documentation had to go for scrutiny and a final date, time and place stamp before a senior officer. There was only one further hiccough. He spoke some English and he checked every item on the inventory.

"Where is the video and the TV?"

"I haven't brought them to Greece."

"But it says here on the permission one television set and one video."

— 243 —

"Yes but that's in case we want to bring them on our next trip." I knew I was wrong to heed the consul's advice.

"Why it says now you bring in TV and you say no TV this time? Why?"

"The permission lasts for six months."

"But you bring everything else now. Why not TV? Video and TV very expensive in Greece. So why not import from England?"

"Maybe next time."

To Nikos. "What means maybe?"

As we took the last crate up to the apartment, Nina appeared and said, "That took you a long time."

Nikos said, "OK, no problem."

I unpacked the buhl desk and set it, to great advantage, almost opposite our front door. Nikos looked and admired it.

"Not gold, eh?" He laughed until he spluttered. "Not gold. Very good."

XXII

The next day we drove to Athens. Everything seemed to be going remarkably well except, just before we got to Argos, Nina remembered that she hadn't turned the oven off. Or had she? Anyway we went back. She had. And so once again via Argos to Athens. Life was pretty good, I thought, taking stock. With Nina's encouragement I had again tried fish, finny and scaly, and survived. Athens, when we got there, was considerably less polluted than we had expected. From our bedroom in the Electra Palace the Parthenon glowed white in the sunshine.

We dined with Athina and Plato. There was a vigorous argument about the likely culpability of Andreas Papandreou. Plato was sure he could not personally be guilty of corruption; most of it was a trumped-up campaign by the right wing. Athina was less sure, or rather she viewed him, and perhaps all politicians, as venal.

"What about the telephones tapping? *And* Koskotas and the Bank of Crete? *And* the Community, the Market. *To sitari* . . ." She waited for a translation.

Plato and I both said "wheat" and Nina asked, "What's all this about the Common Market and wheat?"

Plato explained. "*Yugoslav* wheat was, I think the phrase is passed off as *Greek* cereal. For the EC."

"Yes," said Athina "a Pasok cabinet minister will forge papers and allow it to seem Greek. For money from EC."

"For a subsidy from Brussels," said Plato.

"And," Athina went on, "Greece is found."

"Fined," said Plato patiently.

"Find, found," said Athina triumphantly. "Aorist. Past tense."

"Different verb," said Plato. "Different meaning. And all this has nothing personally to do with Andreas."

"*And* the Mirages," Athina, undeterred, continued her litany. "I suppose Louvaris was not to do with Papandreou. *Etsi then einai?* Isn't it?"

Plato was rising to the bait, Nina was saying that she had forgotten the details and I was trying to explain. Louvaris, a close friend of Papandreou's, had been forced to resign from his post after it had been alleged that arms, planes and missiles had been bought from France at what was said to be considerably more than their market price in return for handsome kickbacks. There was also some other alleged scandal about the selling on of weapons but by then we were all getting tired. We went to bed reassured that Greek politics was alive, kicking and not as clean as all that; and that Aristophanes would have recognized the bones of the conversation. In the event, somewhat later Mr Papandreou was acquitted of the charges levelled at him.

I woke up with an aching foot and a sense of foreboding. By noon I was bored with shopping and rather lame. It was beginning to get very hot. A heatwave, it was rumoured, was on the way.

"Why," said Nina as though she had only just noticed it, and perhaps she had, "do you always make such an exhibition of yourself when we're walking round Athens? I know we've been on our feet for a couple of hours but that's no reason to limp. You haven't got a gammy leg too." Question or assertion? And what did she mean by "too"? I limped on silently, not wincing much above twice a minute. We spent hours, or so it seemed to me, while Nina chose an extremely expensive portable electronic typewriter whose only advantage was that you could change daisy wheels to type in Greek or English. It had become very hot. We paused for a sparse lunch and then mercifully discovered all the shops were closed. A chance to sleep, to take a siesta, *enas mesimerianos ypnos*, in the oasis of our air-conditioned room.

Two hours later, unrefreshed but rested, I tried to get up. My foot was hot, red and shiny. It was painful and it would not fit into my shoe.

"Don't worry," said Nina. "You remember it happened before in Rome?" I muttered neutrally but she went on. "Well, I do, I can tell you. All that fuss. Those poor Lanes. David was busy being ambassador to the Vatican and Sara had to lug you to that nice hospital with the nuns. And after all that, there was nothing on the X-ray and it just went away. Or did you have antibiotics?"

I went to a doctor, both ways by cab; I couldn't walk. He said I had an infection, gave me antibiotics and painkillers and told me to take it easy. I hobbled out to dinner in some loose sandals. I left both undone for the sake of symmetry and kept on losing them and tripping up. Bob McDonald, who had been the BBC correspondent in Athens for most of the Colonels' rule and was on his annual visit to assess the economy, kept my spirits up. Nina's spirits seemed remarkably undiminished.

The following morning it was even hotter and the *nephos* had returned but I felt better, cheerier. Nina was solicitous. What about going to a hospital? A hospital, I said to myself? In this smog? Not if I can help it. I thought it better to return to base.

"Let's go home," I said, and meant Nauplion.

I drove back and we made good time, arriving around lunchtime. The foot was a bit stiff when I got out and grew worse as I went on but I managed to unpack the car and walk upstairs. Then I folded on to the bed, leaving Nina to trudge up and down. I could hear her saying consoling things to herself like "Poor little drudge. Poor little workhorse" but I just floated out, on some other tide.

The next morning Nina told me I had had an appalling night. So had she. I was feverish and the foot was horribly swollen and very painful. While Nina went out to get some fruit juice and probably to escape from my gloom I dismally contemplated my leg. What had been an angry red ankle-sock was now a long scarlet stocking about to cover the knee.

Nina returned with a mixture of bewilderment and determination. She had met the child who had hurt her arm in our cellar and had spoken to her. The mother, said Nina, had given her a look. She had also run into Barbara in the square who had said of course I ought to go to the local hospital. Nina agreed. She entreated. Eventually I yielded.

Our progress was somewhat slow. It was hell getting down the stairs, tricky getting into the car and it was a very, very hot day. Nina drove me to Nauplion General Hospital and waited with me in a crowded corridor. After an hour or so we got moved up the queue.

"Let the foreigner go first. What will he think of us Greeks and our *philoxenia?*" angrily shouted one old man who had clearly been there all morning. It was a touching example of Greek hospitality, of the way to treat strangers.

Meanwhile there was a constant stream of people barging into the consulting room. Usually it was someone who knew the doctor or who thought he knew the doctor or who thought the doctor ought to have known him. It was almost invariably a man: the women sat outside and complained, spasmodically and noisily. Sometimes it was a relative of the patient being examined, forcing his way in. Everything was carried out at a shout. The hospital seemed to be charged with emotion.

Eventually, after another bellow of "Let the foreigner go first", I was hustled in. It was a suite of rooms and there seemed to be three or four doctors, a handful of nurses and a patient or two. I said I couldn't stand and was helped to a chair in front of a youngish doctor who took down my details. Name. Father's name. Age. Home address. Country of birth. Occupation.

Previous diseases. Current medication. Surgical history. Length of stay in Greece. Address in Greece.

I saw the purpose in all this but I was beginning to float away again and found it difficult to keep even a tenuous grip on reality. We were using a bemusing cocktail of languages. At last he asked me what was the matter. I showed him my foot. He touched it and I think I shrieked. The next thing I knew I was lying on the examination couch in the adjoining room with three doctors peering at me and Nina hovering behind them. The senior doctor, he turned out to be the physician superintendent, had some English. He said that I had a high fever and a very strong infection and I must come into hospital now, at once.

A wheelchair appeared a few minutes later and I was steered, at a racing sprint, along corridors and into and out of a lift and finally to a two-bed ward full of people. I was put on the bed next to the window. In the other bed lay an elderly, almost immobile man surrounded by what looked like several dozen relations of varying generations. They kindly made way for Nina and asked me what was wrong. I said my foot. They sympathized. *Ponaei?* Does it hurt? *Ponaei.* It hurts.

A doctor appeared, shooed some of the crowd away and into the corridor, got Nina to help me undress and then with a nurse assisting, examined me again. The scarlet stocking had covered my knee. It was very hot. I couldn't bear to have anyone or anything touch it, not even the light cotton sheet. The doctor said he'd be back in a few minutes with *pharmaka* (medicines). I relaxed. If I didn't move and willed the pain to go to the end of the bed, it retreated a bit, to about my ankle. What would happen when the scarlet stocking reached the groin? Ouch.

Nina said, "Don't be silly. It's not like shingles meeting round the waist. And I don't suppose that's true either."

I grinned feebly and let my guard drop. It was a mistake. With a resounding clatter the wheelchair had returned. I was carried into it and swept off by Speedy Gonzales, at an even faster lick, into the lift and down to the basement. Where was he taking me? *Aktinographia.* I assumed this meant radiography. It was probably sensible to X-ray the foot, though I wasn't much looking forward to the process.

Yes, it was the X-ray department. But no, it wasn't the foot. It was my chest they wanted to X-ray. My *chest?* I pointed to my foot. They were unimpressed and adamant. Words like *pnevmonia* were used, which even in my enfeebled state meant something to do with lungs. I gave up, but worse was to follow. I was pushed to my feet and made to stand upright, a fair amount of brusque adjustments to my position being made, while I was trying through the blaze of pain to explain that standing wasn't quite the thing for my foot. I had to stand to wait for the X-ray to be developed. Incoherent with pain, I then waited for the wheelchair to return.

Back on the bed I remembered Theodoros, a doctor friend of ours who had trained in London, telling me that TB was still endemic in Greece. Ah ha, I said to myself, obviously they take the opportunity of X-raying everyone who comes to hospital whatever their complaint or condition. It didn't make me feel any better but it pleased me that my brain was still working.

It seemed my veins were not doing so well. Two nurses, one on each side, each with a drip, were fighting their respective ways into connecting me intravenously. Nina said it was butchery; I thought it a kind of torture.

"Why *two* drips?" said Nina in a lull. "It's only you. Everyone else has only got *one*."

"Antibiotic," I said, continuing in Sherlock Homes mode. "The other one must be glucose."

"Why should everyone, why should you, be on a glucose drip?"

"Standard practice in Greece. To combat shock and under-nourishment." I was busking on a high.

"Under-nourishment?" said Nina. "You? Under-nourished? Or them for that matter." She looked at various patients all wheeling their mobile drips up and down the corridor and crowding round the open door. I drifted off into an uncomfortable half-sleep to the high-volume drone of Greek exclamatory conversation and the slow repetition by Nina, head deep in a phrasebook, "*O andras mou einai sto nosokomeio.*" My husband is in hospital. "*O andras mou einai sto nosokomeio. O andras mou . . .*"

At some point during the late afternoon the hubbub sub-
sided, and when I looked round there were only two visitors,
one knitting, click-click, click-click, and one reading aloud,
presumably to her companion, bits of a newspaper. The room
was darker and Nina had disappeared. It was also appreciably
cooler. There was no air-conditioning but there was a decent
draft going through the room whenever there was any breeze,
and shutters and curtains kept out the glare and intense heat of
the sun. Despite the outside temperature, the room had not
been uncomfortably hot.

I was, I told myself, very lucky: heat on top of the pain, the
swelling and the fever would have been intolerable. And the
doctors seemed competent and conscientious and careful. The
chief said that if he thought I needed complex surgery he would
advise me to return to England. But as I didn't, and couldn't
travel in any case, I was just as well off in his hospital. For the
moment. How long did he think I'd be there? Till the infection
goes and the swelling diminishes. How long is a piece of string?

Nina says I'm always influenced by the superficial. She made
this remark when I said I thought the doctors were pretty good
and what's more they had proper ward rounds twice a day: a
troupe of white-coated medicos at various stages of training,
experience and age following the chief and conferring over the
patient, all seeming to know what they were doing. It was reassuring, even if they were not sure what had gone wrong with
my foot.

I was not so confident of the nurses. Just before Nina
returned, laden with goodies like pyjamas, short-wave radios,
Greek dictionaries, books, fruit and bottles of cold water, I was
visited by a pair of nurses. It was a routine taking of temperature, under the arm, and a dishing out of pills. Somehow they
managed to dislodge the syringe arrangement that kept one of
the drips feeding into a vein. It hurt momentarily and produced a spill of blood but by the time they had finished fitting
it all together again I was a great deal sorer and immoderately
covered with blood, as was the sheet beneath me.

There was, as Nina observed, not much of a rush to change
the sheet. I said it didn't matter. I was relieved not to be pushed

and pulled for a while, the foot remaining a baleful centre of concentrated pain. But what I did need, fairly urgently, was a bottle, flask or pisspot. I had tried to ask the nurses but evidently without success. Earlier, a nurse who spoke French had told me that if I ever wanted anything just to ring the bell. Ha! I had rung and rung. Nothing. Nobody.

The nurses, I began to understand, were not there to look after the comfort or the bodily functions of the patients. Indeed, as Nina was to say tartly a day or two later, they seemed to be there mostly to drink coffee, smoke cigarettes, gossip and from time to time attend on the doctors. But that was after the crisis of the urine down the drain and Nina was understandably jaundiced.

Later, too late, we discovered that it was possible to hire a sort of auxiliary or practical nurse who did all the boring and disagreeable things and stuck around overnight; it was not only possible, but achievable. Patients without extended and extensive families, or patients whose families did not wish to carry out such menial tasks, were often kitted up with these Mrs Gamps.

Alas we were ignorant, so neither I nor, more to the point, Nina was able to benefit from these angels-of-mercy-for-hire. Instead Nina wore herself to a thread-paper rushing to and from the hospital and I repined in bed, unable to stand or get around.

It was during the longer hiatuses that I began to study and envy the extent of my room-mate's entourage. Mr Poseidon was a fisherman. He appeared to be small, well-weathered and gnarled, in his mid-seventies – his wife said he was sixty-nine, his son seventy-six, a strangely large discrepancy. He had suffered a stroke and his limbs and speech were affected. He looked as though he had given up trying to move any part of his body. He had the air of a man both discouraged and bewildered, until, that is, his daily fish supper appeared, cooked, presented and fed to him by his wife. She was bigger than he seemed to be and had the shape of a heavy cone with a large head balanced on top. She was hirsute, grave, apparently unflappable and kind. Late at night she pulled out a truckle bed from under his bed and went to sleep between him and the door. In fact she stayed with him all day as well, except during the afternoon when she went home. She returned, always dressed in a long black garment, at about seven o'clock, carrying the fish pie, two gardenias for him and two gardenias for me. One of my strongest memories of Nauplion General is the heavy scent of the gardenias, glowing white in a glass on the hospital locker against the dark night.

Nina met our doctor friend Theodoros in the entrance to the hospital. He was almost incoherent with embarrassed apologies. "I'm so sorry," she reported him as saying, "that Austen has been put in with a low-class person." Nina was taken aback. I said I was glad I was sharing with Mr Poseidon and family but, all the same, it was kind of Theodoros to have taken such an interest. I had a distant recollection of his coming into the room when I was half-awake, patting my hand and making comforting noises. Alas, as he said himself, he could be of little use: he was a paediatrician. But he was helpful as well as friendly and sympathetic. Most days he came in and told Nina or me what the consultant physician thought of my progress.

I suppose the Posiedons were rightly described as peasant stock; peasant and somewhat pyknic. Their children were different, taller and less thick-set. The one son came in every morning and shaved his father. He was a petty officer in the harbour authority. The daughter had worked in a bank and her husband had a taverna. The grandchildren had again changed the pattern. It was like a speeded-up cartoon of evolution and social mobility. They were tall and slender, and had been to university, one to Athens, one to Patras, and were now part of the professional classes, a teacher and a lawyer. And then there was a great-grandson.

Thanos was, I suppose, two. He was brought in on the Sunday morning. While everyone else was chattering away he was placed on somnolent Great-Grandad's chest. Suddenly a strange, hoarse but rather sweet voice was heard, singing a nursery song. It was the first time I had heard Mr Poseidon make any noise; it was the beginning of his recovery. Within hours he was trying to bounce the child on his chest and within days he was able to go home, at least half of him working again.

*

Greek hospitals present an animated social theatre. Most of human life is here and none of it understated. Visitors, in numbers, seemed to be around night and day with a slight, a very slight, reduction of activity during the siesta hours. Most patients had relays of friends and relations who not only kept up the noise and interest level but also performed all the useful domestic functions like bedpans, bottles, tidying, waking, washing and feeding. Meanwhile other patients' visitors walked up and down the corridors and peered into the various wards. Often enough they saw someone they knew and, by the sound of it, hadn't seen for years. It was all a great, and mostly jolly, social occasion. From time to time, for example during the consultants' rounds, all civilians were encouraged to leave the room. Not many did. I rather got the impression that, for all the exaggerated respect accorded to them, doctors weren't allowed to get away with anything, like secrecy: everything had to be conducted under the scrutiny of curious, inquisitive and critical family.

In all this thrumming, extended familial activity, I felt deprived, orphaned. Not that Nina wasn't there much of the time, and not that I didn't have visitors, but that I did not have brothers and aunts and cousins and sisters-in-laws. I was not Rabbit and I lacked his friends and relations.

On proper reflection, even at home I was an only child and lost out on the cheerful sibling relationships that kept everybody else's party going. Nor was I easily attuned to the Greek way of illness. Mainly I think because even in hospitals Greeks import their gusty zest for enjoyment and drama. They are as scared of death and pain and decay as the next man; they fear illness and abhor disfigurement, disease and disablement to an excessive extent, witness their attitude to the mentally ill, the retarded, the physically crippled, but they love and relish the rhythm of life, and births and deaths are part of that beat. It is not that Greeks march to a different drum, although I sometimes think they do, but that they carry extra psychological equipment with them, not least a capacity for gaiety, *kephi*. Every Greek carries within himself ready-made construction kits for starting a political party, for high-spiritedly enthusing a party-party, and for full-weight grieving at deaths and any other losses. So here in hospital there was nothing of hushed tones, of whispering gentility or stiff upper lips: everyone, patients and visitors alike, shouted, complained, stormed, laughed and cried unreservedly.

It could on occasions be both tiring and tiresome, as well no doubt as being – had I but had the strength to enjoy it – liberating. My own visitors were not exactly inhibited.

James and Barbara were not above criticizing the nurses and the hospital management and then laying into Mr Papandreou, whose fault everything was, at high volume. I was sure the Poseidons were Pasok supporters and were bristling at every mention of Papandreou's name. Mind you, Nina pointed out to me when I accused *her* of shouting, a certain amount of volume was needed to make yourself heard. Barbara had made a dish of banana and bacon, which Nina and I finished off, and a thermos of iced fruit juice.

Laura arrived with a basket of fruit, a sheaf of American magazines and a chilled bottle of wine. And plenty of scandalous tales about what was going on in Nauplion. Then there was our neighbour from Kapodistriou.

Antigone and one of her sisters walked the not inconsiderable way to the hospital in the extreme heat, bringing me a large bunch of roses. I was bowled over. As far as she was concerned we had hardly been the least troublesome of neighbours. It might well, I thought to myself, have been a writ rather than flowers .

Antigone said I must not worry about the expense of anything. If I needed other doctors she would arrange it. She would take care of anything I wanted. Did I perhaps want to go to a hospital in Athens? Being part of the profession herself, she was a mite more tactful and, of course, more knowledgeable about provincial deficiencies. She looked around before saying that maybe the facilities would be better in Athens. No, no, I cried, she was too kind. I was extremely touched, almost tearful. As they got up to leave, her sister affectionately tweaked the big toe of my swollen foot. I suppose it was irresistible, the whole foot lovely and red and shiny like a polished apple. I levitated.

I had been put on Brufen, an anti-inflammatory drug, largely because the knee was now swollen and hot. It was all extremely uncomfortable and the scarlet stocking had not receded, but nor had it advanced any further in its march up my thigh. I was, as Nina said in approved uplifting fashion, holding my own.

A nurse, bringing the evening dollop of pills, said helpfully that if I had been swimming at the town beach then, of course, I would have picked up an infection. I was aggrieved and, a year later, vindicated when Arvanitia was awarded one of the not altogether numerous EC clean beach and sea awards.

The heat continued. And the drought. For much of the day, and for six hours after midnight, the water in Nauplion was turned off. Nina became more and more tired, traipsing to and from my bedside, and more and more depressed. My spirits were hardly elevated either as day after day the infection remained recalcitrantly, as the doctors put it, strong. How long would I be there? Would it ever get better?

I decided to be Pangloss. "The food's really rather good," I said to Nina when she returned after some essential shopping. "And look. Mr Poseidon can move three of the fingers on his left hand."

"And I'm boiled," she replied, "and exhausted. And the carpet people are coming. And there's no shade anywhere and no water. It's a *horrible* place. I wish we'd never come here and I'm *too hot*."

It was that night that Nina was given a cardboard pot labelled "*Kos. Ostyn*" and instructed, by the tone you might say ordered, to come in early and get me to provide a fasting sample of urine. It was to be placed on the designated table by six-thirty in the morning. Not a minute later. We laughed about it and Nina went off to get an omelette and salad at Noufara and, she hoped, an early night.

She was back at half past six of a shimmering morning, dizzy with exhaustion. It was already hotting up and even with the shutters half-closed and the blinds down I could feel that it was going to be a scorcher. Nina took my bottle and disappeared. She was back within the minute, pallid and thunderstruck.

"I've poured it down the lavatory and pulled the chain," she said, gesturing appalled at the empty bottle. "What can we do?"

I too must have blanched. What would the nurse gauleiter

say? Or do? Would it mean my incarceration for even longer?

"Can't you try and pee some more?"

I tried and couldn't.

"Shall I use someone else's? There are several full pots on the table."

"No," I said. "He might have something terrible wrong with him and they'll think I've got it. And cut me up." By now, the full gravity as well as the heinousness hit me. Tears started up in my eyes. "I'll be here for ever. They'll never find out what's wrong with me."

This had little effect on Nina who was going tearfully along her own path of desperate remedy. Her next suggestion was, "I tell you what. *I'll* use your bottle. They'll never tell the difference."

"How is that going to help them diagnose what's wrong?"

By now my whole leg was hurting fearfully and I was groaning with pain and anxiety. Beside me Nina was crying with frustration, exhaustion and apprehension.

"What are they going to say when I tell them?" She marched bravely off towards the nurses' room brandishing the empty bottle.

I closed my eyes. Why was I behaving in this absurd way? It couldn't be that important. A silly accident. Poor Nina.

She came back what seemed like hours later, laughing – convulsed with laughter. She had gone to the nurses' room. There was a gaggle of them drinking coffee and smoking. No one spoke or understood any English, or French for that matter. Nina had tried to mime giving me the bottle, taking it out to the lavatory, pouring the urine down the pan and pulling the chain. They looked bewildered. They obviously had never played dumb crambo. I don't somehow think party games figure largely in the Greek conspectus. She had tried again, this time miming the whole business, unzipping flies, getting the penis out, fitting it into the neck of the bottle. They caught the drift and laughed but still didn't understand the pouring down the lavatory pan and pulling the chain. Nina found herself miming more and more cloacal details before they got the point. More laughter. "*Then birazee.*" Never mind. "*Avrio.*" Tomorrow.

"But why," she said to me, laughing fit to bust, "couldn't they get the pulling of the chain?" She mimed it all again for my benefit. The Poseidons looked transfixed and then politely looked away again.

"Perhaps they aren't used to doing it," I said.

"Doing what?"

"Pulling the chain."

"Don't be so filthy."

"No," I said, trying to recover my equanimity and the sense of balance and objectivity for which the World Service is world famous. "I mean they went straight from long drops to low-flush suites."

"Ah," said Nina, glad to have a logical explanation, "no wonder. Levers and buttons, not chains."

She went out and came back with warm croissants.

After four days my temperature was down, the red stocking had rolled back below the knee and the butterflies in the backs of my hands which now held the drips were getting extremely uncomfortable, the nurses having somehow run out of convenient veins. It was not their forte. I was, I dare say, becoming a less docile patient as I got better. I was restless and rather depressed. So was Nina. But we were both buoyed up by seeing Mr Poseidon go home. His speech was much recovered, his left arm was moving stiffly but well and only his left leg, which buckled whenever he tried to stand on it, which was often now, particularly in the early morning, curbed his enthusiasm for movement.

I too left the ward in a wheelchair but that was after a week. Mr Poseidon's bed was taken within the hour by a long-faced and moribund figure, his skin the colour of old parchment, who never spoke.

"He looks a goner," said Nina on coming in and finding him in the other bed. The patient's son, daughter and private nurse were conferring.

"How do you know they don't understand English?" I hissed.

"They won't understand slang," Nina said complacently.

"Dated slang," I said.

He had suffered a *megalo* heart attack. I learnt no more about him. His daughter, who I think lived in Nemea and visited for a couple of hours each day, obviously didn't want to talk. His son merely dashed in every evening to shave him. This shamed Nina who went out and bought me an absurdly expensive electric razor. Most of the time now when Nina wasn't there the ward was unwontedly quiet. The private nurse occasionally sang to herself and tried to spur the patient into speech. She washed him twice a day with energy and enthusiasm, paying a lot of attention to his genitals. Jocularity was her style. "Come along my little man. You've seen better days, eh, and places . . ."

After a while, since she was there twenty-odd hours a day, she began to get on my nerves. Seeing the room virtually uninhabited, other more ambulatory patients took to calling in, bringing their mobile drips with them.

"*Ypofero apo tin kardia mou,*" was the general line. "I have a heart condition." It was never quite clear what. And then a cough. "And my lungs." I had realized that the constant comings and goings along the corridor, *to piyain' ela*, was the ebb-and-flow of smokers fighting their way to the fire-escape landing which was a kind of Tom Tiddler's ground, and I did rather question the sense of simultaneously complaining about the condition of their lungs. To be fair, Greece is said to have one of the lowest incidences of lung cancer and almost everyone smokes. I enjoyed these conversations although I had little dramatic to offer in exchange, just my foot. "*Ponaei?*" Yes, it still hurts. "*Pote tha figete?*" I wish I knew when I was leaving.

Several fellow inmates came in to tell me about a new patient in the next ward. He had come not only with private nurse but with a machine, so they said, like a television that monitored his heart all the time. And there was nothing wrong with his heart. And the machine made a horrid noise. And it took up space. His room-mate took to coming in and sleeping the afternoon away in one of the chairs in our room. There was much tutting and *po-po*-ing about the cost of the monitor.

The doctors were pleased that they'd got my temperature down and that the infection was weakening. I thought it might have been a gout that somehow got infected. No, they said, it wasn't gout. It wasn't in the right sort of place and anyway they'd tested for uric acid. They were sorry but more tests were needed. And anyway I couldn't go home yet. Nor was I to try to walk or stand. Stay in bed just for a few more days.

After a consultant's round when I was feeling especially downcast, a lady administrator came briskly along to the ward. A friend was on the phone from Athens. She would ring back in ten minutes. What did I want? She would pay for anything: going to Athens, more doctors, drugs. Everything. The lady, perhaps an almoner – since they still had physicians superintendent, anything was possible, even almoners, if not, given the lack of esteem in which nursing is held in Greece, matrons – was impressed. So was I. It was neighbour Antigone. But I could think of nothing I wanted. I just said to say thank you, it was extremely kind and thoughtful of her. I felt immensely affected: it was an act of great charity and *philoxenia*.

Nina was trying to cope with the continuing furnishing of the apartment as well as constant hospital visiting while the temperature remained remorselessly high. She managed to think of delicacies and jollities, for example a jar of lumpfish, mock caviar. This went very well when mixed with a whitish substance that was a constant on the menu. Nina claimed it was semolina but I reckoned it was some kind of rehydrated potato such as we had during the war which was later marketed, in for all I know an improved version, as POM. For some reason I had been put on a vegetarian regimen and I found the salad and fruit, yogurt and rice, not to mention the semolina-POM, easier to contemplate in the heat than any meat-and-veg. But food was not top of my list of priorities: getting better and/or getting out were.

By the time I got back to Kapodistriou I had been in bed a week and felt pretty feeble. The infection seemed to have gone but the foot was still somewhat swollen, angry and inflamed. I could not put any weight on it. The senior doctor said he was sorry that they had not been able to make a definitive diagnosis. He thought it might be an infective arthritis. But this was rare. He would really rather keep me in for another few days but he understood. I must please go and see a rheumatologist as soon as I got back to London.

Before leaving the hospital I was wheeled into the main office. I had forgotten about things like paying and was suddenly anxious. Perhaps I should have taken Antigone up on her generous offer. I need hardly have worried. The total bill came to £40 and if I had brought the right form with me – reciprocity of national health services within the EC – it would have been zero. Since I was paying, it didn't seem enough and I said so. I was told that it was just for sheets, towels, laundry and food. I was extremely grateful for all they had done for me and tried to say so adequately.

Nina had recruited Barbara's son Peter, a large and strong young man, to help me get up to the top floor. He half-carried me up the stairs and then went off and returned with a folding wheelchair belonging to his mother which he stowed downstairs in the entrance hall. Despite this evidence of my temporary (I hoped) disability, I was delighted to be home. I slumped happily on the multi-seater and looked round. There were changes. New lamps and stools in place. The carpet was laid in the attic although I couldn't get up there to look at it. And through the French windows on the harbour-side I could see two mop-headed figures in the afternoon sun.

"They *are* mops," said Nina. "Gert and Daisy. Gert's the red-headed one. And in case you're wondering why they're stuck in the flagpole holder . . ."

"I know," I interrupted. "There's no broom cupboard."

"You may have forgotten," said Nina, and she was right, "that Kate and her chums are arriving in Tolo tomorrow."

"We must fix something, take them out."

"With you like this?"

I pointed out that our niece Kate and her friends, who were recovering from A-levels, would not want to see us immediately. The day after would do. And I might be more mobile by then.

Nikos came to see how I was. He said he thought he had sold one or two of the flats. We both said, "To whom?"

"Oh," he said loftily, "foreigners. American. English. Italian.

Perhaps a Greek man from Athens. Perhaps French too."

"All of them?" Was he fantasizing, I wondered; hadn't we heard this litany before?

"Not all. Two-three."

"Which?"

"We see." Grin, shrug.

We arranged to fly back in a week's time, to leave the car in Nikos' mother's garage which wasn't used, or rather wasn't used as a garage, and to pay for the attic carpet before we left. Whilst I was lying on my hospital bed, Nina had been constrained to explain that we had run out of cash. No matter, they said. Pay when you can. No hurry. *Then birazee.* Everyone was unbelievably understanding and just plain kind.

Nikos was to make sure that the carpenter had made the desks by the time we returned in September. My foot apart, it all seemed to be tying up nicely. Except, I thought, for someone to look after the place and keep it clean and tidy whilst we were back in England.

"No," said Nina, picking up the drift of my thought, "Janet won't budge. She was very sorry to hear you were in hospital but she's got quite enough on her plate."

"So what do we do? And another thing, do you suppose we have to tell the customs about leaving the car for a couple of months?"

"I went down there with Peter."

"And? Is it all right?"

"Sort of. They really want you to have it sealed and put in bond which means it standing in the sun all day on the docks. Nikos is sure that if you lock it up and keep it off the road till you return, it's OK."

"Fine. But what did the customs actually say?"

"Gobbledegook. Turn a blind eye. If it is doesn't come to their attention, no harm done. No one the wiser. Nudge, nudge, wink and half a wink."

"All this in Greek?" I said disbelievingly.

"No, not really. Peter was doing all the talking. Yes, all right, in Greek. But I was watching. And anyway he told me the nub of the exchange."

We went ahead with the plan to leave the car immobilized with Nikos' mother. I was right to be wary. Customs officials can be excessively legalistic and despite moves towards the single market Greece jealously protects its punitive duty and stringent regulations on the importing of vehicles.

I once brought our car into Patras three days short of the six months it should have been out of the country. Inadvertently. The customs officer looked at my passport. He opened it, turned it upside down and stared at it again. Then he went through all the entries which registered my taking a car in and out of Greece. Having satisfied himself of the facts, he told me that I was three days shy of the six months. Conscious of the long queue of cars and people trying to get out of the port and on with their lives and holidays, I smiled ingratiatingly and said I was sorry.

"A month," he said.

"A month?" I said disbelievingly. "I wanted six months."

"A month."

"The EC," I said firmly. "*EOK. I Evropaiki Oikonomiki Koinototiti.*"

This momentarily fazed him. He turned to his supervisor. She took the passport, looked at me, looked at it, turned it upside down, whipped through the pages and muttered something I couldn't hear. He took the passport back and said, with reassurance, "*Yia ena mina. Mono.*"

So there it was: only for one month. But we were hoping to stay for several months. What could we do? I asked him.

"Look," he said, "it says here you've got a secondary residence in Nauplion." I acknowledged it. "They've got a nice customs house in Nauplion. You go and try them."

I did. It took time. The man I eventually saw held out his hand for my passport and subjected it to the same kind of examination. A quick scan, a peer at it upside down, and then a detailed, and this time itemized on a separate piece of paper, scrutiny of the importing and exporting of cars. Five minutes later, he said, "You're five days short. Not three."

"Why?"

"You left Greece on the nineteenth of October last year and you returned on April the sixteenth. They did a rough and ready six months and it's really one hundred and eighty-two days."

"They've only given me a month. Can't you give me an extension? Till mid-October?"

He looked doubtful, very doubtful. I said what about the latest EC regulations? He said he'd been thinking the same thing. Would I be so good as to pass him that file in the bookcase behind me? No, not that file, the blue one with EOK on the spine.

He went through it carefully. It was clearly the update box with all the amendments and notifications of changes in the regulations. He read it meticulously, copying out various reference numbers and dates.

"Well," he said finally, having collected all his notes, "I can give you till the end of August."

"Oh," I said, "but I was only three, sorry five days short. Can't you give me the rest of the six months?"

"C .i. End of August."

As we had to get back to London by the end of June, it meant taking the car back mid-June. We could have flown back to Greece but I wanted to do some touring and that meant driving out again at the end of August but this time putting the car on Nina's passport. Which is what I should have done to start with.

"In that case," I said, "just give me till the end of June."

"End of August," he said firmly. "I'll put this piece of paper in your passport. Come back just before your one month expires and give it to the responsible person here."

I went back three days before it expired, walked along to the same point on the counter and after a few minutes the same official came up to me.

"Yes," he said. "Is there something?"

I produced my passport with the slip of paper protruding. He took it out and read it as though it contained some new and totally unexpected piece of information. He then looked at my passport, turned it upside down, peered at it, went through the pages, checking the dates and calculations on the slip of paper, asked me to pass him the file behind me, cross-checked the references, and then said, "End of August."

He went back to his desk and rummaged in the third drawer on the right. He came up with a rubber stamp. It was the wrong one. He went to another desk and found the right stamp. He returned to the counter. He carefully inked the stamp and equally carefully pressed it on the page of the passport opposite the landing entry at Patras, rocking his hand slightly to effect the best impression. Alas most of the dotted and many of the solid lines were invisible and others incomplete. He sighed and looked closely at the rubber stamp: it was worn. He went back to his desk and returned with a ruler. He then set about drawing in and repairing the incompletely lined area. It took some fifteen minutes. He then very carefully, very precisely, filled out the details and the dates by hand. Then he had to find the small circular stamp of the Greek Republic to authenticate it. Another colleague had it. He came back triumphant. He carefully inked and stamped the passport. Now the car could stay – but not for long enough. In its way the transaction was beautifully accomplished, even elegant. It was great service, if very time consuming, but low in productivity. Since Greece has over-employment in government and public service, and under-employment generally, socially this low productivity no doubt makes some kind of sense.

I thanked the customs official, although I was still fuming about the absurdity of the regulations. He wished me a happy stay, adding, "Up to the end of August." He was not without humour.

Nor was Phaidon who came to see us bearing a bottle of a wine which was being marketed under a Nauplion label. He wanted to tell us a story he had heard and believed to be true. It was about a shepherd who had come down to Astros, leaving his sheep with his daughter. He had met a Greek-Australian much younger than himself who was visiting Greece for a holiday and who wanted to know what kind of sheep and pasture the old man had. He told the Australian as best he could, the young man having only vestigial Greek; it was his grandfather who had emigrated. In return he asked the young Australian what he did.

He said he also farmed sheep. How many? It was a small station with about 10,000 sheep. The old man, who had 300 sheep

and thought he was doing pretty well, a shepherd of consequence, went into the *Po, po, po* routine and then asked how
many men were employed.

"About six."

"Six?" said the old Greek.

"Yeah, well we have more around during shearing. But
they're freelance, get paid by results. Quick as a flash, off with
the fleece."

But the old man was worried about the six. How could they do
the work? The Australian tried to explain about the size of the
operation and economy of scale but this didn't fool the old man.

"Thousands and thousands of sheep and six men!" he said
again, with marked disbelief. He knew a con man when he saw
one. "And how do you do the milking?"

Plato phoned and brought us up to date on the political
manoeuvring to form a coalition government. He said there'd
be another election before the winter. He said they were
hounding Andreas but they'd never make any charges stick. He
was, to put it bluntly, not guilty as charged. Inflation was going
up, the economy was in tatters, but the government would survive. Just. So what's new?

Athina phoned and said the politics has been in a mess.
Pasok will be guilty and another election was held soon. Prices
are much more last month and next month. And why will we
go home so soon? She thought now that I was out of hospital,
the foot was better. Should she come down to help us? She
had to be in court tomorrow, but perhaps the weekend.

It was difficult getting downstairs, indeed it was difficult
walking at all, even with a stick. Nina had managed to get a
message through to our niece, Kate. We would pick her and her
friends up at their hotel. Nina drove us across to Tolo and
found the hotel, and the three of them, roughly where we'd
been told. They bundled into the back.

Nina drove rather cautiously to Nauplion.

"Other people's children," she said by way of explanation and
turned with studied care on to the road climbing up to the great
fort of Palamidi and onward to the bay of Karathona. She negotiated the sweep up to the castle without letting her eyes stray to

the precipice. She parked immaculately. Knowing how she felt about heights, I said, not patronizing her, "Well done. Sorry I can't do the driving." Nina smiled and I added, "Lucky it's not so hot. There's some cloud for a change. The girls had better take care. They could get badly burnt even with heavy cloud."

They paid no heed and shot out of the car. I stumbled out like some elderly drunk not sure where he would find the ground. Nina shepherded us through the main gate and, my total contribution being the money for the entrance fee, sat me down on a small wall with some large stone cannonballs for company. Nina asked if the girls wanted her to take them on a conducted tour. No; they'd rather find their own way. And off they leapt, tight jeans constraining their jumps, up one of the paths. They were soon out of sight.

Putting aside its grim history Palamidi is a glorious place of fortifications, lookouts, astonishing views, wild flowers, butterflies and tortoises. It was built by the Venetians to be impregnable, and so it looks, but was captured by the Ottomans in 1714 after a siege of nine fearful days. During the Greek War of Independence it was taken by Staikos at the end of November 1822, two Turks having told him that their officers, weakened by starvation, were spending the night in Nauplion after a parley and the garrison was empty.

Sitting on the low wall and looking at the bastions, I found myself musing on why the Venetians lost Palamidi in 1714. Had it been treachery? The castle looked so well-planned and indeed recently French army officers were known to have studied the fortress as a project for a staff course. It had been built late enough to be based on the use of rifle, gun, cannon, mortar and bomb. Perhaps they, the Venetian forces, had been thoroughly demoralized and weakened by the days of siege and starvation. They were an ill-assorted group of Albanians, Croats, Greeks, Slavs and various Italians including a substantial number of Venetians. It was essentially a mercenary force and it was facing a Turkish army of some 70,000 fired with their Islamic faith and determined to wipe out the defeat of thirty years earlier. This time the Turks conquered the whole of the Morea, the Peloponnese, in just over two months. The garrison in Palamidi probably numbered no more than three to four thousand men. And it was said that they were bickering and fighting amongst themselves long before the Turks appeared. Still, the fortress was eminently defensible. So had they just crumbled from despair? Or disaffection? Or lack of courage, or belief? In the end, they panicked.

I looked around. A dramatically lowering sky had appeared with the suddenness of sorcery, reflecting my sombre thoughts, or causing them. The weather had broken, the long heat-wave ended. A splendid electric storm began to erupt, lightning playing round distant peaks and a low, accompanying murmur of rolling thunder. It started to rain, a sprinkle first, then a splatter of larger raindrops, and then a full downpour, with hard little missiles, perhaps (could it be?) hail, bouncing off the ground. The storm came closer, the thunder louder, the lightning brighter. I toyed with the idea of trying to get up but everything looked wet and slippery and a bit of rain wasn't going to hurt me. I stayed where I was but picked up my stick.

Nina had moved towards the thick-walled arch that led to the entrance gate and provided the only shelter within reach. Out of the corner of my eye I saw the three girls come hurtling down the hill and dart towards the arch with great whoops and shrieks, determined, I imagined, to save their jeans and carefully distressed hair from the rain.

At that moment there was an enormous flash of blinding light and a clap of thunder like the crack of doom. I saw, in negative as it were, the girls and Nina converging, and the arch; and then nothing except the searing brightness. It was directly overhead. The explosions seemed to go on and on like untidy gunfire.

When I could see again, Nina was lying on the ground, not moving, and the girls had disappeared. I tottered to my feet, or rather foot, and hobbled over. By the time I got there others had rushed out from under the arch and were crying for water, in Greek, and holding up Nina's head. I thought she must have slipped, hit her head and knocked herself out. She looked pale, pale enough to be drained of blood, and unconscious. For a dreadful moment, I feared her dead. Suddenly, her eyelids flickered and she slowly opened her eyes, peered heavenwards, and then looked around bewildered. One of the attendant ladies mopped her forehead with a moistened cloth. Others stood under the arch, chattering loudly. It was still raining. "That one, the foreigner, she is lucky. May God preserve her. *Xhtipietai apo keravno.*"

Struck by lightning, they said. All of them. *Keravnovolimeni.* I tried to help Nina to her feet but I was little use as a prop since I couldn't put my still swollen foot to the ground. The girls came running over. Kate supported Nina back to the car.

"What happened?" said Kate. "I didn't see. Did you fall over?"

"They all say she was struck by lightning," I said, unsure. Wouldn't she have been burnt? Wouldn't I know? I was only a few yards away. Had the girls perhaps collided with Nina? I ran the scene back and was no wiser.

"I *was* struck by lightning," Nina said. "It knocked me out. I don't remember anything."

I unlocked the car and then realized that of course Nina couldn't drive; she had hurt an arm, a wrist and an ankle. None of the girls drove. I hopped in and experimented. It was an automatic gearbox. If I could manage to get my left foot across to control brake and accelerator, all would be well. I couldn't: there was nowhere to put bandaged and throbbing right foot. Perhaps if I put the car in bottom gear and used the handbrake, I could get us back home.

We set off very slowly indeed, I didn't use the accelerator at all, I couldn't if I'd wanted to. But it's a steep road and by the time we got down, towards the outskirts of the town, I was having to use the handbrake all the time to reduce speed. When we and the road finally flattened out the trouble began, with impatient cars hustling behind me. I was going at no speed at all and the road was wet and slippery; car after car would buzz up behind me, brake and skid and then angrily and noisily overtake me with lots of rude gestures. I was a silly old dodderer and shouldn't be allowed out in a car. And a foreign driver to boot. I could hardly explain our unlikely predicament or our sacred trust; other people's children. The rain was still hurtling down but the thunder and lightning had become a distant sideshow somewhere towards the other side of the bay.

We got into the house without further mishap. The girls ran upstairs, Nina and I slowly limped or hopped. It took some time. We let the girls in and tried to show them around, but neither of us was up to much. Not up to snuff, I found myself saying; not up to snuff at all. Nina was looking pale and remote, brushed by Death's wing. Kate told us to sit down. She would make us a nice cup of tea, thoughtful girl that she is. Except, of course, that she didn't know where the tea was kept or the teapot. Nina got up and showed her. I dangerously tried to open the fridge, get out some milk and then balance it as I hopped. Kate rescued it and then told us both to sit down again, which we did.

We heard comforting noises of cups being put on saucers, a teapot being rinsed in hot water and the kettle being switched on.

"Oh," said Kate a few minutes later, "I don't think the kettle's on." It wasn't. "Oh," she added, "I think there's been a power cut."

This time it wasn't a strike. A sub-station had been hit, put out of action somehow, by the electrical storm. No tea, no hot water, no bath, no shower: alcohol the only comforter.

Not all of Nauplion was in the dark. The square seemed to be lit up. We bandaged Nina's wrist and put the arm in a sling. Kate and the other two girls got my wheelchair out into the street and put me into it. Kate wheeled me, at a sober pace, into the little square of Agios Spyridon. It slopes down and debouches, after a steep incline, into the busy Staikos Staikopolou. I am somewhat heavy. Kate I would judge to be pretty light. The surface of the stones was wet and very slippery. We – Kate, the wheelchair and I – swept into the street at no mean speed. Luckily there were few bystanders and the shopkeepers were quick enough to jump aside. I craned my neck round when we slowed down just in time to see Nina, supported by one of Kate's friends, skid uneasily down the bottom of the slope. She didn't fall over and we arrived in the *plateia* without any more accidents. But only just.

The *plateia* is deliciously paved with marble slabs. It has an air of mature elegance and provides a splendid surface for games of football, children on bicycles and skateboards. In or after rain it is a deathtrap. Kate started to lose control shortly after she wheeled me into the square. The wheelchair accelerated on the wet marble and rather than let go, Kate ran to keep up with it. I consigned my fate to whatever Greek deity, and whichever Orthodox saint, looks after travellers in a like plight. Towards the far end of the square, Kate still running to keep pace with the slowing chair, there was a tree. We seemed to me to be approaching it too fast and too certainly for any hope of intervention. I debated whether it was better to throw my weight sideways and roll the chair over or to wait stoically until we hit the tree. But how would I get my foot out of the way?

With a dextrous lunge Kate swung us away from the tree less than a foot before collision. She whooped with triumph and did what might be called a lap of honour before taking me to the table at which Nina, the girls and Peter, who had come to join us, were sitting. I noticed the rest of the population, and the square was quite full, was watching us silently. The conversations, the shouting, the shrieks of the children, the wails of the babies, the *volta*, the parading to and forth, all started up again, like an electric switch being thrown, as I gratefully, very gratefully, got on to a proper chair.

Jenny from the book and newspaper shop, Odysseus, came up to find out how we were. Barbara had phoned her to say that someone in her village, remote and six or seven miles away, had told her that an Englishwoman had been struck by lightning up at Palamidi. And she, Barbara, had known at once that it must have been Nina.

Ari, whom we had not seen since we visited, and did not buy, his cousin's house with the giant toadstool lights, also came up to us. How delighted he was to have the chance of meeting us again. And what had I done to my leg? And Nina to her arm? We *had* been in the wars, hadn't we. And how splendid it had been to watch me being wheeled at such speed round the *plateia*. It was jolly game of me. And how lucky I was to have such a beautiful and, if he might say so, so black-skinned a charioteer to drive me.

He sat down and joined us, immediately summoning up another litre of wine. Since neither Kate nor Peter touched alcohol and the other two girls were restrained in their enthusiasm for retsina, Nina and I had already drunk more than our share. But no matter; being struck by lightning deserved copious draughts of retsina.

Turning to Kate, Ari said, "It occurs to me that I have been oddly discourteous. To mention the colour of your skin, I mean. But you must forgive me. I do not see many black people and none so beautiful, black or white, as you." He bowed his neck and then went on to ask whether they had seen Mycenae yet, or Tiryns. Just the castle? Ah well, perhaps the sea and the beach was more to their liking, at their age; and why not?

"You know," he said, turning to me, "like most Greeks I love the archaic and the classical and the Byzantine. But we carry our history, like the donkey an over-heavy load, uncomfortably. It depletes our energy for the present. Let alone the future." He sipped his wine. "I do hope I haven't bored you. Altogether too jolly depressing. Must be off now. No peace for the wicked. Or is it wicket, eh? You see I've even watched cricket. How's that!"

He went off, chuckling. Peter said he'd take the girls to a disco in Tolo and see them back to their hotel. But first he wheeled me back, uphill, and helped us back to our apartment.

The next day we took Nina to Nauplion General. My foot was easier; I could drive after a fashion.

"I bet they're delighted," said Nina as we sat in the crowded corridor that served as a waiting-room. "They've no sooner got rid of you and your foot than I come in with an injured wing. A right pair of fools."

"Let the foreigner go first," said the same old man. He clearly either had a season ticket to, or shares in, the hospital. "They say she has been struck by lightning."

"You've really blown our anonymity," I said.

"And the *kyrios*," the old man continued, "you will remember has an infected leg and spent many days in our good hospital."

"*Episis*," said Nina whose Greek vocabulary was doubling

every week. Likewise. And the same to you, with knobs on.

Nothing was broken. A nasty sprain and bruise, and generally a bit shaken up. Only to be expected. Take it easy. Don't
use the hand. Aspirin if it continues to hurt.

As we got back to Kapodistriou we saw Phaidon ringing the
bell. He was carrying two beautifully wrapped parcels which he
presented, one to Nina, one to me. Home-made chocolate
cookies to sustain Nina on the journey and a bottle of ouzo to
comfort me in the cool of England.

"Laura says you were struck by lightning, Nina. Perhaps the
Gods were trying to say something. Since Zeus didn't kill you,
he must have been telling you to stay. But not to take Greece or
Greeks lightly, eh. And you, Austen, all I hear about all day is
you being wheeled about the *plateia* very fast by a beautiful
young woman. Is your leg better? Are you really going back in
a day or two?"

"Yes," we both said. "Alas."

"Nauplion will miss you. *Kalo taxidhi*. Have a good voyage.
Come back soon."

"We will, "I said, near to tears.

"In September," said Nina, sniffling into a minuscule handkerchief.

"We'll miss all of you," I said.

He went down the stairs. We heard the front door slam and
then the entryphone rang.

"I forgot. Laura said to tell you she saw Janet and Janet says
with all your difficulties she'd better fit you in. She'll come round
at about one-thirty, quarter to two. Before lunch. *Yeia sas*."

Nina danced a little jig, until she became conscious of her
slung arm. She was high on her entanglement with lightning-
hurling Zeus.

"If Janet's really coming we'd better see if the extension bit we
ordered for the Hoover has come in, and do a quick clean up,"
said Nina. "We don't want to give Janet a bad impression."

So, in effect, we started on our rounds to say goodbye, beginning with Alexandros and his father who kept an electrical
shop two streets down. The Hoover accessory was there, waiting for us. But Alexandros and even more his father were taken

aback by Nina's arm in a sling. They were prepared to see me still limping and indeed congratulated me on my recovery, but Nina's mishap was a surprise, a shock.

"You have been in the wars," said Alexandros who had only recently returned to Nauplion from taking a degree in electrical engineering at Nottingham.

His father, who spoke no English, looked and sounded worried.

Alexandros translated. "He says you are not taking precautions against the evil eye. He says where is the charm you ought to be wearing round your neck, Mrs Nina? The little eye. He says you never know. Someone may have given you the evil eye. The verb is *matiazo* in Greek. *To matiasma*, the spell. *To kako mati*, the evil eye." Like everyone we knew in Nauplion, Alexandros was thankfully always happy to instruct us. "Of course I don't really believe in any of this superstition but my father and all the older generation do. But it's a very little thing and what have you got to lose? You don't know: it might do some good. You have had rather a chapter of accidents."

"Yes, yes," said Nina. "I'll go and get a little eye at once. I used to have one but . . ." She paused. She had been going to say she'd bought it in Turkey years ago and lost it but decided the Turkish connection might have led to complications.

They wished us a good journey and a quick return. We went to the *plateia* and found a charm in one of the jeweller's shops. Nina had it put on her neckchain.

"Well," she said rather defensively as we walked across the square, "I don't believe in it, you know."

She was fingering it as we went into Dimitri and Jenny's book and newspaper shop. *Kyria* Nitsa was behind the counter, Dimitri's mother; she used to tell Nina about being a refugee from Asia Minor in the 1920s, believing Nina understood most of what she said. Now she was saying that she was glad that Nina had the little eye. After her encounter with the bolt of lightning, she would need it. Another woman, overhearing, said that if it was a question of the evil eye, she knew a knowledgeable woman near Argos who was better than most at doing the . . . She mumbled something. It sounded like *xemetrima*. I

rushed in and said we were going back to England. Would *Kyri'*
Nitsa please say goodbye to Jenny and Dimitri.

"That was all very Greek," said Nina. "Did you understand
it?"

"Not altogether. She was recommending a wise woman to
take off the spell."

"Obviously. But what is it?"

"The *xemetrima?* I don't know. It's a secret prayer. White
magic."

Greeks seem closer to the ancients, to sorcery and magic, and
to their own country-roots. I remember years ago meeting an
acquaintance by chance, at Nicosia airport. He was a diplomat
at the Greek embassy and I asked him where he was going. To
Athens, he said. His mother had just died. We talked about
death and bereavement. I asked how long he would stay in
Greece. Long enough to go to Volos to see a soothsayer he
knew. To help him or his mother? Both, sort of.

Two nights later, our last in Nauplion that trip, another side
of Greece was opened up for us. We had gone to The Boatyard
for a stirrup-cup after eating prawns at Savouras. It was a story
Phaidon had kept for me.

"Did you read about the nun at Ayia Moni?"

"No," I said. "Is that our monastery?"

"Yes. It's up the mountain from Areia. Where the spring is
that they say can restore virginity."

"Oh, that monastery," I said.

Ayia Moni Areias is on the outskirts of Nauplion and is
really a nunnery. In fact it seems to have been a nunnery in
1143 when Leo, Bishop of Argos and Nauplion, founded it.
The next year it was converted to a monastery and thereafter
had a long and distinguished history: during the various lengthy
periods of occupation it kept the Orthodox flag flying despite
Latin and Muslim rulers. It was knocked about during the
Greek War of Independence and later reverted to a nunnery. It
is a marvellous oasis of Byzantine calm and beauty.

Some Athenian acquaintances of Phaidon's had introduced
a German couple, friends who were touring Greece. They had
been to all the obvious sites, archaeological and touristic.

Where to now? Phaidon had said why not go to Ayia Moni. It was cool, beautiful and had some excellent Byzantine church architecture. And lace which the nuns sold.

The weeks went by and Phaidon had forgotten about the German pair when the Athenians told him, startled, that their friends had been arrested at the airport for trying to smuggle out an icon. On being questioned they said that they had bought it from a nun at the monastery. The nun was arrested and said she didn't know what all the fuss was about. It was a dark, dirty old thing. Nobody wanted it. Except perhaps these foreigners. And everyone knows about foreigners and their funny ways. On being told it was a fifteenth-century icon she was unimpressed and said she had thought of throwing it on the bonfire. She was released to the prioress and the Germans went home.

Months later the Germans returned to Salonika where they were brought to trial. Because they had believed the nun's assertion that it was neither wanted nor particularly old – and why shouldn't they, Phaidon asked: she was a nun after all, a holy woman – the case was dismissed.

"What happened to the nun?" I asked.

"The case was dismissed against her too. If the Germans hadn't committed an offence, then logically she couldn't have committed an offence either. It seems fair to me. She's back at the monastery now."

"And the icon?"

"They're going to return it to the monastery."

A voice piped up, "So she can sell it again."

"And again," said someone else, and the bar shook with laughter.

The next morning we set off. As we finished packing the car and shut the front door a neighbour came across, her apron full of walnuts. For our journey, she said.

The mops, Gert and Daisy, were standing in place of a flag-pole when we left. They were still there when we returned, part of the landscape.